Educating
the Net Generation

Diana G. Oblinger and James L. Oblinger, Editors

ISBN 0-9672853-2-1
© 2005 EDUCAUSE. Available electronically at
www.educause.edu/educatingthenetgen/

An EDUCAUSE *e-Book*

Educating the Net Generation

ISBN 0-9672853-2-1

An EDUCAUSE *e-Book*

CHAPTER 1

Introduction

Diana Oblinger
EDUCAUSE

James Oblinger
North Carolina State University

It started with our children. Trying to get them to study without the TV and radio was rarely successful. (We succeeded—temporarily—when the house had been struck by lightning and almost all the household electronics were "fried.") Trying to concentrate with the stereo on drove us crazy, but didn't seem to have any impact on them. None of our dire predictions about poor grades materialized. We probably rented as many games from Blockbuster as we did videos. At one point we thought we'd better find out what these games were all about. They let us try a game—something to do with Grand Prix auto racing. We both drove the car right into the wall. One dose of humiliation was enough to convince us that our visual-spatial skills would be no match for theirs, no matter how much we practiced.

The youngest used to arrive home after school and shout, "Hi, Mom, I'm home. Are you on the Internet?" Those were the days of dial-up, of course. I had to get offline so he could get on. He wouldn't go outside with his friends until he'd checked e-mail and chatted with his online pals. It seemed odd, but to many parents, the teenage years are just that—odd.

Sometimes we'd ask them about information technology. We've gotten used to seeing the semi-surprised look on their faces when we'd ask what seem to be reasonable questions about technology. They were polite enough not to say, "Are you serious?" but we could tell they thought that by looking at them. And, like many parents, when it comes to getting consumer electronics information—a new cell phone plan, for example—we'd ask the kids to figure it out for us. You don't need to ask who set up the VCRs, remote controls, and DVD players in our house, do you?

Many of you have probably had similar experiences with your children, nieces or nephews, or even grandchildren. These situations often lead us to say, "That's not how it was when I was growing up."

But it all started to make more sense on Sundays. On Sunday nights we have the tradition of getting the family together for dinner. We thought we could use these occasions to help the children hone their critical thinking, powers of persuasion, and appreciation of the world around them. Well, perhaps we did. But we are the ones who learned the most.

We learned about technology. Even our least technologically inclined son could tell us things about graphics and images that we didn't know. He has a digital literacy that eludes us. We heard about experiential learning. Each one of the kids has talked about wanting—and needing—hands-on experiences to learn. At first we thought it was due to all those hours with LEGOs when they were young. We now think it is something more significant. We learned many other things as well. What we assumed was impatience is something they consider immediacy—responses are supposed to be fast. The list goes on and on.

The relevance of what we were hearing applies to more than parenting, though. We probably speak for most educators when we say that not only do we not really understand our children, but we don't really understand our students the way we'd like to.

This is a book for educators. Those who have chosen to be educators are generally dedicated to students. But, sometimes we don't quite understand what we are seeing. We hope this book will help educators make sense of the many patterns and behaviors that we see in the Net Generation but don't quite understand.

The first chapter surveys much of the literature in an effort to distill a picture of Net Generation learners—students who were born in the 1980s and later. Although no two individuals are alike, the characteristics help establish the contrast between generations. While we at colleges and universities routinely collect demographic information on our learners, we may not be asking the questions that will help us design and deliver programs that are optimal for current learners.

Having Baby Boomers talk about the Net Generation is not nearly as good as listening to learners themselves. Greg Roberts from the University of Pittsburg–Johnstown, along with Ben McNeely and Carie Windham, both from North Carolina State University, help us understand the Net Gen perspective on technology and higher education. Their insights help us appreciate that even our definitions of technology are different. They also emphasize the importance of interactivity and learning-by-doing.

Joel Hartman, Patsy Moskal, and Chuck Dziuban from the University of Central Florida have experience with different generations of learners in online, blended, and face-to-face situations. Their research highlights an assumption we often make: that younger students are likely to have the strongest preference for technology. Reflecting what the student authors told us, technology is simply a means to an end. The expectation for involvement with faculty and other students overrides a desire to use technology.

Even though technology may not be the entire focus, colleges and universities make massive technology investments based on what they believe students need, want, and already have. Bob Kvavik reports on the first EDUCAUSE Center for Applied Research study that details what technology students have, how they use it, and the benefits they believe result. Clearly, there is room for improvement in higher education's use of learning technologies as we move from course management systems to more interactive approaches.

Interactive instruction is the focus of Judith Ramaley and Lee Zia's chapter, based in large part on their work at the National Science Foundation. Virtually all those who study the Net Generation believe that their preference for experiential, hands-on learning is a distinguishing characteristic. The chapter details different types of interaction (for example, people to people, people and tools, people with concepts), along with examples of projects that put these interactions into practice. Beyond individual courses, how should institutions think about the curriculum, particularly if the desire is to prepare students for the 21st century? Alma Clayton-Pedersen and Nancy O'Neill use the Association of American Colleges and Universities' Greater Expectations initiative as a starting point for exploring how the curriculum can be adapted to better meet the needs of today's learners and how technology can be used in service to learning.

Although we often think of students and the classroom, an array of services and support are necessary to ensure that students succeed. Jim Wager from The Pennsylvania State University describes how student services professionals think of today's students and technology. Although he concludes that it is not about technology, technology has an important role to play in making services more convenient and in better integrating them into the campus experience.

If faculty and students have different perspectives, there should be a process to help faculty understand those different perspectives, as well as effective approaches to teaching their students. Anne Moore, John Moore, and Shelli Fowler describe programs designed to enhance the faculty's fluency in information technology—and better meet the needs of the Net Generation. Virginia Tech's program for faculty, the Faculty Development Institute, as well as one designed for future faculty, the Graduate Education Development Institute, provide valuable models of faculty development.

If the Net Generation values experiential learning, working in teams, and social networking, what are the implications for classrooms and the overall learning environment? Malcolm Brown from Dartmouth University explores the implications of the Net Generation, learning theory, and information technology on learning spaces. Keeping learning principles in mind, he contends that learning spaces for the Net Generation will be described more by the activities they enable than the technology they contain.

Just as our notion of classrooms may need to be expanded to learning spaces, the concept of the library is evolving. Students mention Google more often than going to the library. Although content, access, collections, circulation systems, and online catalogs will always be part of the library, Joan Lippincott of the Coalition of Networked Information challenges us to realign library programs, services, and spaces with the Net Generation. Citing numerous examples from institutions around the country, she provides both a theoretical context and practical suggestions for colleges and universities to consider.

All in all, a number of changes are implied if higher education is to adapt to the Net Generation. Carole Barone of EDUCAUSE asserts that a new academy must form if higher education is to remain relevant and responsive in changing times. She describes the interplay of culture and technology along with new cultural values and a new style of leadership as some of the characteristics of the new academy. She calls on us to have the institutional resolve needed to transform higher education, starting with understanding the Net Generation.

As colleges and universities adapt to the Net Generation—and as technology continues to change—institutions must also ask, "What's next?" Chris Dede of Harvard University describes how emerging media are fostering neomillennial learning styles. Multiuser virtual environments and ubiquitous computing will allow users to move beyond the desktop interface to much more immersive environments that enhance learning. In turn, learning styles will evolve based on mediated immersion and distributed learning communities. Dede details the implications of neomillennial learning for investments in physical facilities, technology infrastructure, and professional development.

For us, it started with our children. You may have developed an interest in the Net Generation as a result of a different experience. However you began, we hope you will join us in actively exploring the intersection of the Net Generation and higher education. We consider this collection of chapters as a start. As more institutions begin thinking about the Net Generation, asking questions, and exploring options, we will learn more.

Because this is an area of active exploration, we have chosen to make our thoughts available in electronic format rather than as a traditional printed book. Not only will our understanding of the Net Generation change over time, but our expression of it is limited if we use text alone. We hope you will visit the Web site (http://www.educause.edu/LibraryDetailPage/666&ID=pub7101) for additional examples, video, and other material that enriches the text. Please share your observations with us as well.

Educating the Net Generation is a privilege and a challenge. They expect a great deal of us, just as we do of them. To find the right balance point, we need to understand each other well. We hope this book helps as you educate the Net Generation—and as they educate us.

CHAPTER 2

Is It Age or IT: First Steps Toward Understanding the Net Generation

Diana Oblinger
EDUCAUSE

James Oblinger
North Carolina State University

Introduction

A junior at the university, Eric wakes up and peers at his PC to see how many instant messages (IMs) arrived while he slept. Several attempts to reach him are visible on the screen, along with various postings to the blog he's been following. After a quick trip to the shower, he pulls up an eclectic mix of news, weather, and sports on the home page he customized using Yahoo. He then logs on to his campus account. A reminder pops up indicating that there will be a quiz in sociology today; another reminder lets him know that a lab report needs to be e-mailed to his chemistry professor by midnight. After a few quick IMs with friends he pulls up a wiki to review progress a teammate has made on a project they're doing for their computer science class. He downloads yesterday's chemistry lecture to his laptop; he'll review it while he sits with a group of students in the student union working on other projects. After classes are over he has to go to the library because he can't find an online resource he needs for a project. He rarely goes to the library to check out books; usually he uses Google or Wikipedia. Late that night as he's working on his term paper, he switches back and forth between the paper and the Internet-based multiplayer game he's trying to win.[1]

Information technology is woven throughout Eric's life, but he probably doesn't think of it as technology. One generation's technology is taken for granted by the next. Computers, the Internet, online resources, and instantaneous access are simply the way things are done. Eric is a member of the Net Generation; he's never known life without the Internet.

Children and Teenagers

Today's Net Gen college students have grown up with technology. Born around the time the PC was introduced, 20 percent began using computers between the ages of 5 and 8. Virtually all Net Gen students were using computers by the time they were 16 to 18 years of age.[2] Computer usage is even higher among today's children. Among children ages 8 to 18, 96 percent have gone online. Seventy-four percent have access at home, and 61 percent use the Internet on a typical day.

Exposure to IT begins at very young ages. Children age six or younger spend an average of two hours each day using screen media (TV, videos, computers, video games), which nearly equals the amount of time they spend playing outside (1:58 hours versus 2:01 hours). Both significantly exceed the amount of reading time (39 minutes). Half of the children in this age group have used a computer; among 4-to-6-year-olds, 27 percent spend over an hour a day (1:04) at the keyboard. "It's not just teenagers who are wired up and tuned in, it's babies in diapers as well." While earlier generations were introduced to information through print, this generation takes a digital path.[3]

Home digital media use (computer, games, Internet) is approaching the amount of time spent watching TV. Thirteen-to-17-year-olds average 3.1 hours a day watching TV and 3.5 hours with digital media. Note that students may use more than one medium at a time. Consistent with the multitasking found in older students, it is the norm for children and teenagers to be online while simultaneously watching TV, talking on the phone, or listening to the radio. A sizable percentage of kids report visiting a site mentioned by someone on the phone, seen on TV, or mentioned on the radio.[4]

Children may be developing greater digital literacy than siblings who are just a few years older. For example, over two million American children (ages 6–17) have their own Web site. Girls are more likely to have a Web site than boys (12.2 percent versus 8.6 percent).[5] And, the ability to use nontext expression—audio, video, graphics—appears stronger in each successive cohort.

Access to computers for the majority of children and teens is through the home. However, home access to technology is not uniform across populations. One possible variable is race. Ninety-six percent of whites report they have gone online, compared to 95 percent for Hispanics, and 92 percent for African-

Americans (ages 8–18). The figures are similar (within two percentage points) when making comparisons based on parental education or median family income. When considering Internet access at home the differences are greater (80 percent for whites, 67 percent for Hispanics, and 67 percent for African-Americans). For children whose parents have a high school education or less, 68 percent have Internet access at home. This contrasts with 82 percent for those whose parents completed college. The distribution based on median family income is similar: 84 percent of families with incomes over $50,000 have Internet access at home; for those making less than $35,000, the percentage is 66.[6]

Whether or not students have access to computers and the Internet from home, they consider such access important. When high school students were asked why technology is essential to their education, responses included:

▶ It's part of our world.
▶ Technology is so embedded in our society, it'd be hard not to know how to use it.
▶ It's really helpful—it makes things faster.
▶ Abstract concepts are often easier to grasp when technology is used effectively as a teaching tool.
▶ Some students at my school who weren't great students are better ones now thanks to computers.
▶ Technology allows us to learn as much as we want to about virtually any topic.
▶ I usually connect with friends either to get help or to help others.[7]

By the teenage years, students use the Web extensively for school research (94 percent) and believe it helps with schoolwork (78 percent).[8] Although technology is used heavily, students seem to keep technology in perspective. In their words:

▶ Teachers are vital to the learning process. Tech is good, but it is not a perfect substitute.
▶ Computers can never replace humans.
▶ Learning is based on motivation, and without teachers that motivation would cease to exist.
▶ A major part of school is building social skills. If we were to always communicate through technology and not in person, then the way we would view life would change dramatically.[9]

Perhaps because home computers and the Internet have become almost as prevalent as the telephone, instant messaging is a common communication and socializing mechanism. Not only is IM accessible, it can support multiple, simultaneous conversations. Seventy percent of teenagers use IM to keep in touch, slightly less than those who use e-mail to stay in touch with friends and relatives (81 percent). Still, nearly 13 million teenagers use IM. "Talking to buddies online has become the information age way for teens to hang out and beat boredom."[10] A separate study found that 74 percent of teenagers use IM as a major communication tool compared to 44 percent of online adults.[11] Once they leave for college many will use IM to stay in touch—oftentimes daily—with high school and childhood friends. Forty-one percent of teenagers indicate they use e-mail and instant messaging to contact teachers or schoolmates about class work. Greater than half (56 percent) prefer the Internet to the telephone.[12] In fact, students in grade 7–12 know more screen names than home phone numbers.[13]

When teenagers are asked what they want from the Internet, the most common response is to get "new information." Close behind, at about 75 percent, is to "learn more or to learn better." The use of the Internet to learn is not limited to school work. Students are often informal learners, seeking information on a variety of topics, such as personal health. Other common activities involve participating in online communities, showing others what they can do, or voicing their opinions.[14]

College Students

The characteristics of traditional age (18-to-22-year-old) college students—a group sometimes called the Millennials—have been described by Howe and Strauss as individuals who:

▶ Gravitate toward group activity
▶ Identify with parents' values and feel close to their parents
▶ Believe it's cool to be smart
▶ Are fascinated by new technologies
▶ Are racially and ethnically diverse; one in five has at least one immigrant parent
▶ Are focused on grades and performance
▶ Are busy with extracurricular activities

When asked about the biggest problem facing their generation, many respond that it is the poor example that adults set for kids.[15]

Individuals raised with the computer deal with information differently compared to previous cohorts: "they develop hypertext minds, they leap around."[16] A linear thought process is much less common than bricolage,[17] or the ability to or piece information together from multiple sources. Among other differences are their:

▶ **Ability to read visual images**—they are intuitive visual communicators
▶ **Visual-spatial skills**—perhaps because of their expertise with games they can integrate the virtual and physical
▶ **Inductive discovery**—they learn better through discovery than by being told
▶ **Attentional deployment**—they are able to shift their attention rapidly from one task to another, and may choose not to pay attention to things that don't interest them
▶ **Fast response time**—they are able to respond quickly and expect rapid responses in return[18]

Although many observations can be made about the Net Generation, several merit special mention because of the potential impact on higher education.

Digitally Literate

Having grown up with widespread access to technology, the Net Gen is able to intuitively use a variety of IT devices and navigate the Internet. Although they are comfortable using technology without an instruction manual, their understanding of the technology or source quality may be shallow.

The Net Gen are more visually literate than previous generations; many express themselves using images. They are able to weave together images, text, and sound in a natural way. Their ability to move between the real and the virtual is instantaneous,[19] expanding their literacy well beyond text. Because of the availability of visual media, their text literacy may be less well developed than previous cohorts.

Students are more likely to use the Internet for research than the library (73 percent).[20] When asked, two-thirds of students indicated they know how to find valid information from the Web. However, they realize that the Web does not meet all their information needs.[21]

Connected

"As long as they've been alive, the world has been a connected place, and more than any preceding generation they have seized on the potential of networked media."[22] While highly mobile, moving from work to classes to recreational activities, the Net Gen is always connected. According to one student, "I like how cell phones work—you can always get ahold of someone, and it goes with you wherever you go." The particular device may change depending on circumstance (for example, laptop, cell phone), but they are constantly connected and always on.

Immediate
Whether it is the immediacy with which a response is expected or the speed at which they are used to receiving information, the Net Gen is fast. They multitask, moving quickly from one activity to another, sometimes performing them simultaneously. They have fast response times, whether playing a game or responding to an IM. In fact, more value may be placed on speed than on accuracy.

Experiential
Most Net Gen learners prefer to learn by doing rather by being told what to do. The role having grown up with video games plays in this preference is unclear, but Net Gen students learn well through discovery—by exploring for themselves or with their peers. This exploratory style enables them to better retain information and use it in creative, meaningful ways.[23]

Social
"Prolific communicators, they gravitate toward activities that promote and reinforce social interaction—whether IMing old friends, teaming up in an Internet game, posting Web diaries (blogging), or forwarding joke e-mails."[24] The Net Gen displays a striking openness to diversity, differences, and sharing; they are at ease meeting strangers on the Net.[25] Many of their exchanges on the Internet are emotionally open, sharing very personal information about themselves. The Net Gen has developed a mechanism of inclusiveness that does not necessarily involve personally knowing someone admitted to their group. Being a friend of a friend is acceptable. They seek to interact with others, whether in their personal lives, their online presence, or in class. (Sometimes the interaction is through an alternative identity. Significant numbers of teens assume an online identity that is different from their own.)[26] Although technology can't change one's personality, introverts, for example, use the Internet as a tool to reach out. These social connections through e-mail might not have happened before. Extroverts can make their circle of friends even larger.[27]

The Net Gen also exhibits learning preferences that are closely related to their characteristics. For example, their social nature leads aligns with their preference to work in teams or interact peer-to-peer. Net Gen learning preferences that may impact higher education include the following.

Teams
The Net Gen often prefers to learn and work in teams. A peer-to-peer approach is common, as well, where students help each other. In fact, Net Geners find peers more credible than teachers when it comes to determining what is worth paying attention to.[28]

Structure
The Net Gen is very achievement oriented. "They want parameters, rules, priorities, and procedures ... they think of the world as scheduled and someone must have the agenda."[29] As a result, they like to know what it will take to achieve a goal. Their preference is for structure rather than ambiguity.[30]

Engagement and Experience
The Net Gen is oriented toward inductive discovery or making observations, formulating hypotheses, and figuring out the rules. They crave interactivity. And the rapid pace with which they like to receive information means they often choose not to pay attention if a class is not interactive, unengaging, or simply too slow.[31] The Net Gen may need to be encouraged to stop experiencing and spend time reflecting.

Visual and Kinesthetic[32]
The Net Gen is more comfortable in image-rich environments than with text. Researchers report Net Gen students will refuse to read large amounts of text, whether it involves a long reading assignment or lengthy instructions. In a study that altered instructions from a text-based step-by-step approach to one that used a graphic layout, refusals to do the assignment dropped and post-test scores increased. The Net Gen's experiential nature means they like doing things, not just thinking or talking about things.

Things that Matter
The Net Gen readily takes part in community activities.[33] Given a choice, they seem to prefer working on things that matter, such as addressing an environmental concern or a community problem. They believe they can make a difference and that science and technology can be used resolve difficult problems.[34]

Nontraditional Learners

At the same time that colleges and universities are graduating their first Net Generation learners, most campuses are experiencing an influx of nontraditional students. Three-quarters of all undergraduates are "nontraditional," according to the National Center for Educational Statistics. Nontraditional students are defined as having one or more of the following characteristics:

▶ Delayed enrollment—did not enter postsecondary education in the same year they graduated from high school
▶ Attend part-time, for all or part of the academic year
▶ Work full time—35 hours or more—while enrolled
▶ Financially independent as defined by financial aid
▶ Have dependents, other than a spouse, which may include children or others
▶ Single parent, having one or more dependent children
▶ Lack of a high school diploma[35]

The more nontraditional characteristics students possess, the less likely they are to persist in college after the first year or to graduate. Nontraditional learners tend to be concentrated in specific types of institutions. In community colleges, for example, nearly half the students have delayed beginning postsecondary education. Half also had two or more persistent risk factors. In contrast, 91 percent of students in four-year colleges enrolled immediately after high school; 85 percent had no persistent risk factors.[36]

Adult learners represent a significant category of nontraditional learners:

▶ 35 percent of undergraduates are adult learners
▶ 70 percent of all adult learners are female
▶ 38 is the median age of undergraduate adult learners
▶ 80 percent of adult learners are employed[37]

The motivation for going to college is often different for adult learners compared to the Net Gen. Among adult learners 70 percent have a degree as their goal; the other 30 percent are seeking a certificate or a specific set of skills.[38]

Product of the Environment

It is often said that we see the world through our own eyes. Our experiences and the environment around us shape how we think, behave, and act. Consider birthplace. If you were born in the south, you might have a southern accent; if raised in Canada, you would speak differently. Tastes in food and clothes might differ, as would customs and expressions. We are all products of our environment—and technology is an increasingly important part of that environment.

Few generalizations are entirely correct. However, generalizations—such as those about generations—highlight trends. Today's generations can be described as follows.[39]

	Matures	Baby Boomers	Generation X	Net Generation
Birth Dates	**1900–1946**	**1946–1964**	**1965–1982**	**1982–1991**
Description	Greatest generation	Me generation	Latchkey generation	Millennials
Attributes	Command and control Self-sacrifice	Optimistic Workaholic	Independent Skeptical	Hopeful Determined
Likes	Respect for authority Family Community involvement	Responsibility Work ethic Can-do attitude	Freedom Multitasking Work-life balance	Public activism Latest technology Parents
Dislikes	Waste Technology	Laziness Turning 50	Red tape Hype	Anything slow Negativity

Other attributes show generational trends as well (for example, attitude toward changing jobs or locus of community). One of the most striking attributes is the attitude toward the Internet. For the Net Gen, the Internet is like oxygen; they can't imagine being able to live without it.[40]

Not Just an Age Phenomenon

Although these trends are described in generational terms, age may be less important than exposure to technology. For example, individuals who are heavy users of IT tend to have characteristics similar to the Net Gen. In fact, the pervasiveness of technology—in our professions and in our personal lives—virtually ensures that most individuals gradually assume some Net Gen characteristics. For example, ask yourself:

▶ Are you more comfortable composing documents online than longhand?
▶ Have you turned your "remembering" (phone numbers, meetings, and so on) over to a technology device?
▶ Do you go to meetings with your laptop or PDA?
▶ Are you constantly connected? Is the Internet is always on whether you are at home or work? Is your cell phone is always with you?
▶ How many different activities can you effectively engage in at one time?
▶ Do you play video or computer games?[41]

The differentiating factor may not be so much one person's generation versus another; the difference may be in experience. Generational issues are relevant to higher education because the faculty or administrator perspective may be considerably different from that of our students.

Implications

Whether the Net Generation is a purely generational phenomenon or whether it is associated with technology use, there are a number of implications for colleges and universities. Most stem from the dichotomy between a Net Gen mindset and that of most faculty, staff, and administrators.

It's Not About Technology

It is an almost instinctive assumption to believe that Net Gen students will want to use IT heavily in their education; they certainly do in their personal lives. However, if you ask Net Gen learners what technology they use, you will often get a blank stare. They don't think in terms of technology; they think in terms of the activity technology enables. In general, the Net Gen views the Internet as an access tool—a medium for distribution of resources rather than a resource with limitations.

When asked about technology, students' definitions centered on new technologies. For example, a cell phone with a new feature was considered technology; a cell phone with standard features was not. What we might consider "new technology," such as blogs or wikis, are not thought of as technology by students.[42]

The activity enabled is more important to the Net Gen than the technology behind it. For example, instant messaging wasn't considered a technology; IMing is treated as a verb—it is an action, not a technology. Students often use the word "talk" when they describe text messaging or instant messaging. Software blends into the background; it enables certain activities to occur, but it is not new, novel, or customizable—all part of the Net Gen's definition of technology.[43]

Student satisfaction with online learning exemplifies our assumptions about online learning. Since Net Geners spend so much of their time online, it seems reasonable to expect that they would have a strong preference for Web-based courses. The reverse is actually true, as illustrated by a study from the University of Central Florida. Older students (Matures and Baby Boomers) are much more likely to be satisfied with fully Web-based courses than are traditional-age students. The reason relates to the Net Gen desire to be connected with people and to be social as well as their expectations of higher education. Traditional-age students often say they came to college to work with faculty and other students, not to interact with them online. Older learners tend to be less interested in the social aspects of learning; convenience and flexibility are much more important.[44]

In response to a student technology survey the majority of students preferred a moderate amount of IT in their classes. Students appreciate the convenience provided by online syllabi, class readings, and online submission of assignments.[45] They also want face-to-face interaction, however:

> Year after year, face-to-face interactions are ranked by all students in either first or second place. This replicates the results of many distance education studies that show students often feel that something important to their learning is missing when all interactions are mediated, whether asynchronous or synchronous.[46]

The implication is that colleges and universities should not assume that more technology is necessarily better. Technology that enables certain types of activities is likely to be appreciated. For example, wireless networking enables learner mobility and makes it possible to be constantly connected. The majority of wireless network use, however, may be outside the academic realm. Using technology to increase customization, convenience, and collaboration is well received; however, its integration into most courses or curricula is not as deep as into students' personal lives.

Communities and Social Networks

The Net Gen exhibits a tendency to work in teams or with peers and will move seamlessly between physical and virtual interactions. It is not uncommon to find students working together and still sending IMs—even though they are a few feet away. Their communities and social networks are physical, virtual, and hybrid.

Personal does not always mean "in person" to the Net Gen. Online conversations may be as meaningful as one that is face-to-face. Interactions with faculty need not be "in person" to be valuable and personal.

Net Geners use technology extensively to network and socialize. In their personal lives, buddy lists, virtual communities, and social networks such as Flickr or Orkut are heavily used. "When we poll users about what they actually do with their computers, some form of social interaction always tops the list—conversation, collaboration, playing games, and so on. The practice of software design is shot through with computer-as-box assumptions, while our actual behavior is close to computer-as-door, treating the device as an entrance to a social space."[47]

Net Geners are emotionally open and use the Internet as a social technology to reveal their feelings, to express their views, to meet new people, and to experience different cultures. Many of the online exchanges by Net Geners reveal a great deal of personal information—not just facts but emotions.

Computer games provide a social outlet for large numbers of Net Geners. Students play games in groups; online communities form around games; and players add to existing games, sharing their work with others. "Games encourage collaboration among players and thus provide a context for peer-to-peer teaching and for the emergence of learning communities. ... Look up any popular game on the Internet and you find robust communities of game players debating games, sharing game tips, or offering critiques to designers."[48]

First-Person Learning

Learning is participatory; knowing depends on practice and participation. Digital resources enable experiential learning—something in tune with Net Gen preferences. Rather than being told, Net Geners would rather construct their own learning, assembling information, tools, and frameworks from a variety of sources.

Digital repositories can provide raw material for learning. For example, *The Valley of the Shadow* archive (http://www.iath.virginia.edu/vshadow2/) allows students to draw their own conclusions about the Civil War using original records from two counties—similar in all aspects except one was Confederate and the other was Union. Census data, agricultural records, newspaper articles, church records, and letters from soldiers and their families constitute the original source material that allows students to engage in "first-person learning." The site also serves formal and informal learners. It is the most heavily accessed Civil War site on the Web, according to Google.[49]

Online laboratories and remote instruments enable students to collect data that can be analyzed and manipulated with the tools of the profession. For example, iLab uses a Web interface to link students with a circuit analyzer. Thanks to the online interface, the instrument is available not only to MIT students but also to students at several other institutions whenever and wherever they choose to do their experiments.[50]

Simulations and visualizations allow students to explore and draw their own conclusions—another form of first-person learning. Games and role playing provide students with the opportunity to assume another persona and learn by "being there" rather than by being told. For example, the game Civilization III serves as the impetus for students to use traditional sources of learning material. Rather than replacing traditional resources such as maps, texts, or educational films, the game encourages students to use those media to do better. Students must deal with a range of complexities—political, scientific, military, cultural, and economic—over 6,000 years to win the game, and they must synthesize and integrate information from multiple disciplines to succeed at the game.[51,52]

Interaction[53]

The social nature Net Geners, as well as their desire for experiential learning, implies that interaction is an important technique for colleges and universities to employ. The importance of interaction is not new; learning science has consistently demonstrated that students learn more when they interact—with material, with each other, and with faculty. The "talk, text, test" approach to teaching is not highly effective with most learners. Students do best when they actively construct their own knowledge. In addition, there is a positive correlation between interaction and student retention.[54]

The level of interactivity in a traditional lecture is low. Estimates are that students ask 0.1 questions per hour in a traditional class; faculty ask 0.3 per hour. Technology makes it possible to provide learners with anytime, anywhere content and interactions. Computer-based instruction, however, increases the number of questions posed from less than 1 per hour to 180–600 per hour.[55]

The short attention spans of Net Geners also point to interaction as an important component of instruction. They "crave interactivity—an immediate response to their each and every action. Traditional schooling provides very little of this compared to the rest of their world."[56]

Digital Natives accustomed to the twitch-speed, multitasking, random-access, graphics-first, active, connected, fun, fantasy, quick-payoff world of their video games, MTV, and Internet are bored by most of today's education, well-meaning as it may be. But worse, the many skills that new technology [has] actually enhanced (for example, parallel processing, graphics awareness, and random access)—which have profound implications for their learning—are almost totally ignored by educators.[57]

Interaction is not limited to classroom settings. Informal learning may comprise a greater share of students' time than learning in formal settings. The type of interaction, peer-to-peer instruction, synthesis, and reflection that takes place in informal settings can be critically important. In fact, "the full range of students' learning styles is undercut when interaction is limited to classroom settings."[58]

Immediacy

"Digital natives are used to receiving information really fast. They like to parallel process and multitask…. They thrive on immediate gratification."[59] The expectation of immediacy holds true for access to friends, services, and responses to questions. According to one student, "The ever-increasing speed of the Internet is one thing I really like because I like my info now, not later."

Although the Net Gen expects constant connections and immediate responsiveness, this is often an unrealistic expectation. Faculty may find it helpful to set expectations about e-mail turnaround; rather than instant response, it may take up to 48 hours for a response on the weekend.

Multiple Media Literacy

The Net Gen has been exposed to multiple media types from a young age. Prensky estimates that by the time individuals reach age 21, they will have spent twice as many hours playing video games as reading (10,000 versus 5,000).[60] The Net Generation is more visually literate than earlier generations. Many are fluent in personal expression using images; they are comfortable in an image-rich rather than a text-only environment.

For some time educators have realized that although reading text may be the preferred mode of learning for faculty, librarians, and other academics, it is not the preferred mode for most of the population. Students on average retain 10 percent of what they read but closer to 30 percent of what they see. Much of the reading done by the Net Gen has been on the Web, where they are more likely to scan than to read.[61]

In fact, overreliance on text may inhibit Net Gen participation. Net Geners "prefer their graphics before their text rather than the opposite."[62] In one course (Library 1010 at CSU–Hayward) significant numbers of students would not process extensive written directions. They would either try to infer the directions or they would turn in incomplete assignments. When the homework was altered, presenting pictures first rather than words, refusals to do the assignment dropped (by 10–14 percent) and student scores increased (an improvement of 11–16 percent); pretest versus post-test scores gained 4–9 percent.[63]

Asking the Right Questions

It is easy to assume that we understand our students, but there is often a difference in perspective between the Net Generation and faculty/administrators. As a result, it is important that colleges and universities ask the right questions and not simply assume that the current student cohort is like we were. Important questions for colleges and universities to ask include the following.

▶ **Who are our learners?** Although the institution may have demographic information (date of birth, home town, gender, ethnicity, and so on), we may not understand how students view the world, what is important to them, or even how they learn best. It is increasingly important that colleges and universities engage learners in a dialogue to better understand their perspective. Institutions make massive investments (IT infrastructure, residence halls, recreational facilities) for the sake of meeting students' wants and needs; basing these decisions on assumptions is risky.

▶ **How are today's learners different from (or the same as) faculty/ administrators?** Although the Net Generation may be different in many ways from Baby Boomers, some things stay the same. Students still come to college to meet people, to socialize, and to interact with faculty. Many of the measures of student engagement have consistently shown the importance of interaction with faculty and other students, as well as a supportive campus environment. Student preferences for how they receive information are likely different, however—they favor more graphics, a rapid pace, and immediate responses. If faculty and administrators can understand the factors that lead to student success—which persist and which differ from their own college experience—they will be able to more effectively develop programs and target investments.

▶ **What learning activities are most engaging for learners?** It isn't technology per se that makes learning engaging for the Net Gen; it is the learning activity. If today's students are experiential learners, lectures may not be an optimal learning environment. If they are community oriented, providing opportunities for peer-to-peer experiences or team projects may be preferable to individual activity. There are significant individual differences among learners, so no one-size-fits-all approach will be effective. Even so, learning science and the habits of the Net Generation provide some clues as to how we can improve learning.

▶ **Are there ways to use IT to make learning more successful?** Learning science indicates that successful learning is often active, social, and learner-centered. However, with the multiple responsibilities of faculty, staff, and administrators, as well as the large numbers of students most campuses serve, ensuring successful learning without the support of IT may be impossible. Individualization and customization are laudable goals for instruction; they are also time intensive. With the appropriate use of technology, learning can be made more active, social, and learner centered—but the uses of IT are driven by pedagogy, not technology.

Educating students is the primary goal of colleges and universities. However, reaching that goal depends on understanding those learners. Only by understanding the Net Generation can colleges and universities create learning environments that optimize their strengths and minimize their weaknesses. Technology has changed the Net Generation, just as it is now changing higher education.

Acknowledgments

The authors would like to thank Vicki Suter and Jean Kreis for conducting focus sessions with students and for sharing their observations.

Endnotes

1. Adapted from *The Key to Competitiveness: A Guide for College and University Leaders* (Washington, D.C.: American Association of State Colleges and Universities), <http://www.aascu.org/book/default.htm>.

2. Steve Jones, "The Internet Goes to College: How Students Are Living in the Future with Today's Technology" (Washington, D.C.: Pew Internet & American Life Project, September 15, 2002), <http://www.pewinternet.org/reports/toc.asp?Report=71>.

3. Kaiser Family Foundation, "New Study Finds Children Age Zero to Six Spend as Much Time with TV, Computers, and Video Games as Playing Outside" (Menlo Park, Calif.: Kaiser Family Foundation, 2003), <http://www.kff.org/entmedia/entmedia102803nr.cfm>.

4. Peter Grunwald, *Children, Families, and the Internet* (Bethesda, Md.: Grunwald Associates, 2004), <http://www.grunwald.com/>.

5. Peter Grunwald, "Two Million American Children Have Their Own Web Sites, Broad New Internet Survey Shows" (Bethesda, Md.: Grunwald Associates, December 4, 2003), <http://www.schooldata.com/ssm-grunwald-internet.htm>.

6. Kaiser Family Foundation, "The Digital Divide Survey Snapshot" (Menlo Park, Calif.: Kaiser Family Foundation, 2003), <http://www.kff.org/entmedia/loader.cfm?url=/commonspot/security/getfile.cfm&PageID=46366>.

7. Threshold/ISTE Youth Forum, "Future Chat," *Threshold*, Summer 2004, <http://www.ciconline.com/NR/rdonlyres/e4z3cf2ylkjj6o5jnjpdr5pvsrh6okzwx5fokgw5slt2idy6om36rff4bzfusqrhqhhdt2ry7sbnjrggxv3nnf5kz2h/T-Sum-04-FutureChat.pdf>.

8. Amanda Lenhart, Maya Simon, and Mike Graziano, "The Internet and Education: Findings of the Pew Internet & American Life Project" (Washington, D.C.: Pew Internet & American Life Project, September 2001), <http://www.pewinternet.org/pdfs/PIP_Schools_Report.pdf>.

9. Threshold/ISTE Youth Forum, op. cit.

10. Amanda Lenhart, Lee Rainie, and Oliver Lewis, "Teenage Life Online: The Rise of Instant-Message Generation and the Internet's Impact on Friendships and Family Relationships" (Washington, D.C.: Pew Internet & American Life Project, June 20, 2001), <http://www.pewinternet.org/pdfs/PIP_Teens_Report.pdf>.

11. NetDay, *Voices and Views of Today's Tech-Savvy Students: National Report on NetDay Speak Up Day for Students 2003* (Irvine, Calif.: NetDay, 2004), <http://www.netday.org/downloads/voices%20and%20views%20final.pdf>.

12. Lenhart, Simon, and Graziano, op. cit.

13. NetDay, op. cit.

14. Peter Grunwald, "Key Technology Trends: Excerpts from New Survey Research Findings," Exploring the Digital Generation, Educational Technology, U.S. Department of Education, Washington, D.C., September 23–24, 2003.

15. Neil Howe and William Strauss, *Millennials Rising: The Next Greatest Generation* (New York: Vintage Books, 2000).

16. Marc Prensky, "Digital Natives, Digital Immigrants, Part II: Do They Really Think Differently?" *On the Horizon*, vol. 9, no. 6 (December 2001), pp. 15–24; available from <http://www.marcprensky.com/writing/>.

17. John Seely Brown, "Growing Up Digital," *Change*, vol. 32, no. 2 (March/April 2000), pp. 10–11, <http://www.aahe.org/change/digital.pdf>.

18. Prensky, op. cit.

19. Jason Frand, "The Information-Age Mindset: Changes in Students and Implications for Higher Education," *EDUCAUSE Review,* vol. 35, no. 5 (September/October 2000), pp. 15–24, <http://www.educause.edu/apps/er/erm00/articles005/erm0051.pdf>.

20. Jones, op. cit.

21. Online Computer Library Center (OCLC), "How Academic Librarians Can Influence Students' Web-Based Information Choices," OCLC white paper on the information habits of college students, June 2002, <http://www5.oclc.org/downloads/community/informationhabits.pdf>.

22. Scott Crittenden, "Silicon Daydreams: Digital Pastimes of the Wired Generation," *virginia.edu,* vol. VI, no. 2 (fall 2002), <http://www.itc.virginia.edu/virginia.edu/fall02/daydreams/home.html>.

23. Don Tapscott, *Growing Up Digital: The Rise of the Net Generation* (New York: McGraw Hill, 1998).

24. Crittenden, op. cit.

25. Lenhart, Rainie, and Lewis, op. cit.

26. Ibid.

27. Crittenden, op. cit.

28. Kate Manuel, *Teaching Information Literacy to Generation Y* (New York: Haworth Press, 2002), <https://www.haworthpress.com/store/ArticleAbstract.asp?ID=32857>.

29. Kathleen Phalen, "Self-Assured, Stressed, and Straight: Millennial Students and How They Got that Way," *virginia.edu,* vol. VI, no. 2 (fall 2002), <http://www.itc.virginia.edu/virginia.edu/fall02/student/home.html>.

30. Howe and Strauss, op. cit.

31. Prensky, op. cit.

32. Manuel, op. cit.

33. Jeffrey R. Young, "A New Take on What Today's Students Want from College," *Chronicle of Higher Education,* January 31, 2003; available by subscription at <http://chronicle.com/weekly/v49/i21/21a03701.htm>.

34. Howe and Strauss, op. cit.

35. U.S. Department of Education, National Center for Education Statistics, *The Condition of Education 2002,* NCES 2002–025 (Washington, D.C.: U.S. Government Printing Office, 2002), <http://nces.ed.gov/pubs2002/2002025.pdf>.

36. U.S. Department of Education, National Center for Education Statistics, *Teaching Undergraduates in U.S. Postsecondary Institutions: Fall 1998,* NCES 2002–209 (Washington, D.C.: U.S. Government Printing Office, 2002), <http://nces.ed.gov/pubs2002/2002209.pdf>.

37. W. S. Swail, "Higher Education and the New Demographics: Questions for Policy," *Change,* July/August 2002, pp. 15–23; see also the listserv posting at <http://lists.eou.edu/archive/ctl-group/d20034/0019.html>.

38. Carol Aslainian, personal communication, 2002.

39. Rita M. Murray, personal communication, 2004.

40. Tammy Savage, personal communication, 2003.

41. Vicki Suter, NLII presentation, 2002.

42. Greg Roberts, personal communication, 2004.

43. Ibid.

44. See chapter by Hartman, Moskal, and Dziuban.

45. See chapter by Kvavik.

46. Chris Dede, *Planning for "Neomillennial" Learning Styles: Implications for Investments in Technology and Faculty* (unpublished paper).

47. Clay Shirky, "Clay Shiky's Writings About the Internet: Economics & Culture, Media & Community, Open Source" (e-mail from Larry Johnson, November 9, 2004).

48. Kurt Squire and Henry Jenkins, "Harnessing the Power of Games in Education," *Insight,* issue 2003 (2003), <http://www.iaete.org/insight/articles.cfm?&id=26>.

49. Edward Ayers, personal communication, April 4, 2003.

50. J. A. del Alamo et al., "Educational Experiments with an Online Microelectronics Characterization Laboratory," 2002, <http://science.donntu.edu.ua/konf/konf7/o102.pdf>.

51. Wendy Rickard and Diana Oblinger, *Higher Education Leaders Symposium: Unlocking the Potential of Gaming Technology* (Redmond, Wash.: Microsoft Corporation, September 9–10, 2003), <http://www7.nationalacademies.org/itru/Gaming%20Technology.pdf>.

52. Squire and Jenkins, op. cit.

53. An entire chapter is devoted to the importance of interaction for the Net Generation.

54. George D. Kuh et al., "Student Learning Outside the Classroom: Transcending Artificial Boundaries," *ASHE-ERIC Higher Education Report No. 8* (Washington, D.C.: The George Washington University, School of Education and Human Development, 1994), <http://www.ericdigests.org/1996-4/student.htm>.

55. Dexter Fletcher, *Higher Education Leaders Symposium: Unlocking the Potential of Gaming Technology* (Redmond, Wash.: Microsoft Corporation, September 10, 2003).

56. Prensky, op. cit.

57. Ibid.

58. Dede, op. cit.

59. Prensky, op. cit.

60. Ibid.

61. Manuel, op. cit.

62. Prensky, op. cit.

63. Manuel, op. cit.

About the Authors

Diana Oblinger is vice president for the EDUCAUSE teaching and learning initiatives and directs the National Learning Infrastructure Initiative (NLII). Previously, Oblinger served as the vice president for information resources and the chief information officer for the 16-campus University of North Carolina system and as a senior fellow for the EDUCAUSE Center for Applied Research (ECAR). She was the executive director of higher education for Microsoft Corporation and led the Institute for Academic Technology for IBM. Oblinger was on the faculty at Michigan State University and the University of Missouri–Columbia, where she also she served as an academic dean. She is a graduate of Iowa State University.

James L. Oblinger is the chancellor of North Carolina State University, a research-extensive land-grant institution with 30,000 students and approximately 2,200 full- and part-time faculty. Previously, he served as provost and executive vice chancellor, dean and executive director for agricultural programs of the College of Agriculture and Life Sciences, and associate dean and director of academic programs at NC State. Oblinger is also a professor of food science and has held positions at the University of Missouri–Columbia and the University of Florida. Oblinger received his bachelor's degree in bacteriology from DePauw University, his master's in food technology from Iowa State University, and his doctorate in food technology from Iowa State University.

CHAPTER 3

Technology and Learning Expectations of the Net Generation

Gregory R. Roberts
University of Pittsburgh–Johnstown

Introduction

I am a member of the Net Generation. The Internet and related technologies have had a major influence on my generation's culture and development. Many, if not most, Net Generation students have never known a world without computers, the World Wide Web, highly interactive video games, and cellular phones. For a significant number, instant messaging has surpassed the telephone and electronic mail as the primary form of communication. It is not unusual for Net Geners to multitask using all three communication methods at once, while still surfing the Web and watching television.

Higher education often talks about the Net Generation's expectations for the use of technology in their learning environments. However, few efforts have been made to directly engage students in a dialogue about how they would like to see faculty and their institutions use technology to help students learn more effectively. Through a series of interviews, polls, focus groups, and casual conversations with other students, I gained a general understanding of the Net Generation's views on technology and learning.[1]

Technology Expectations of the Net Generation

To better understand what the Net Generation expects from technology in support of learning, we must first understand how the Net Generation defines technology. In one-on-one interviews, I asked my fellow students at colleges and universities across the country to complete the sentence, To me, technology is _____.[2] The following responses reflect the wide range one would expect from such a broad group; they also provide some common threads that hint at a shared perspective.

To me, technology is...

▶ "Reformatting my computer system and installing cutting-edge software that allows me to do what I want, when I want, without restrictions, viruses, and the rules of Bill Gates." —Jody Butler, Junior, Idaho State University

▶ "The ability to adapt and configure an already established program to [something that] benefits me daily, be it customizing WeatherBug to state the weather in my particular region or formatting my cell phone pad to recognize commonly used phrases in text messaging." —Christopher Bourges, Senior, Duke University

▶ "Any software and hardware alike that gives me the power to do what I need to do faster than ancient methods of conducting things, such as e-mailing versus writing, messaging three people versus buying a three-way calling package, digital research versus traveling to a well-stocked library, et cetera." —Lindsey Alexovich, Senior, American University

These comments reflect two consistent themes that appeared across the range of responses I received from students regarding their views on technology:

▶ The definition of technology is not confined to computers or the Internet. Technology is viewed as any electronically based application or piece of equipment that meets a need for access to information or communication.

▶ Customization is central to the definition of technology for Net Geners. Technology is something that adapts to their needs, not something that requires them to change.

The first theme is reinforced by the results of a poll conducted with 25 students at The Pennsylvania State University, where students were asked to indicate whether they considered a set of applications or hardware to be technology. Overall, the average response to whether Web browsing, instant messaging, and the Internet constitute technology was neutral.[3] For Net Geners, technologies that are still considered transformative by their parents' and grandparents' standards (for example, instant messaging) are a basic part of their everyday lives; they are only considered technology in the broadest sense of the term. In light of what these students did not consider technology, their definition of what constitutes technology is fascinating, and it emerged as a third major theme: For the Net Generation, technology is "what's new," and the time between new and old can be quite brief when viewed from a perspective other than the Net Generation's.

"Everything new and different is automatically technology because it's usually branded as 'hard to understand,'" explained Lauren St. John, a senior at the University of Pittsburgh–Johnstown. "For example, [take] voice over the Internet. This seems like a new concept, but really we've been using this for years. Anyone with a mike on their computer would just press the 'talk' icon on instant messenger and there you have it—voice over the Internet."[4]

Together, these three themes pose interesting questions for colleges and universities:

▶ How will institutions define and develop technology-enabled learning when students view technology as encompassing a wide range of mobile options beyond the traditional classroom?

▶ Do student expectations regarding technology and customization constitute a barrier to effective teaching and learning with technology?

▶ What does it mean when students consider an institution's "advanced technology" as "so yesterday?"

To address these questions, we have to look at the learning expectations of the Net Generation.

Learning Expectations of the Net Generation

The Net Generation's learning expectations begin with the expertise and passion of the faculty member. The following student comments represent the general perspective of students interviewed for this process:[5]

▶ "To me, my success in the classroom depends on the teacher. If the teacher is prepared and knowledgeable about their particular field, I know I can expect to learn from their knowledge as well as know what is expected of me." —Joseph Gerocs, Junior, San Diego State University

▶ "I love when I come back from a class where my professor's knowledge of a particular field is astonishing." —Samuel Bass, Junior, Southwest Missouri State University

▶ "It's great when the professor is passionate about the field. They are usually knowledgeable about their field. In turn, that knowledge and passion rubs off on me, and that's my ideal class environment!" —Thomas McMillian, Senior, Texas Tech University

These students still view expert faculty members who are committed to teaching as the key ingredient for learning success. However, the data collected for this project also suggest that Net Generation students have high expectations for faculty members' technology knowledge and skill. For example 25 students at the University of Pittsburgh–Johnstown were asked to rate the following three items in terms of their importance to successful learning (scale of 1 as least important to 10 as most important):

1. The professor's experience and expertise.
2. The professor's ability to customize the class using the current technology available (for example, Courseweb, BlackBoard, and so forth).
3. The professor's ability to professionally convey lecture points using contemporary software (for example, PowerPoint).

Consistent with the anecdotal results identified above, the highest average score (8 out of 10) went to Option 1; the students view faculty expertise as paramount. However, the average scores for Options 2 (7.64) and 3 (7.68) were barely below that of Option 1. For this group of students, less than a half point separated the importance of the faculty member's general academic expertise from the importance of the ability to use technology effectively to communicate that expertise (Option 3) and customize the learning experience for students (Option 2).[6]

Student expectations regarding technology customization in the classroom are closely linked to faculty knowledge and skill. The Net Generation's views on technology in the classroom include the expectation that professors will use technology to better communicate expert knowledge. Additional feedback indicates that Net Generation students may consider a balanced use of technology in the learning environment essential. For example, members of another group of 25 University of Pittsburgh–Johnstown students were asked to rate their preference for the level of interactivity in the learning environment, with various forms of technology understood as key enablers of interactivity. The options were:

▶ 100 percent lecturing
▶ 75 percent lecturing and 25 percent interactive
▶ 50 percent lecturing and 50 percent interactive
▶ 100 percent interactive

The vote wasn't even close—all 25 students gave the highest rating to a balanced, 50-50 environment.[7]

The judicious use of PowerPoint emerged as a commonly cited component of faculty technology use from the student perspective. Victoria Kyes, a sophomore at Middle Tennessee State University, spoke for many members of the Net Generation when she stated, "Using PowerPoint increases a teacher's ability to convey essential information."[8] Lacy Kniep, a junior at Central Washington University, highlighted that it is the appropriate use of PowerPoint that helps a faculty member improve learning. From her perspective, PowerPoint is

> a software package developed to provide power to a particular point. For example, if I am the professor and I want my students to understand the definition of a distribution channel, I will place various information about distribution channels on a PowerPoint slide to drive home this particular point; however, I would not place my entire course lesson on marketing techniques on every slide.[9]

Thus, student views regarding faculty use of PowerPoint help illustrate the Net Generation's desire for the use of technology to support learning, as long as faculty members have the technological—and pedagogical—knowledge and skill necessary to use it appropriately.

It is interesting to note that the student focus on PowerPoint may signal that the Net Generation still holds relatively modest expectations for what constitutes leading-edge technology in the learning space. For example, none of the students surveyed regarding the important contributors to successful learning pushed back on the identification of BlackBoard as "current technology" and PowerPoint as "contemporary software";[10] however, many people—Net Generation and non-Net Generation alike—might consider those applications as well-established features of the current higher education landscape. It may be that Net Generation students have seen so few examples of advanced technologies applied to learning that those options do not come to mind when they think about teaching and learning with technology. The window of opportunity for colleges and universities to avoid the negative impact of increased expectations may be narrowing, however, as expressed by Nivedita Bangerjee, a junior at the University of Pittsburgh:

> I love when my profs take us through virtual 3-D programs to help explain a particular topic. As a visual learner in my major [biology], learning through seeing is very useful. With all the programs available in today's age, I think all professors should use technology in the classroom. It will only help drive home key points.[11]

Conclusion

The views expressed by the Net Generation students interviewed and surveyed for this chapter suggest that the Net Generation defines technology broadly. It is not just computers and the Internet, but whatever digital devices or applications that help a student meet his or her needs. A key component of the Net Generation's definition of technology is customization, or the ability to adapt technology to meet individual needs, rather than vice versa.

Given the technology expectations of Net Geners, it is no surprise that they may also have significant expectations regarding the use of technology to support learning. However, those expectations appear tied to faculty members and their ability to use technology correctly. In this study, PowerPoint registered as the most common example of faculty use of technology. Students praised PowerPoint's ability to help faculty members convey specific information when used appropriately. On the other hand, they expressed significant frustration with faculty members who simply transferred their lecture notes to PowerPoint slides and expected quality learning to occur.

The feedback from this select set of Net Generation students does contain some good news. It indicates that the Net Generation's general expectations regarding leading-edge technology have not fully impacted its expectations about the use of technology to support learning. This may signal a failure in the responsiveness of colleges and universities in terms of keeping pace with the rapidly changing technological landscape. However, it may also indicate that the opportunity to catch up with the Net Generation has not been lost. Higher education must continue to engage the Net Generation in a dialogue regarding its expectations about technology and learning to assess how wide the window of opportunity may still be, as well as how quickly it may be closing.

Endnotes

1. This research initiative relied on one-on-one interviews (in person and by phone), focus groups, and random polling using the University of Pittsburgh–Johnstown network in late 2004.

2. This information resulted from two focus groups at the University of Pittsburgh–Johnstown, one in late September 2004 and the other in mid-October 2004.

3. From a focus group held in late September 2004 at the University of Pittsburgh–Johnstown.

4. These quotations came from telephone interviews on October 8, 2004.

5. Data from random polling conducted October 8, 2004, using the University of Pittsburgh–Johnstown network; 25 students responded.

6. Data from random polling conducted November 5, 2004, using the University of Pittsburgh–Johnstown network; 25 students responded.

7. Data from random polling conducted October 8, 2004, using the University of Pittsburgh–Johnstown network; 25 students responded.

8. From a telephone interview with Victoria Keys on October 1, 2004.

9. From a telephone interview with Lacy Kniep on October 1, 2004.

10. From one-on-one interviews on October 11, 2004.

11. From a one-on-one interview with Nivedita Bangerjee on September 24, 2004.

About the Author

Gregory R. Roberts is the residence director of the Living/Learning Center, a 456-person residence hall at the University of Pittsburgh–Johnstown. He is a senior in business management who has served as president of Chi Lambda Tau Honorary Leadership Fraternity and on the executive board of the Alpha Kappa Psi Professional Business Fraternity, the Student Judicial Board, the Student Council of World Affairs, the Student Senate, and the Academic Integrity Review Board. Roberts has worked as a junior intern program coordinator in the White House Drug Policy Office, strategic team intern at the Department of Defense–Military Traffic Management Command, research intern for the House of Representatives Judiciary Committee, and policy intern for EDUCAUSE. Future plans include a master's in business administration and a doctorate in global studies.

CHAPTER 4

Using Technology as a Learning Tool, Not Just the Cool New Thing

Ben McNeely
North Carolina State University

I fully realized the digital age when I first spoke to my grandparents over the "talk" feature on AOL Instant Messenger. How cool is it, I thought, to have grandparents that not only have a computer, but know how to use it? What was more striking was that my grandfather, a man who never had much formal technical education, built not one, but two, computers from parts—motherboard, disk drives, hard drives, and so forth—with the help of my cousin. He has high-speed Internet access, sends and receives e-mail, burns CDs, and chats online using IM. He even built a computer for my grandmother, who uses it to check the obituaries daily on the *Winston-Salem Journal* Web site and does online jigsaw puzzles. She can no longer do real ones, as the pieces are too small for her to see and grasp.

Growing Up with Technology

In kindergarten, I was introduced to the Apple II computer. We were herded into the library and seated in front of a big-screen television. There, the librarian demonstrated the computer and its uses. She even showed us a game: The Oregon Trail—arguably the most popular computer game of our generation. It was simple, informative, and interactive. I can't tell you how many times I got my wagon stuck in the mud or how many teammates I killed off with cholera or malaria.

For my classmates and me, computers were just tools to get things done. Mastery of technological skills was a way to show we were advancing further than our classmates. In middle school, my family bought our first home computer. We also were hooked up to the Internet for the first time. It was a dial-up connection, slow compared to the instantaneous broadband speeds nowadays, but nonetheless, we were surfing the Net.

As a Boy Scout, my troop would participate in scout shows at the local mall. While other troops demonstrated traditional scouting skills, like pitching tents and lashing up towers, my troop set up a computer cluster and took digital pictures of people in the mall. Using Photoshop, we cut their images out of the pictures, placed them on backgrounds of their choosing, and gave them printouts.

My brother, a senior in high school, now uses WebAssign to complete homework problems for chemistry class. A Web-based learning application developed at North Carolina State University (NCSU), WebAssign is used across disciplines as a way for teachers to assess their students and offer supplemental information outside the lecture. He even applied to college using an online application.

As a member of the Net Generation, I have been surrounded by advances in digital technology, almost to the point where I cannot do my work as a journalist without it. In university, I have used assessment tools such as WebAssign and WebCT in classes as supplements to lecture and textbook. But now technology is advancing at such a rate that traditional ways of teaching and learning are not pushing students and teachers to their full potential. By using IT properly in the classroom, teaching and learning are enhanced and given a new dimension. Before curricula can be created to challenge the Net Generation, though, faculty must know how Net Geners learn and interact with each other, with technology, and with life in general. Remember that word—*interact.*

How the Net Gen Learns

Are you interested in knowing how Net Geners learn? Let me illustrate using my friends, me, and my grandfather.

Learning by Doing

Patrick Clarke, graphics editor for a student newspaper, sits down at a computer and launches Adobe InDesign. He opens a template for the news page and pulls in graphics, pictures, and text. He manipulates the blocks on the virtual newspaper page, moving back and forth between two other Adobe products, Photoshop and Illustrator. By the time the page is sent to the printer for printing, the elements on the page would have been manipulated, edited, and reedited at least a dozen times. Patrick is a creative and dynamic designer, but he is not a design major—he's in computer engineering.

Chris Reynolds is a business major and wants to open a music store when he graduates. In his spare time, he is a DJ musician. He spins and mixes his own beats, using a computer, sound-editing software, turntables, and a keyboard. He teamed up with a friend to make a how-to video on spinning. They used digital video and professional editing software to create the video. Because he is a DJ, he worries about court cases involving the music industry. A recent case where the use of "sampling" was ruled illegal hit him hard, as sampling is widely used by DJs when they create their music.

Jake Seaton is a big arts and entertainment fan. He lives and breathes for music, movies, and anything Hollywood. He can tell you about film and music history and can quote even the most obscure lines from zombie movies (his favorite). He also is up-to-date on the latest in computer and console gaming. He chose a multidisciplinary degree in music journalism and has taken distance-education courses. In high school he won a state architecture award and has taught himself to use Photoshop and InDesign.

These are representatives of the Net Generation. They all use computers in their class work and in their hobbies. They have a wide range of interests, outside their chosen area of study. They are not locked into one thing, although all are highly motivated and pursue their interests with passion. They use the latest in technology, whether cell phones, computers, PDAs, MP3 players, or digital cameras. They expect things to work properly and work fast. They get bored if not challenged properly, but when challenged, they excel in creative and innovative ways. They learn by doing, not by reading the instruction manual or listening to lectures. These are the learners that faculty must reach.

When I first came to NCSU in 2000, I came to a public university dedicated to technology. There were numerous computer labs all over campus, and professors actively used assessment tools like WebAssign and WebCT in their classes. In an experimental psychology class, I used SAS statistical software to crunch data I collected from experiments. I used online message boards to post ideas and criticism in my opinion/editorial writing class.

In my technical document design class, I experienced the best use of technology in a class: hands-on, experimental, and interactive. This course covered the fundamental designs of technical documents: instruction manuals, memos, resumes, and so forth. Taught in a computer lab, the class sat one student to a computer. We learned to use Adobe Pagemaker, the most popular desktop publishing program at the time. With basic exercises from the instructor and trial-and-error assignments with broad guidelines, I learned not only how to use the program but also design fundamentals—by doing the actual design, not by reading it out of a book.

This is how the Net Generation learns: by doing. Many of my peers have emerged as the leaders of my generation. They will go on to become the leaders of our nation in many different roles—politicians, business executives, artisans, scientists, and journalists. Much like how we learn by doing, we lead by doing; that is, by practicing the art and science of our chosen paths.

Human Interaction

Generational differences in learning techniques are apparent in how people of different ages approach technology. It has been said that we, the Net Generation, are closer to our grandparents—the Greatest Generation—in our work ethic and optimism about the future than to our parents' generation. But how we approach problems is totally different.

My grandfather is a tinkerer—he figures out how things work by trial and error. He is very mechanically inclined and has spent his life working on many kinds of machinery. But when it comes to computers, he approaches it one thing at a time, step by step.

Every time I come home from college, he has a new problem for me to fix on his computer. He will fiddle and fiddle with a program until he is befuddled. Usually it is because he missed a step somewhere. If I show him and write down steps, he takes the information I've given him and works it out for himself. Even though the computer's parts are more complex than a carburetor or gear drives, the skills my grandfather used to put it together came from decades of tinkering with machines. He still uses a step-by-step thinking process used in mechanical arts to figure out software and basic functions like e-mail and Internet browsing.

Similarly, Patrick sits down with a new piece of design software and tinkers with its features. "Usually, if it is from a software company I know, I can figure out a new program easily," he said. He has fundamental knowledge about how certain software should work. By tinkering, he can figure out shortcuts and pick up the gist of the program quickly.

Even though Patrick uses step-by-step problem-solving skills, he also is pulling information from his own memory, experience, and base knowledge to master the new program. Patrick has had almost two decades of experience working with computers—almost to the point that it is second nature. My grandfather, on the other hand, has only had about five years of computer experience. Because they have been wired since grade school, Net Geners are likely to grasp technological concepts faster.

But the same "tinkering" practice applies in the classroom: doing hands-on work and working in groups, students get a better grasp of concepts the professor is trying to teach. Using technology only enhances the hands-on experience; it does not—and cannot—replace human interaction. There's that word again.

Interaction, Not Isolation

Distance education is the popular option for nontraditional learners. With many traditional industries such as manufacturing and textiles going offshore, 20-year veterans of the workplace are being laid off and going back to school to learn a new trade. Distance education—through Internet and video courses—helps those who have to work a job and go to school at the same time better schedule their learning opportunities. These people are usually older, in their 30s or 40s, and are learning to use technology, like the Internet and computers, while training for a new career. In theory, the Net Generation should learn better through Internet courses because they have been surrounded by computers all their lives and know how to use the technology already.

Just the opposite is true. Net Geners like the social interaction that comes with being in class with their peers. While they may use technology in their daily lives, relationships are a driving force in the learning process.

Jake Seaton, as a part of his multidisciplinary degree, took a video course through distance education—and didn't like it. "I needed the structure of going to class. I would go to my other classes and then come home and have another class to watch on TV," he said. "I didn't like it. At the end of the day, I wanted to be done, not have to work at a class at home."

This is typical among Net Geners: learning through social interaction is important. Feedback from the professor is vital, and working in groups is the norm. Arman Assa, MBA candidate and president of PackMUG—the Mac Users Group at NCSU—said that learning technology has not advanced enough to replace the social interaction in the classroom. "Historically, communal learning has always been the most effective way for educating the student and generating thought-provoking discussion in class. I don't believe technology has reached a point where we can duplicate that effectively on a computer," Assa said. "Some instructors argue that chat rooms, message boards, and instant messaging are good substitutes, but they are by no means replacements for the exchange of tacit knowledge.

"Does this mean that interactive technology is bad for the classroom? No. It means that it should simply augment what is already there," Assa continued. "For instance, one of my human resource classes in the MBA [program] has regular classroom discussion, but the instructor augments it with message board interaction. It was a very effective tool for helping introverts who don't talk in class to join the discussion."

Cut-and-Paste Culture

Technology is everywhere. Net Geners cannot remember a time in their education where a computer was not used for some learning experience. Because of this "tech-savviness," traditional educational practices and ethics are coming into question. Cheating, for example, always a major academic infraction, is on the rise on college campuses—and technology is helping with cheating. Talk to students and any one of them will tell you that cheating is prevalent and part of the culture, especially in technical disciplines. That is, if you use the strict definition of cheating.

NCSU uses WebCT and WebAssign extensively. Since a faculty member cannot directly supervise students and only the answers are recorded in WebAssign, not how the student came up with them, students often work together on their assignments. But students must submit their own answers. In computer engineering, students must write a program and submit it as a part of learning different coding languages. Patrick says these programs are worked over with a fine-tooth comb. "The TAs and instructors run the programs line-by-line to see if any code was copied," he said. "There may be opportunity to cheat, but you will get caught." He adds that there is not much opportunity to cheat during exams.

Plagiarism is the academic infraction of choice. How can it not be, though? Information is easily available from the Internet, especially from sites like Wikipedia. Old term papers are being sold online. Because the Internet provides easy information fast, the temptation to click "copy/paste" and pull in quotes from a Web site without attribution is great. But students still get caught because faculty members can search for familiar phrases or quotes to root out plagiarism.

Cheating is on the rise in universities. Is it because students aren't learning the material? Or is it because their learning and work ethic are so different from their professors that working together to solve a problem is no longer that serious an infraction? Remember that teamwork has been emphasized to Net Geners since the first day of kindergarten. Businesses are also looking for graduates who can work effectively in teams.

Based on the very social nature of Net Geners and the tremendous amount of information available to students these days at the touch of a button, the traditional definition of cheating is changing. How faculty assess students is changing as well. Faculty still give written exams (in English, it is still a certainty), but they must be ever more vigilant to catch the cheating student. Cell phones and text messaging have allowed students to text back and forth between each other, conferring through the airwaves on exam questions. Because of emerging technologies, faculty are having to adapt their classes and how they assess students in order to uphold academic integrity.

Challenges for Higher Education

So what do Net Geners want from learning technology? Interactivity—whether it is with a computer, a professor, or a classmate. They want it; they crave it. Traditional lectures are not fulfilling the learning potential of typical students today. Distance education and online courses don't work well with Net Geners—the social component of learning is required. As technology in the classroom progresses, more and more students are going to demand it be included. This will pose challenges, though.

Funding

First, technology costs money. What else is new? Faculty members can receive grants for using technology in the classroom and developing new learning technologies. This is fine on the department level, but for a university to implement learning technology on a massive scale will take an act of Congress. State legislatures are listening and meeting the basic technological needs for public universities. But it takes bond referendums for state-of-the-art classrooms in order to implement technology on a university level. And bonds are paid by the taxpayers because the referendums are voted upon by the taxpayers. No vote, no bonds. So it goes, I suppose.

Access and Skills

Second, students need to be able to use the technology. In North Carolina, students must pass a computer competency test in the eighth grade before being promoted to high school. They are tested on the most fundamental computer skills: word processing, creating a spreadsheet, using Web browsers, and e-mail. Beyond that, students either pick up skills on their own, take a class outside the primary educational setting—say at a community college or library—or don't learn at all. Users—even Net Geners—will only learn so much when operating a computer. The average student will use a computer for homework, online chatting, checking e-mail, and surfing the Internet. The more advanced users will know how to write a simple Web page, update a ready-made blog site, or download music and movies—perhaps illegally—and burn CDs. But for the most part, users have no knowledge about how to set up a local area network or how to troubleshoot their own computer for minor problems.

On a more fundamental level, there is such a thing as a "digital divide." Technology is expensive, and the only way for some school systems to afford computer labs is if computers are donated. These computers often are refurbished and several years old. While they are useful in teaching fundamental skills, like those tested for in the North Carolina standardized computer test, they will not be able to support the latest technology. Once a computer or software is released on the market, it is usually replaced in 18 months. How can a Pentium II running Windows 95 properly prepare a high school or college student for the working world, which uses Windows XP? It can't. These computers ideally should be relatively up to date and able to provide students with not only fundamental skills but also the chance to learn intermediate and advanced skills as the "cool new thing" rolls out of the factory.

There are students who cannot afford a personal computer in their homes and must rely on technology in their schools or local libraries. There are even students whose first real experience with technology will come when they go to college. How can they possibly survive in the high-tech college world if they don't know the basics?

Colleges need to teach students computer skills beyond fundamentals. Skills such as digital document archiving, Web page design using Dreamweaver or Flash, setting up wireless networks, and using a firewall are quickly becoming the norm, where in the past they were considered advanced knowledge. Even basic upkeep and troubleshooting is still left up to tech-support hotlines, often located halfway around the world. These are the skills students need to know to be competitive. Many colleges offer introductory courses in computer science that are available as electives in many disciplines. Updating the intro course curricula—or even the state standardized tests—will go a long way in fostering computer skills.

While usability has gotten better as operating systems have progressed, you still hear comments like "I can't use a Mac, I use Windows," or "I only know how to word process on my computer, I can't use MS Word on a Mac." Even though the Net Generation learns quickly, the old adage "You can't teach an old dog new tricks" still applies. The inability to move between platforms—and the lack of accelerated fundamental skills—is a major hindrance to learning technology. The workforce is so competitive that the difference in knowing how to set up a simple network and basic computer troubleshooting over knowing just document preparation could mean a job down the road. It will be a challenge to overcome, but it isn't impossible.

Interaction

Third, technology must be relevant and interactive to the coursework. A faculty member who uses PowerPoint in a lecture is not using technology interactively. Students need a practical use for technology, whether to manipulate data or to explore the inner recesses of the human body without cutting up cadavers. Students need to communicate quickly with each other, but in a centralized manner. That is why message boards are great. Members-only message boards allow students and faculty to communicate with each other. Plus, faculty members can use the course lockers during lectures and provide information outside lecture for students to explore at their own pace.

Relevance

Fourth, technology must be used for a practical purpose—that is, taking the fundamentals and technology learned over a semester and applying it to a final project, where creativity and uniqueness is required and rewarded. In my technical document design class, we had to create a useful technical document: write the text and design a technical document using Pagemaker. My group designed an instruction booklet for a video game. Chris Reynolds used his sound-editing software to help a friend with a music project. They wrote a short piece of music, recorded and edited it, and burned it to a CD for the professor to evaluate. Chris was excited because it gave him a chance to "play" with his software. While he doesn't use his music software in his business courses, he is learning skills that could be marketable after college. Plus, his friend got an "A" on the project.

Using technology for some practical purpose, and not for the sake of using technology, must be the clear objective. "Students are often the guinea pigs in

'IT-enabled' classes as faculty test out whether the latest innovations actually help learning," Assa said. "Some faculty, in an effort to use the latest buzzword or receive the next big grant, are testing technology simply for the sake of technology, rather than using technology as a tool for learning, such as paper and pencils. When people focus too much on technology, they lose sight of the true purpose of technology, which is to facilitate learning in the classroom."

The Next Generation

Turn on the TV on Saturday mornings and watch cartoons for an hour. Count how many commercials there are for interactive toys for toddlers and young children. Even babies have "learning centers," with flashing colored lights and music. Whether or not the "Mozart Effect"—the theory that musical stimulation increases IQ scores—exists, parents have latched onto the idea that it does, and toy makers are obliging and capitalizing on their belief.

These new learners are exposed to technology—even on a rudimentary scale—from nearly the womb onward. My mother's kindergarten class uses the computer for learning games that reinforce counting and spelling skills. A quarter of the population has a computer at home, and many more have access to a computer—and the number continues to grow every year.

The next generation of learners will meet and surpass the Net Generation's expectations of educational standards. Those standards will only be met if faculty and administrators today establish the infrastructure of learning technology in the classroom. And not just using PowerPoint in the lecture hall, but understanding how technology can be used to reach the most people in an effective way. It will take great effort on both sides—students and faculty alike—to learn and use technology effectively. But the benefits will be well worth the effort.

About the Author

Ben McNeely is the managing editor of Technician, the student newspaper at North Carolina State University. A senior in English, Ben hosts a talk show on WKNC-FM and also contributes to the yearbook and to the online magazine Americana. As an officer in PackMUG, the Macintosh Users Group at NC State, he was instrumental in bringing Steve Wozniak, cofounder of Apple Computer, to campus as a speaker. McNeely, an aspiring journalist and Eagle Scout, is interested in technology's impact on today's society and its implications for the future.

CHAPTER 5

The Student's Perspective

Carie Windham
North Carolina State University

Introduction

We sat across from one another, he in his cracked leather desk chair and me in a wooden chair taken from the hallway. He leaned back, arms crossed, eyes peering over wire-framed glasses. I strummed my fingers nervously on the chipped wood of the chair's arm.

"I e-mailed you the proposal last week," I said. "I don't understand why the topic change came as a surprise."

"I didn't get it," he said simply.

"I sent it a week ago. Maybe it came back; I don't know."

"I'll be honest; I don't check my e-mail."

I paused.

"Ever?" I asked.

"Ever. Can't stand it."

"Right. Should I have called?"

"I don't check voicemail either."

My brow furrowed as I contemplated my next move.

"So how exactly do you stay in touch with your students between classes?" I asked.

"Well, I expect that they'll hunt me down on campus if they need anything."

I sank back in the chair and stared at his desk, scattered with haphazard Post-Its and torn notebook paper. A cassette-tape answering machine gathered dust in the corner. An overstuffed planner bulged near my seat. I thought of my own desk at home—neat, sterile, a laptop and a Palm Pilot.

"So you're serious? No e-mail and no voicemail? Do you even use the Web?" He just smiled.

Though we sat just four feet away from one another, the distance suddenly felt light years apart. I would find out, in subsequent conversations, that my professor—a relic of the Greatest Generation—did, indeed, surf the Web when it was necessary. But he preferred the newspaper over CNN.com, the weatherman over WeatherBug, and face-to-face visits over e-mail exchanges. He dusted off journals from the 1980s and flipped through their pages, and, if you asked him, he actually knew how to load one of those microfiche machines on the second floor of the university library. He represented, for me, a world I could scarcely remember—a world before driving directions on MapQuest, book buying on Amazon.com, and making plans on Instant Messenger—a world when tasks were managed one by one instead of all at once on multiple Web browser windows.

I am a member of the Net Generation. I've surfed the Web since the age of 11, and it has increasingly taken over every facet of my personal and academic existence. I can barely recall making plans before the advent of IM and have rarely attended a campus meeting without setting it up over e-mail first. I get my news, my weather, my directions—even my clothes—from the Web. And, as my peers and I continue to flood the gates of the nation's colleges and universities, I am a puzzle to many of the faculty and administrators who will try to teach me. They will either try too hard to transform education into the virtual language I understand or too little to accommodate for the differences between us. Just as with past generations, however, all that is required is a basic understanding of what being a Net Gener really means and how it translates to the classroom.

Meet Generation Y Not

It's easy to call myself a Net Gener—to talk about the pains of growing old in the Net Generation, to trade glib remarks with my peers about those fossils who grew up tied to their landline existence. Defining what all of it means, however, is another story.

As a future historian, I've learned that everything in time must, eventually, fit neatly into a series of ages, categories, or generations: the Baby Boomers, the Bronze Age, the Silent Generation, the Renaissance. So, naturally, countless hours of history lecture were dedicated—in my head—to the role that my generation would play in future history texts. Would students in 2105 find us materialistic? Self-absorbed? Would we be defined by September 11 or the War on Terrorism? Quite frankly, I didn't know.

Luckily, where my history musings fell short, the social sciences dedicated countless hours and volumes to dissection. And fortunately, the prognosis was good. Though the youngest among our ranks are barely teenagers and the oldest have just entered the workforce, it seems posterity will forever remember the Net Generation as the Next Greatest Generation. Or, if we fail to measure up, the Generation That Could Have Been the Next Greatest.

According to Neil Howe and William Strauss, authors of *Millennials Rising: The Next Greatest Generation,*[1] my friends and I are nothing like our immediate predecessors in Generation X. We are academically driven, family oriented, and racially and ethnically diverse. We are committed to telling the truth and traditional values, yet we refuse to accept our elders' speeches or sermons at face value. We are not politically active, but community centered. We truly believe we have the tools and the desire to solve the lingering problems that our parents' generation has left behind.

In my own experience, both as a Net Gener and as a student leader and journalist at North Carolina State University, Howe and Strauss and their colleagues are not entirely off base. But the generalities require greater exploration, especially in the role they will play for college faculty and administrators in determining how best to reach the next generation of learners.

Driven to Succeed

Net Geners, for the most part, are not just driven by the notion of achievement—they are consumed by it. Drilled by guidance counselors, parents, and teachers about the importance of attending college in determining our own self-worth and success potential, the race for the top began for some of us in middle school. We quickly learned that a 4.0 grade point average is no longer sufficient to get a foot in the door of a good school and that every applicant would be able to claim honor roll as an achievement. To distinguish ourselves, therefore, we load our schedules with honors, advanced placement, and international baccalaureate coursework. We take classes from community colleges. A portion of us even enter college with sophomore standing.

And achievement is no longer limited to the classroom. College-bound students learn early that extracurricular activities, leadership development, athletics, and community service are not only to be enjoyed but exploited. In a world where high school transcripts increasingly look more uniform in their perfection, a role as president of SADD—Students Against Destructive Decisions—might be enough to tip the scales in your favor. And you know it.

Even at the university level, we feel pressure that our degree simply will not be enough. We've watched the economy falter and jobs disappear. We sat through the dot-com bust (feeling fortunate we were still in college, at least) and heard analysts share horror stories about students with four-year degrees and nowhere to go. Those fears have driven Net Geners outside the normal confines of the classroom and made them desperate to add both value and experience to their degrees. Internships are taken during the summer, co-ops throughout the year. Clubs are joined and community service embraced. It is enough, by junior year, to leave us wondering at what point all the preparation for life ends and enjoyment actually begins.

For college administrators and faculty, it means that each class of incoming freshmen will be more stressed than the last. The average college-aged Net Geners sitting in the back of the classroom will have more than the weight of a 15-hour course load on their shoulders. Instead, most will be juggling a position or role in a campus organization, a part-time internship, an independent research project, and applications for summer jobs and graduate school. They will be masters of multitasking and—by the time they graduate—will leave with a suitcase of experience and an ulcer lying in wait.

Driven by Compassion

Our capacity for community service and engagement is not entirely tied to our desire to succeed, however. From a very early age, my peers and I have been exposed to opportunities for service and examples of servant leaders in the community and in history. Community service is not just an opportunity to the Net Generation, it is a responsibility.

The average American high school encourages community service through service clubs, service awards, service requirements, or service-learning courses. Religious groups and national humanitarian organizations, bolstered by the falling prices of international travel, are taking youth on more trips around the world to teach the importance of a "global citizen" and a dedication to worldwide service. The nation and the media consistently praise and hold up examples of youth in service. It has become increasingly "cool" to give back.

Beyond high school, colleges and universities have increasingly become community centers for civic responsibility and community giving. Beyond a host of service organizations, most universities have departments on campus to coordinate service projects, plan service trips for extended university breaks, and support service organizations. Other student bodies, like that at NC State, coordinate mass days of service that often draw thousands of volunteers to work with service groups around the community.

This acceptance of and emphasis on social responsibility has also changed the way the Net Generation looks at careers. Priority within our ranks is placed less on monetary value and fame than happiness and "doing something good." We join programs like the Peace Corps, AmeriCorps, and Teach for America in record numbers and repeatedly express an interest in a career that will—somehow—impact the future and other people.

Driven by Hope

It is true, as Howe and Strauss indicated, that the Net Generation is an overly optimistic generation. We have not seen the corruption of power or felt the fear of the Cold War. Instead, we've watched technology solve problems and alleviate the rigors and stresses of our everyday lives. Just as society often views technology as a vessel for progress, we see ourselves as the future navigators.

There is an unspoken sentiment within our ranks that the problems of the world have largely been deposited at our feet. With the hole in the ozone layer growing, peace shattering, and disease raging, many of us feel that older generations have simply stepped aside to make room for our ingenuity and creativity. And, largely, we feel that we are up to that challenge. In our eyes, our technological savvy makes us smarter, easily adaptable, and more likely to employ technology to solve the problems of past and present generations.

Father Google and Mother IM

Perhaps the greatest indicator of the Net Generation, however, has less to do with our habits and values than our namesake: the Internet. I met the Internet for the first time from my second-row seat in Mrs. Kingsley's fourth grade class. We sat transfixed as a golden highway unfurled across the TV screen in a 30-minute film about the future of society. Soon, a voice promised, we would be able to talk to children across the world, access medical advice from our home computers, and search libraries across the country. The possibilities would be endless, the vaults of knowledge limitless.

After class, two friends and I stood in awe at the single PC in the back of the classroom. From that little box, we thought, we would soon access the world.

One friend picked up a yellow cable from the back. "Do you think this is it? Do you think this is the highway?"

I rolled my eyes. "They said the highway isn't complete yet. It's like cable—you probably have to wait until they dig the highway in your neighborhood," I remarked.

It took years before I realized that the approaching Information Superhighway was nothing more than an interconnected system of networks. It would take many more before I realized the way the Internet had permeated almost every facet of my life.

Technological Masters

Growing up alongside the wheels of Web-based progress has instilled a feeling within the Net Generation that technological understanding is a necessity for current life and future existence. We cannot succeed in this world, we reason, without an understanding and command of technological advances. This feeling is reinforced by the emphasis on computer literacy in public school curriculums and the nagging feeling that few jobs in the future will not rely on some form of computer technology.

To keep pace, Net Geners have become some of the most technologically adept members of society. Our cell phones often serve as Web browsers, digital phones, and game consoles. We keep our schedules and addresses in Palm Pilots and our music in MP3 players. We program our televisions to record movies while we watch a game on another channel. We strive to stay ahead of the technology curve in ways that often exhaust older generations.

This drive to keep pace with current trends is not fueled by society's ability to educate and teach these technologies. Instead, we are a generation of learners by exploration. My first Web site, for example, was constructed before I had any concept of HTML or Java. I simply experimented with the commands until the pieces fit together. I have installed every addition to my computer myself, often with just my instinct and eyesight to guide me. Likewise, many of my peers rarely pick up the instruction pack to learn programming or a technique. Instead, spurred by our youthful exploration of the Internet, we tend to learn things ourselves, to experiment with new technology until we get it right, and to build by touch rather than tutorial.

Filling the Attention Deficit: Reaching the Net Generation in a Traditional Classroom

In middle school, my second-period health class took a break from memorizing the food groups to learn healthy study habits. Flipping idly past images of red-shirted, blue-panted stick figures seated upright in desk chairs in our text, we were told that the best way to study was to isolate ourselves from the television, the tape player, and the busy sidewalks outside the window. We were to clear a nice study corner with a comfy chair, good lighting, and ample work space.

If Harcourt Brace were to evaluate my college study space, it would—no doubt—be the antithesis of healthy study habits pictured in one of their textbooks. There would be no clear desk, no silent cocoon, no harsh lighting. Instead, *Law and Order* reruns would be playing in the background. To my left, a trail of jumbled cords would stretch from my bedroom to a laptop on the couch cushion. My IM buddy list would be minimized on the screen, but noise alerts would be turned on to tell me when friends signed on or off the Internet. A collage of browser windows would remain open, one directed to CNN.com to read the day's news between chapters, another to my e-mail to know exactly when the next piece of mail arrived, and then another to Google, in case the text raised any questions. Somewhere in the middle would be me and a history textbook turned to page 149.

My study space—which could be found in the average dorm room suite—is characteristic of my life. With information and accessibility lying effortless at my fingertips, I have grown accustomed to juggling multiple tasks at once, at lightning speed. In the average online conversation with a friend, for instance, I am likely to be talking to two others, shopping online at Barnes & Noble, laughing out loud at *Friends* reruns, and printing off notes from a chemistry lecture. It is only in the classroom, therefore, that my mind is trained on one subject. To keep it in place requires some flexibility and creativity on the part of the professor and an understanding of the basic principles that guide the Net Generation.

Interaction

Though online communication is often seen as the opposite of personal and the antithesis of contact, for the Net Gen it is certainly not seen as such. Instead, the Internet has become a vehicle for interaction. It allows us the opportunity to communicate with friends, to participate in chat room discussions, and to stream video from around the world. In short, it allows interaction with a variety of people and material.

In the classroom, we crave much of the same. An online society may increase the means of communication, but it does not diminish the human need for connection. Instead, many Net Geners often leave the computer screen craving actual conversation and interaction with their classmates. To capitalize on this need, faculty should encourage interaction both within and outside the classroom. Group work should be emphasized alongside required one-on-one meetings with professors. Students should be given the opportunity to interact with faculty and researchers outside the confines of the curriculum and to develop meaningful relationships with them.

Exploration

Just as we want to learn about the Web by clicking our own path through cyberspace, we want to learn about our subjects through exploration. It is not enough for us to accept a professor's word. Instead, we want to be challenged to reach our own conclusions and find our own results. Lessons last longer, in our minds, if we understand the relevant steps to reach them.

Therefore, a need to explore is implicit in our desire to learn. Rather than discussing bias, for instance, a journalism professor once asked my class to analyze several articles and discuss their diction. We arrived at the conclusion that the authors' bias was implicit in their work with little direction. We left class that day with both a sense of accomplishment and a deeper understanding of the journalistic themes the professor had hoped to explore.

Relevancy

In a world where technologies change daily and graduates armed with four-year degrees are entering the workforce in record numbers, there is an increasing fear among the Net Generation that a four-year degree will be neither relevant nor sufficient preparation when it becomes time to enter the work force. Consequently, students are consistently looking for practical applications of their studies in a real-world context.

Establishing relevancy in the classroom is not as simple as it sounds. It does not equate to presenting a laundry list of future occupations or examples of a field in the news. Instead, more and more curricula are focusing on the notion of extension, or applying the lessons learned in the classroom to real-life problems, institutions, or organizations in the community. For the Net Generation, such curricula speak to two of its values: community service and interaction. Extension is an opportunity to help a community while learning the real-world application of taught material and acquiring relevant skills and experience.

As a history major, for example, I spent a semester researching a cultural heritage site on the North Carolina coast. Beyond simply teaching documentary skills, the experience helped glue together the pieces of four years of courses to demonstrate how my degree would eventually translate into marketable skills.

Multimedia

Turn on the nightly news and it is clear that no medium is one-dimensional. Prose is supplemented by song. Photographs are accompanied by video. Issues are even turned into online polls and discussions. For the Net Gen, nearly every part of life is presented in multimedia format. Even my study space, as I detailed before, is a hodgepodge of digital, audio, and text information. To keep our attention in the classroom, therefore, a similar approach is needed. Faculty must toss aside the dying notion that a lecture and subsequent reading assignment are enough to teach the lesson. Instead, the Net Generation responds to a variety of media, such as television, audio, animation, and text. The use of a singular unit should be kept short and alternating, producing a class period as diverse in structure as it is in content.

In my four years of courses, the best example of a multimedia classroom comes from a three-hour seminar I participated in on the Vietnam War. Though the prospect of spending three hours in the same cramped classroom was daunting, the professor employed a variety of media to keep our attention. Class began with a song from the period, and film clips were used throughout to illustrate key themes or replicate events. The lecture alternated discussion interspersed with photographs, tables, and graphics. As a result, most of us were more alert and interested in this class than in previous 90-minute classes, despite the considerably longer class time.

Instruction

It's easy to deduce that all this technology has made the Net Generation lazy. We don't pick up dictionaries anymore—we go to Dictionary.com. We don't walk to the library—we search online journal databases. We wouldn't know an archive if we stumbled into it on the way to the fax machine. Though the Internet is attempting to phase out these standard methods of research, they are important, nonetheless.

The average college student, however, has no clue how to navigate or investigate the modern library. Instead, students increasingly rely on Web sites and Internet archives for information—increasing the likelihood that they will stumble across and cite false or incorrect information. For those reasons, modern classrooms, faculty, and libraries must still teach and demonstrate basic research skills such as finding journals, evaluating primary sources, digging through archives, or even perusing library shelves. Today's students may believe they can learn solely on the Internet, but they cannot.

A Virtual Education: Crafting the Online Classroom

Philosophy: my nemesis. For five semesters I had cleverly evaded its call—pointedly skipping over the requirement with the dim hope that a registration glitch might fill the spot without my actual participation. But as graduation grew closer, the empty spot next to its name hadn't budged. So, with a sinking feeling of dread, I decided to budge instead.

My only consolation, as I dutifully joined the roll for Philosophy 205, was that Introduction to Philosophy was finally being offered in a Web-based course. I had never tried an entirely "virtual" classroom before, thinking such endeavors were better suited to distance education students or those with full-time jobs. But philosophy? That could be an exception.

The class was set up with sincere trust and respect for the student. Reading assignments from an assigned text were listed on the course Web site. For grading, we were asked to periodically turn in homework questions from the text and to take occasional quizzes and exams. Every exam was open note and open book with a three-hour window of time. The homework was loosely graded.

For the first exam, I read every chapter and highlighted the notes from the study guide. I finished the test in less than 30 minutes. For the second, with the full weight of a 16-hour semester upon me, I did the reading but skipped the highlighting. I finished in an hour. For the next exam, with two test experiences under my fingertips, I skipped reading altogether and simply searched for the answers in the text. The test took nearly two hours. Each time, the grade was the same. By the end of the semester, I couldn't tell the theory of relativity from utilitarianism. But speed reading? I was a master.

The professor had assumed, while crafting his course, that putting philosophy on the Web would give his students more flexibility to shape their own learning experience. We could read at our own pace. We could respond to message threads at our leisure. We could even take tests with the full support of our text, our notes, and—in my case—our quick darting eyes.

What he hadn't expected, perhaps, is that the advent of the Internet and the opportunity of the online classroom had not diminished the need for traditional educational principles like discipline, engagement, and interaction. Instead, my online course had turned learning into exactly what I despised—a one-dimensional exercise in learning and regurgitating facts.

Take, as a counterexample, a course in Latin American History offered on the Web. Like my philosophy course, we were asked to read from an assigned text.

Instead of quizzes and tests, we were asked to periodically turn in essays and papers. The main difference, however, was that each week we were required to participate in online discussions relevant to our text or reading found on the Web. Some weeks we were required to simply post our own responses. Other times, part of the class was to counter the arguments made by another part. During some weeks, we were to evaluate and critique our classmates' arguments. Though it seemed effortless at the time, the exercises were a thinly veiled attempt to hold us accountable for the reading and to engage us in the material.

As technology improves and the "virtual classroom" becomes more popular, there is a tendency on the part of institutions and students to turn to online courses. They save resources and can accommodate more students. They are more flexible for busy schedules or commuters. But as these examples demonstrate, the online classroom must be created with the same care and expectations as the traditional one.

Students still crave interaction with their fellow students, even if they cannot see them. Otherwise, the online classroom seems cold and disconnected. To keep students engaged in the material and passionate about the subject matter, therefore, the professor must find a way for the students to interact with one another. Discussion forums are a natural solution and can be facilitated by posing questions for students to respond to or as simply a "free for all" for student discussion. The professor must be an active participant and facilitator, however, or students will diminish the exercises' importance. Another solution is virtual group work. Asking students to collaborate on projects or assignments forces them to meet and exchange ideas with their peers and fulfills their need for group interaction without actually meeting in a classroom.

Students also want diversity in both content and content media, a desire that should not be stifled by the assumed one-dimensionality of online coursework. While most online courses create a class Web site for posting assignments and logging in to take tests, these sites could be used as portals for multimedia exploration. One of the great benefits of the Web is its use of multiple media formats: users can stream video, listen to audio, and peruse photographic archives. It is important, therefore, to incorporate a variety of formats into the online classroom to keep content fresh and to appeal to the sensory habits of a variety of learners.

The Web-based course, unlike the traditional classroom, is also at an advantage visually. Net Gen learners are more likely to respond to visual images than a form of straight text. From childhood, we are bombarded by images on television, on billboards, in magazines, and on the Web. A quick survey of newspaper evolution reveals the increased reliance on images—rather than text—to tell the story over time, and Net Gen learners have evolved alongside this phenomenon. To teach the Net Generation, therefore, requires the use of visual images in conjunction with text, a feat easily accomplished through animation and diagrams on the Web.

It's a common misconception that students take online courses to avoid the rigor and workload of a traditional classroom. In many cases, that's simply not true. When students choose an online classroom, they still want to be challenged. They still want exploration. And they still want creativity. Net Gen learners are not likely to excel in an environment where they are simply handed material and expected to recite it. Instead, most log on to online courses because they despise this traditional format of lecture and regurgitate. Instead, they feel they learn better in an environment where they can teach themselves. With that in mind, the online professor must find ways to offer students a method of exploration and research within the curriculum. Students might be asked, for example, to abandon the course Web page to search an archive or journal for information on their own. They might be asked to weave current events within the context of the taught material. Or they might employ their own technical savvy to construct research Web pages or blogs.

The simple rule is engagement—moving students beyond being mere participants in the class to become active learners and discoverers.

E-Life: The Net Gen on Campus

"Do you have a check? You could pay in a check."

I scratched my head as I stood at the counter. Check... Check... I vaguely remembered seeing an unused checkbook tossed carelessly in the trunk of my car that morning. But even if I could locate it, I couldn't be sure it was in the right sequence. Or that I could even remember how to use the darn thing.

"Are you sure you can't take a debit card? Or maybe a credit card? I have Visa. Or Mastercard. Is that better?"

She smiled sympathetically and pointed to the sign behind her: CASH AND CHECKS ONLY.

I sighed and grabbed my application from the countertop. I needed to add money to my campus account but didn't have the energy to walk across campus to the ATM or to fish my checkbook from my trunk. Dejected, I pushed my way out the door. Just as I left, I heard familiar words from the counter.

"Cash? I have a debit card. Or could you take my credit card?"

It should be noted, in our defense, that most Net Geners use technology to navigate even the most mundane chores in life. Thanks to online banking, we no longer balance our checkbooks. Because of ATM cards, few of us know what that memo line on checks is even for. We pay bills online. We order books online. If it were a possibility, we would probably order our pizza online. The thought of doing anything in person, therefore, is not just scary, sometimes it's downright confusing.

Each new class of Net Geners will have technology to thank for removing one more obstacle from their everyday lives. My older sister, for instance, remembers sleeping outside the registrar's office to be first in line to register for courses during her sophomore year. I have only registered for courses online—in my pajamas—from the comfort of my dorm room. As technology replaces these exercises in our daily life, we expect our colleges and universities to follow suit.

To make campus and student services more accessible and accommodating for the Net Generation, university staff and administrators must first realize the depth to which technology has revolutionized daily life for us:

▸ **Plastic or plastic?** Cash is disappearing rapidly from our wallets, to be replaced by credit and debit cards. We use these cards for purchases in stores, to pick up tabs in restaurant, and even to swipe at drive-through restaurants. We pay our bills with them and do our shopping with them. In many cases, in fact, students will simply avoid establishments that refuse to accept them.

▸ **For customer service, press Ctrl+Alt+Delete.** Thanks to the marathon waiting times for customer service hotlines and the lack of tasteful elevator music, the Net Gen would much rather log on than call to fix problems or seek advice. Surfing Internet help lines for assistance solves two of our problems: speed and accessibility. It's much faster to find the solution in an online troubleshooter, oftentimes, than to wait for an operator to read from a textbook. It's also more likely that online help can be found any day, at any time. There are no closing times online and no hours of operation.

▸ **Dear Dr. Jones.** It's not that we can't use the telephone or find an office, it's that it's just so much more difficult. Using e-mail to set up meetings, ask simple questions, or send in excuses for absences has become so commonplace in the modern classroom that few students turn to anything else. E-mail is less personal and less frightening. You don't have to worry about saying the wrong thing or getting flustered. You can carefully craft your message and spell-check the result. It's much easier to take risks and push the envelope without hearing disapproval or confronting anger. For that reason, the Net Gen will turn to e-mail for everything from job inquiries and applications to meetings with administrators. (As a former college editor, I was shocked to learn that my reporters had even resorted to conducting interviews entirely over e-mail.)

▶ **ATTN: School's Closed.** When breaking news hits, students in the Net Generation are more likely to log on to a news Web site for the latest information than to turn on CNN. When we get dressed in the morning, we check WeatherBug or the local television's Web site for the day's weather prediction rather than wait for a forecast on the morning news. When we need information, we expect it immediately and seek it ourselves.

Implications

We aren't expecting, when we enter college, that campus will be the technological equivalent of a science-fiction movie. What we hope, however, is that student services will evolve alongside our own society to reflect the changes we have undergone as passengers on the Information Superhighway.

▶ **Cashless on campus.** It is unlikely on today's campus that a random wallet search of a hall of freshmen would reveal more than $100 in cash. Instead, these students would say they only carry their debit, credit, or ATM card. By refusing to accommodate these students, universities place them in a perilous position, stripped of resources when they might need to pick up supplies, run a few copies, or purchase a meal on campus. A number of universities have caught on to the reality of a "cashless campus," installing ATM machines, allowing student ID cards to double as debit cards, or offering secure online transactions with credit cards. But some universities still fail to realize the needs of enrolling Net Geners. In the future, more campus services such as student ticket sales, printing kiosks, and campus eateries should accommodate debit or credit cards.

▶ **Immediate communication.** Because we have learned to seek and expect information at the touch of a button, it is simplest to disseminate information in a similar fashion. When inclement weather strikes, for instance, a mass e-mail will reach students before a ticker on the bottom of the local network news. Students will check their e-mail before class before they will check their voicemail or a classroom door for notes posted there. School systems, therefore, must evolve to place less emphasis on phone lines or verbal communication and more on using e-mail and Web sites for the rapid distribution of news, warnings, and alerts.

▶ **Constant access.** Whether it be news, shopping, or paying bills, technological advances have made it possible for the Net Gen to access services anytime, anywhere. They have grown accustomed to doing business after midnight or shopping after two o'clock in the morning. Late classes and schedules bulging with club activities, jobs, and study sessions often mean working late into the night. As a result, they have come to demand 24-hour access to university services such as health care, dining, Internet troubleshooting, and libraries. Whether in person or on the Web, current student habits demand a new evaluation of hours of operation and staff accessibility.

▶ **Face time.** The Internet has enabled faculty, students, and administrators alike to communicate with more people on a daily basis while only having to physically see a few. As an administrator once lamented, "I can help 30 students each day over e-mail exchanges, but I rarely get the opportunity to meet them." While some might assume the Net Gen loathes face-to-face interaction, the opposite is true. The constant glow of a computer screen and the cacophony of clicking keys has only left the Net Generation longing for more face-to-face interaction with faculty and administrators. Despite the ease of online communications, therefore, faculty and administrators must continue to make a concerted and sincere effort to offer real face time to students and to arrange meetings so that genuine, real-time discussions, which are often stifled online or over inbox communication, can occur.

Outlook for the Future

I arrived home in December to meet a sullen, unresponsive teenage boy: my brother. As I watched him plant himself in front of the computer each night and rush between chores to "check his buddy list," I couldn't help but pull rank.

"You know, in my day, we used to actually call our friends over winter break. And we had to actually have our friends over to play games, we couldn't just do it on the Internet," I said.

He rolled his eyes. "Right, right, I know," he said. "And your cell phones only made phone calls."

Suddenly, I felt quite old. The truth is, I haven't called a friend just to chat since my freshman year in college. But the technology that revolutionized my college experience has transformed my younger brother's middle and high school experience. The technology that captivated my imagination as a teenager is a "fossil" in his eyes.

The next generation of learners, therefore, will only raise more questions on college campuses. Their lives will be more reliant on technology, their attention spans that much shorter. They will have little concept of checkbooks and scant recollection of landline telephones. Their needs and their values will require a reevaluation of the concepts noted here and a fresh look at the needs and expectations of our nation's college freshmen. By then, the Net Generation will be relics of the first generation of Internet youth, when the Web was still new, page loading still slow, and telephones still in use.

But I'll just read about all that on the Internet.

Endnotes

1. Neil Howe and William Strauss, *Millennials Rising: The Next Greatest Generation* (Vintage Books: New York, 2000).

About the Author

Carie Windham is a senior studying history at North Carolina State University. When she is not Googling her own name or instant messaging her friends, she is active in student government, the University Honors Program, and the Center for Student Leadership, Ethics, and Public Service. While at NC State, she has been a member of Phi Beta Kappa and Phi Kappa Phi and recipient of the Park Scholarship. She spends her free time volunteering at Noah's Landing, a nonprofit nature center, and plans to attend graduate school in Northern Ireland on a Mitchell Scholarship in fall 2005.

CHAPTER 6

Preparing the Academy of Today for the Learner of Tomorrow

Joel Hartman, Patsy Moskal, and Chuck Dziuban
University of Central Florida

Introduction

Predicted to be America's first generation to exceed 100 million persons,[1] the wave of Net Geners entering colleges and universities brings a blend of behaviors, attitudes, and expectations that creates opportunities—as well as challenges—for higher education. Opportunities arise from students' familiarity with technology, multitasking style, optimism, team orientation, diversity, and acceptance of authority. Challenges, on the other hand, include the shallowness of their reading and TV viewing habits, a comparative lack of critical thinking skills, naïve views on intellectual property and the authenticity of information found on the Internet, as well as high expectations combined with low satisfaction levels. Not surprisingly there is an increasing gap between most institutions' IT environments and the technologies the Net Gen uses. These factors lead, in turn, to the greatest challenge for higher education leaders, faculty, and staff—nearly all of whom belong to earlier generations: to understand the Net Generation learner and through this understanding provide the learning environments, services, and facilities needed to help these students achieve their potential.

Most institutions profess intense interest in the academic, social, and personal needs of their students. Yet, generational differences are not often used to gain a better understanding of students' behaviors, attitudes, and expectations. Perhaps this is because generations represent a historical perspective, better illuminating the past than the present or future. Change and adaptation within the academy proceed at a slow, deliberate pace. Adapting institutional processes and services to the needs of a specific generation of students requires advance planning and action; the timeframe for planning and deliberation may exceed the time the learners are enrolled. Planning is complicated because personal characteristics are not homogeneous within generational groupings; for example, individuals born late in the Gen-X cohort may think and behave more like Net Geners, making it difficult to take a standardized approach. Unfortunately, the generational literature fails to predict the characteristics of future generations.

Institutional leaders need to find ways to think about generations in designing campus and individual student initiatives, as well as to discern trends that will allow future-directed planning.

Generations and Technology

The technologies available as a generation matures influence their behaviors, attitudes, and expectations. People internalize the technologies that shape information access and use, as well as the ways they communicate. Matures (born 1946–1964) were exposed to large vacuum-tube radios, mechanical calculators, 78 rpm records, dial telephones, and party lines. Baby Boomers grew up with transistor radios, mainframe computers, 33? and 45 rpm records, and the touch-tone telephone. Gen-Xers matured in the era of CDs, personal computers, and electronic mail. For the Net Generation, the prevailing technologies are MP3s, cell phones, and PDAs; they communicate via instant messaging, text messaging, and blogs. For each successive generation "technology is only technology if it was invented after they were born."[2]

Technology has experienced its own series of generations. In computing, the nexus has shifted from the mainframe to the minicomputer to the personal computer, and now to mobile devices. In line with Moore's Law, computing and communication devices have radically decreased in size and increased in performance. Connectivity has experienced a similar transition across generations, from no connectivity to proprietary device-to-device cabling, to globally interconnected local area networks, and now to wireless. Computers were initially developed as number crunching devices. The early emphasis on processing numbers, then words, has been joined by multimedia: graphics, images, video, sound, and interactive games. Prevalent among today's applications are interpersonal and group communication tools. The use of early computers was batch-processing-oriented and required programming skills and arcane commands. Today's graphical user interfaces and the Web make the operation of computers highly interactive and achievable by nearly anyone. The Internet has led to the kind of global village of information and communication envisioned by Marshall McLuhan.[3]

Behaviors of the Net Generation are expressed through technologies to an extent not observed in previous generations. At one level, Net Geners are the beneficiaries of decades of technological development that preceded them; at another level, as students they use these technologies in new ways, and in so doing are redefining the landscape in higher education and perhaps beyond. The behaviors of the Net Gen (multitasking, always-on communication, engagement with multimedia, and the like), as well as the capabilities of modern technologies (personal, multifunctional, wireless, multimedia, communication-centric), are in close harmony. To a great extent, the behaviors of the Net Gen are an enactment of the capabilities afforded by modern digital technologies.

According to a report from the Pew Internet & American Life Project,[4] one in five of today's college students began using computers between the ages of 5 and 8; by the time they were 16 to 18, all of them used computers. Nationwide, nearly 90 percent of college students have gone online, compared with about 60 percent of the general population. Use of the Internet or campus networks is nearly universal in higher education. Eighty-five percent or more of college students own a computer, and nearly all of the rest have ready access to one. Sixty percent of college students regularly play computer or online games, and they are twice as likely to have downloaded music as the general population. The Net Generation students exhibit technology-related behaviors that may be unfamiliar to many in the academy: social networking, photo sharing, swarming, blogging, instant messaging, and text messaging. As continuous multitaskers, the Net Geners are adept at context switching, often engaging in several activities at the same time (in the classroom, this behavior can be disconcerting to instructors). Four out of five students believe that Internet use has had a positive impact on their academic experience, and three out of four say they use the Internet for research more than they do the library.[5]

Students are very familiar with the top online commercial sites such as amazon.com and ambercrombie.com; they hold these sites to be the standard against which they judge colleges' online services. And, of all of the generational groups, the Net Generation is least satisfied with their higher education experience.[6]

Net Geners have access to affordable multifunctional devices (for example, cell phones equipped with digital cameras and Web browsers that can play digital audio and video recordings, as well as send and receive e-mail and text messages) that readily support their interpersonal communication needs and multitasking behaviors. Between classes, students bustle about with cell phones attached to their ears. Silberman described the prevalence of cell phones among Net Geners in Finland, and how cell phones' voice and short messaging capabilities allow them to move in synchronization "like schools of fish … on currents of whim."[7] This behavior has since become well established in America, where it is known as *social swarming* or *smart mobs.*[8,9]

Emerging Patterns

The mobility enabled by wireless communication, combined with an expanding class of wireless-equipped portable computers and PDAs, is leading to new instructional and social patterns. No longer do students need to go to a specific place, or even be seated, to use a computer. An array of multifunctional PDAs capable of wireless communication is allowing such devices to follow their users wherever they go, serving as "prosthetics for information, memory, or creativity."[10] This is challenging the very definition of learning spaces because learning can now occur both in and out of the classroom, in both formal and informal settings, and by lone scholars or among groups.

Net Gen students not only use technology heavily, they also trust it implicitly. They are as likely to get their news online as from a newspaper and conduct research through Google as visit a library. Their belief that anything accessible online should be free leads many to download or share music, movies, or software they have not purchased. The extent of this activity has surprised many institutions; campus networks often became saturated when students returned to school in the fall. In some cases this is followed by copyright violation notices from organizations such as the Recording Industry Association of America.

The interactive and exploratory way the Net Generation uses technology is also a break with the past. The French anthropologist Claude Lévi-Strauss described the process of bricolage—tinkering—through which individuals learn by exploring and manipulating objects around them.[11] Turkle[12] and Brown[13] described how changes in technology and its use have moved from a rigid, top-down environment to a new bottom-up style in which the mode of interaction and learning has shifted from programming and commands to exploration and bricolage. The Net Gen approaches computers and other technologies as environments for communication, socialization, learning, and game playing, not as machines to be programmed.[14]

A challenge for campus planners is the increasing gap between the institutional IT environment and the technology environments Net Geners have created for themselves. To be sure, today's students are avid users of Web, e-mail, telephones, and other IT resources; however, their rapid adoption of instant messaging, cell phones, blogs, wikis, social networking Web sites, and other resources that are not generally part of the core campus infrastructure leads to a host of new concerns. There is increased potential for incompatibilities between the technologies adopted by students and campus standards. Other problems such as excess bandwidth consumption, inappropriate use of intellectual property, or security threats are becoming more prevalent. An existing institutional context for the use of these technologies is unlikely, leading to frustration and decreasing satisfaction on the part of both students and faculty.

Although it may be desirable in some instances, it is not necessary that institutions rush to become providers of instant messaging, blogs, wikis, computer games, social networking sites, or any of the array of students' favorite technologies. The real opportunity lies in observing and talking to today's students to learn more about how they conceptualize and use these new tools. With this knowledge institutions can create contexts for technology use that enhance learning, improve student services, and enrich students' social lives.

Assessing the Generations in Online Learning

The Research Initiative for Teaching Effectiveness (RITE) at the University of Central Florida (UCF) regularly conducts formative and summative surveys of students' online learning experiences. These data become transformative because they are instrumental in modifying the organization, structure, and processes of our distributed learning initiative. We believe that both qualitative and quantitative research yield a more valid assessment of students in the online learning environment. When we ask respondents to complete objective statements followed by a reflective narrative, we obtain a more authentic characterization of their attitudes, beliefs, and behaviors.

In the latest survey conducted at UCF, students used a series of 5-point Likert-scale questions to evaluate their online learning experience around two components previously identified through extensive numerical work.[15] The first domain—learning engagement—encompassed six items where students indicated their:

▶ Overall satisfaction with online learning

- Ability to integrate technology into their education
- Ability to control their own learning
- Ability to study efficiently
- Ability to meet their educational objectives
- Willingness to take another online course

The second domain—interaction value—asked students to evaluate their online learning experience in regard to:

- Ease of interaction
- Amount of interaction with students
- Quality of interaction with students
- Amount of interaction with the instructor
- Quality of interaction with the instructor

In addition, the survey protocol asked the learners to state their opinions on whether they changed their approach to learning because of their online experiences (nominal yes–no format). This was followed with a request for an explanation of any reported change. To obtain a directly interpretable measure for assessment, the authors designed a scoring protocol for student responses to learning engagement and interaction value compared to the maximum possible value. For example, if a student scored 66 on learning engagement, his or her positive perception was 66 percent of the maximum possible.

Using the Generations as a Basis of Comparison

At a metropolitan research institution such as UCF, a substantial portion of students represent diverse generations—principally Baby Boomers (born 1946–1964) and Generation X (born 1965–1980). These two cohorts provided the backdrop for our analysis of Net Gen (born 1981–1994) students' learning engagement, interaction value and changed learning approach. There is an important additional generation on the UCF campuses: the Matures (born prior to 1946). Because our demographic and survey work suggests that they represent less than 2 percent of UCF's online population, we have not included them in the comparisons.

Baby Boomers

Through sheer numbers, Baby Boomers have impacted nearly every aspect of American society. They experienced rapidly expanding economic circumstances that led to a sense of financial security. An enduring optimism permeates Baby Boomers, who are process-oriented, preoccupied with convenience, and willing to go into debt. They populate high positions in all sectors of American culture and attract attention for their likely impact on the nation's economy when they retire.[16, 17, 18]

Generation X
The Generation Xers were the first "latch key" generation and strongly influenced by emerging technological developments. Financially, they experienced wide-scale job loss and runaway inflation that led to their sense of economic and social skepticism. These events shaped their hallmark characteristics: they mistrust most of society's organizations and institutions, and they believe that stabilizing influences such as job security are a myth. They seem impertinent because of their confrontational style. For Generation X, versatility is the key to stability.[19, 20, 21]

Learning Engagement, Interaction Value, and Enhanced Learning in the Generations
The current UCF survey yielded 1,489 online student responses, representing a return rate of approximately 30 percent. Figure 1 depicts the generation membership of the respondents. The sample contained a majority of Generation

Figure 1. Generations of Online Students

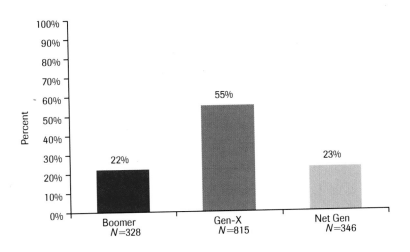

X students with approximately equal proportions of Baby Boomers and the Net Gen. This finding reinforces the expectation that there is substantial age diversity in the distributed learning population in metropolitan universities.

As Figure 2 illustrates, older learners reported more positive learning engagement. The Net Gen, with 73 percent of maximum, shows a steep decline compared to Boomers' 85 percent rating. The positive narratives for all three groups stressed flexibility, convenience, and self-paced learning for their online experiences. Those points converge on reduced opportunity cost for obtaining an education thanks to online learning. The less positive perceptions of the generations showed extensive variability. Baby Boomers lamented the lack of face-to-face interaction in the online environment, a comment consistent with this generation's tendency to discuss and tell stories. Generation X was uncomfortable with the continual connectedness of online learning that contradicts their penchant to "get to the point" and "move on with it." The Net Gen respondents were disappointed; they perceived a lack of immediacy in their online courses and felt that faculty response times lagged behind their expectations.

Figure 3 presents the trend in interaction value from one generation to the next. Again, a comparison of the three generations shows a high of approximately

Figure 2. Percent of Maximum Scores on Learning Engagement for the Generations

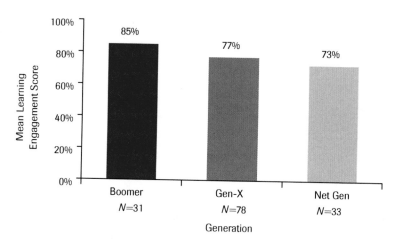

63 percent for the Boomers, 56 percent for Generation X, and 50 percent for the Net Gen. The narratives for interaction indicated that the Boomers judged communication patterns in online classes to constitute one-on-one attention. Gen-Xers responded well to the constant availability of interaction. Net Geners enjoyed the ability to form interactive communities among their peers. On the less positive side, Baby Boomers preferred some face-to-face encounters with their instructors; Generation X students reported substantial, pointless interaction in class; and the Net Gen students felt that the interaction mechanisms designed by their instructors were much less adequate than their personal technologies.

Generational differences were also found in whether students changed their approach to learning as a result of their online experience (see Figure 4). The downward trend by age cohorts continues for this measure. More than half of the Boomers claimed that they modified their learning techniques; the Net Geners decreased to a low of 23 percent. The narratives showed that Baby Boomers enhanced their technology skills and integrated them into their modified student roles, Gen-X students improved their ability to manage time effectively, and Net Geners felt a heightened sense of responsibility and motivation.

Figure 3. Percent of Maximum Scores on Interaction Value for the Generations

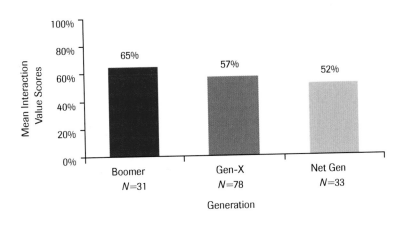

Responding to Results

These differences in student generations present an opportunity for the institution to work toward instruction that addresses the varying needs of students. At UCF, faculty members who teach online or blended courses participate in a faculty development course designed to guide them in both technological and pedagogical approaches to Web instruction. Through a series of interactive sessions with instructional designers and Web faculty veterans, beginning faculty are encouraged to redesign their courses to focus on being student centered and interactive. Beyond the course structure faculty learn to integrate formative and summative assessment mechanisms, both for themselves and for students. The focus is on faculty facilitating instruction and students becoming active and interactive learners.[22]

Blended learning provides a unique opportunity to bridge generations, providing the face-to-face contact requested by Baby Boomers, the independence preferred by Gen-Xers, and the interaction and sense of community desired by Net Geners. Extensive use of e-mail, discussion groups, and live chat increases communication and collaboration among students as well as between students and the instructor.

Figure 4. Students Who Changed Their Approach to Learning by Generation

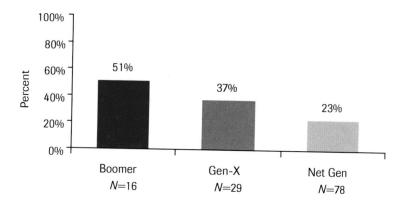

Excellent Teaching

From our exploration of generational issues, an important question evolved: Can students distinguish characterizations of excellent teachers independent of generation, learning style, course modality, and technological sophistication? Data collected at UCF, with more than half a million student responses, suggest an answer.[23] We have identified six characteristics that students attribute to the best faculty—characteristics that are independent of age, gender, and academic achievement. Interestingly, these characteristics correspond to the seven principles of good practice in undergraduate education[24] and to the national study of student engagement.[25] Although students' behaviors, attitudes, and expectations are generally shaped by their generation, what constitutes good teaching appears to be universal across these generations. Students believe that excellent instructors:

▶ Facilitate student learning
▶ Communicate ideas and information effectively
▶ Demonstrate genuine interest in student learning
▶ Organize their courses effectively
▶ Show respect and concern for their students
▶ Assess student progress fairly and effectively

This seemingly paradoxical way in which students determine teaching excellence through the lens of their instructors clarifies how universities must accommodate students' needs, realizing that these needs are universal, yet greatly mediated by the Net Generation.

Conclusion

The Net Generation possesses sophisticated technological adaptability and a remarkable capacity to incorporate multitasking into day-to-day academic activities. However, there is also a growing discrepancy between institutional infrastructure and these students' personalized facility with information. Freeland[26] described a corresponding trend emerging in higher education that he called practice-oriented education—the combination of liberal and professional studies. He foreshadowed the students' tendency to learn through bricolage and the university's reticence to respond: "After 1945 it [the academy] became steadily more open... [but] as its clientele became more 'modern,' higher education became more traditional."[27] As we move into the next decades, the resolution of that polarization compels colleges and universities to examine, and perhaps redesign, their strategic direction.

If today's students do not represent the constituency that our higher educational system is designed to teach as asserted by Prensky,[28] how do we remedy that situation? Possibly, by studying how students interacted (politically, economically, culturally, socially, and technologically) with institutions' instructional climate in the past. By monitoring technology developments and their impact on the student population, we will be better able to anticipate the needs of the class of 2025. This approach will thrust institutions into a forward-thinking posture rather than a reactionary one in response to incoming student cohorts.

From an instructional design perspective, we realize that knowing our students gives us many more options for engaging them in the learning process. Throughout the generations, colleges and universities have attempted to tailor instructional protocols to accommodate students' preferences for acquiring knowledge, enhance learning, reduce ambivalence, facilitate maturation, and maximize success. The audacity with which the Net generation has burst on the academic scene has accelerated our need to understand its learning characteristics. A conundrum accompanies that solution, however: adaptation for the present generation may not be adequate for the next.

Endnotes

1. Neil Howe and William Strauss, *Millennials Rising: The Next Greatest Generation* (New York: Vintage Books, 2000).

2. Alan Kay quoted in Marc Prensky, *Digital Game-Based Learning* (New York: McGraw-Hill, 2000), p. 38.

3. Marshall McLuhan and Bruce R. Powers, *The Global Village: Transformations in World Life and Media in the 21st Century* (New York: Oxford University Press, 1999).

4. Steve Jones et al., "The Internet Goes to College: How Students Are Living in the Future with Today's Technology" (Washington, D.C.: Pew Internet & American Life Project, September 15, 2002), <http://www.pewinternet.org/reports/toc.asp?Report=71>.

5. Ibid.

6. Charles D. Dziuban, Patsy Moskal, and Joel Hartman, "Blended Learning" (Boulder, Colo.: EDUCAUSE Center for Applied Learning, research bulletin, issue 7, 2004), <http://www.educause.edu/ir/library/pdf/ecar_so/erb/ERB0407.pdf>.

7. Steve Silberman, "Just Say Nokia," *Wired Magazine,* issue 7.09 (September 1999), p. 2.

8. Joel Garreau, "Cell Biology: Like the Bee, This Evolving Species Buzzes and Swarms," *Washington Post,* July 31, 2002, p. C01, <http://www.washingtonpost.com/ac2/wp-dyn?pagename=article&node=&contentId=A23395-2002Jul30>.

9. Howard Rheingold, *Smart Mobs: The Next Social Revolution* (Cambridge, Mass.: Perseus Books Group, 2002).

10. Bryan Alexander, "Going Nomadic: Mobile Learning in Higher Education," *EDUCAUSE Review*, vol. 39, no. 5 (September/October 2004), pp. 30, <http://www.educause.edu/pub/er/erm04/erm0451.asp>.

11. Claude Lévi-Strauss, *The Savage Mind* (Chicago, Ill.: University of Chicago Press, 1968).

12. Sherry Turkle, *Life on the Screen: Identity in the Age of the Internet* (New York: Touchstone, 1995).

13. John Seely Brown, "Growing Up Digital," *Change*, vol. 32, no. 2 (March/April 2000), pp. 10-11, <http://www.aahe.org/change/digital.pdf>.

14. Turkle, op. cit., p. 60.

15. Dziuban, Moskal, and Hartman, op. cit.

16. Diana Oblinger, "Boomers, Gen-Xers, and Millennials: Understanding the 'New Students,'" *EDUCAUSE Review*, vol. 38, no. 4 (July/August 2003), pp. 37-47, <http://www.educause.edu/apps/er/erm03/erm034.asp>.

17. Howe and Strauss, op. cit.

18. Robert W. Wendover, *From Ricky & Lucy to Beavis & Butthead: Managing the New Workforce* (Aurora, Colo.: The Center for Generational Studies, Inc., 2002).

19. Oblinger, op. cit.

20. William Strauss and Neil Howe, *Generations: The History of America's Future, 1584 to 2069* (New York: William Morrow and Company, Inc., 1991).

21. Wendover, op. cit.

22. Dziuban, Moskal, and Hartman, op. cit.

23. Charles D. Dziuban, Morgan D. Wang, and Ida J. Cook, "Dr. Fox Rocks: Student Perceptions of Excellent and Poor College Teaching" (unpublished manuscript, 2004).

24. Arthur W. Chickering and Zelda F. Gamson, "Seven Principles for Good Practice in Undergraduate Education," *AAHE Bulletin*, vol. 39, no. 7 (March 1987), pp. 3-7, <http://aahebulletin.com/public/archive/sevenprinciples1987.asp>.

25. George D. Kuh, "Assessing What Really Matters to Student Learning," *Change*, vol. 33, no. 3 (2001), pp. 10-19.

26. Richard M. Freeland, "The Third Way," *The Atlantic Monthly*, vol. 294, no. 3 (October 2004), pp. 144-147, <http://www.theatlantic.com/doc/prem/200410/freeland>.

27. Ibid., p. 141.

28. Marc Prensky, "Digital Natives, Digital Immigrants, Part I," *On the Horizon*, vol. 9, no. 5 (October 2001); available from <http://www.marcprensky.com/writing/>.

Further Reading

Charles D. Dziuban et al., "Three ALN Modalities: An Institutional Perspective," in *Elements of Quality Online Education: Into the Mainstream*, volume 5 in the Sloan-C series, John Bourne and Janet C. Moore, eds. (Needham, Mass.: Sloan-C, 2003), <http://www.sloan-c.org/publications/books/vol5summary.pdf>.

Charles D. Dziuban, Patsy Moskal, and Joel Hartman, "Higher Education, Blended Learning, and the Generations: Knowledge Is Power—No More," in *Elements of Quality Online Education: Engaging Communities*, volume 6 in the Sloan-C series, John Bourne and Janet C. Moore, eds. (Needham, Mass.: Sloan-C, in press).

Jay W. Forrester, "System Dynamics and the Lessons of 35 Years," *The Systemic Basis of Policy Making in the 1990s*, Kenyon B. De Greene, ed. (Cambridge, Mass.: MIT Press, 1991); see <http://sysdyn.clexchange.org/sdep/papers/D-4224-4.pdf>.

About the Authors

Joel L. Hartman is vice provost for information technologies and resources at UCF. As the university's CIO, he has overall responsibility for library, computing, networking, telecommunications, media services, and distributed learning activities. He previously served as treasurer and chair of the EDUCAUSE Board of Directors and currently serves as chair of the EDUCAUSE National Learning Infrastructure Initiative (NLII) Planning Committee. He also serves on the Florida Digital Divide Council, the Microsoft Higher Education Advisory Council, and the board of directors of Florida LambdaRail. Hartman graduated from the University of Illinois, Urbana–Champaign, with bachelor's and master's degrees in journalism and communications, and received his doctorate from UCF.

Patsy Moskal is the faculty research associate for RITE at UCF, where she has been a faculty member since 1989. She received an EdD from UCF specializing in instructional technology and research methods and holds bachelor's and master's degrees in computer science. Since 1996, she has served as the liaison for faculty research of distributed learning at UCF. Moskal specializes in statistics, graphics, and applied data analysis. She has extensive experience in research methods, including survey development, interviewing, and conducting focus groups, and frequently serves as a consultant to school districts, industry, and government organizations.

Charles Dziuban is director of the Research Initiative for Teaching Effectiveness (RITE) at the University of Central Florida (UCF), where he has been a faculty member since 1970 teaching research design and statistics. He received his PhD from the University of Wisconsin. Since 1997, he has directed the impact evaluation of UCF's distributed learning initiative, examining student and faculty outcomes as well as gauging the impact of online courses on the university. Dziuban has received funding from several government and industrial agencies, including the Ford Foundation and the Centers for Disease Control. In 2000, he was named UCF's first-ever Pegasus Professor for extraordinary research, teaching, and service.

CHAPTER 7

Convenience, Communications, and Control: How Students Use Technology

Robert B. Kvavik

EDUCAUSE Center for Applied Research and
University of Minnesota, Twin Cities

Introduction

Much has been made about the new generation of technology-savvy students currently in and entering college. These students possess unprecedented levels of skill with information technology; they think about and use technology very differently from earlier student cohorts. They are characterized as preferring teamwork, experiential activities, and the use of technology. Prensky calls them "digital natives," referring to the fact that they have grown up with technology as opposed to "digital immigrants" who did not.[1a,b]

Jason Frand observed that today's young students take technology for granted and that staying connected is a central part of their lives. Doing is more important than knowing, and learning is accomplished through trial and error as opposed to a logical and rule-based approach.[2] Similarly, Paul Hagner found that these students not only possess the skills necessary to use these new communication forms, but there is an ever increasing expectation on their part that these new communication paths be used.[3]

The assumption of the technology literate undergraduate student population needs to be demonstrated with quantitative data. Much of the work to date, while interesting and compelling, is intuitive and largely based on qualitative data and observation. A study by the EDUCAUSE Center for Applied Research (ECAR), using both quantitative and qualitative data, addressed four questions:

▶ What kinds of information technologies do students use, and what are their preferences?

- With what levels of skill are they using these technologies?
- How does this use contribute to their undergraduate experience?
- What value does the use of information technology add in terms of learning gains?

Student Demographics

This study presents the responses of 4,374 students who replied to a 2004 survey. The students were mostly traditional-age college students from 13 institutions in five states. Ninety-five percent of the students were 25 years old or younger. Ninety-five percent were enrolled full-time; the other 5 percent were enrolled part time. Students surveyed were either freshmen or seniors. Forty-five percent of the students surveyed reported living on campus.

The institutions included in the survey were
- Colgate University
- Drexel University
- University of California, San Diego
- University of Minnesota, Crookston
- University of Minnesota, Twin Cities
- University of Wisconsin–Colleges
- University of Wisconsin–Eau Claire
- University of Wisconsin–La Crosse
- University of Wisconsin–Madison
- University of Wisconsin–Milwaukee
- University of Wisconsin–Oshkosh
- University of Wisconsin–Stout
- University of Wisconsin–Whitewater

Student Use of Technology

There is an inexorable trend among college students to universal ownership, mobility, and access to technology.

Ownership

Fully 93.4 percent of 4,374 students surveyed at 13 higher education institutions in 5 states owned a computer. We found that 70.7 percent of the senior respondents and 57.1 percent of the freshmen respondents reported ownership of a personal desktop computer; 38.5 percent of the senior respondents and 52.7

percent of the freshmen respondents owned laptop computers. Personal digital assistants (PDAs) were owned by only 11.9 percent overall, with male students more likely to own a PDA than female students. Cell phones were owned by 82 percent of the students, with females (84.7 percent) more likely to own one than males (77.7 percent).

Internet Access
All of the students in this study had access to the Internet. Freshmen students, who most often reside on campus, access the Internet using university networks (82.2 percent). Seniors used commercial access most often (56.4 percent). More than 81 percent of students had access to broadband service, either through commercial or university sources, while 18.5 percent used modems.

Use of Technology
Students were asked about the applications they used on their electronic devices. They reported that they use technology first for educational purposes, followed by communication. Students reported using computers for writing documents (99.5 percent) and e-mails (99.5 percent), followed by surfing the Internet for pleasure (97.2 percent) and for classroom activities (96.4 percent). Students reported using technology for creating/editing video and audio and for creating Web pages the least.

Hours of Technology Use
By a wide margin, students said that they used a computer first for doing classroom activities and studying (mean of 4.01 on a scale where 1 represents "do not use," 2 represents less than one hour weekly; 3 represents 1–2 hours; 4 represents 3–5 hours; 5 represents 6–10 hours, and 6 represents 11 or more hours per week). Students used the computer approximately 2–5 hours a week for writing documents, surfing the Internet for pleasure, e-mailing, using instant messaging, using an electronic device at work or downloading/listening to music or videos. Other activities such as completing a learning activity, playing games, creating spreadsheets, and creating presentations (including Web sites) occupied an average student's time less than 2 hours per week (see Table 1).

These findings are supported by the qualitative data. When interviewed, students reported making heavy use of a computer for communication, but that was secondary to their use of the computer for schoolwork.

Table 1. Activities and Hours Spent

Activities	Mean*
Classroom activities and studying using an electronic device	4.01
Writing documents (word processing)	3.76
Surfing the Internet for pleasure	3.47
Creating, reading, sending e-mail	3.47
Chatting with friends or acquaintances using instant messaging	3.45
Using an electronic device (computer, Palm device) at your place of employment	3.31
Downloading or listening to music or videos/DVDs	3.15
Completing a learning activity or accessing information for a course using course management systems	2.48
Using a university library resource to complete a class assignment	2.46
Playing computer games	2.39
Creating spreadsheets or charts (Excel)	2.07
Online shopping	2.06
Creating presentations (PowerPoint)	1.82
Creating graphics (Photoshop, Flash)	1.79
Creating Web pages (Dreamweaver, FrontPage)	1.39
Creating and editing video/audio (Director, iMovie)	1.34

*Scale: 1 = do not use, 2 = less than an hour, 3 = 1–2 hours, 4 = 3–5 hours, 5 = 6–10 hours, 6 = 11 or more hours

We found that the highest computer use was in support of academic activities and that presentation software was driven primarily by the requirements of the students' major and the curriculum. Students reported strong use and skill levels in support of communications and entertainment. As one student commented, "I would feel very disconnected and lost if my laptop and cell phone were taken away from me. However, had I never been introduced to them, I may not rely on them as much as I do now. Still, I believe they are very useful tools, especially for communication."

Factors that explain hours of use fall into the following categories: academic requirements, class status, gender, and age. Academic usage is strongly related to the student's academic major and class status (senior/freshman). Communications and entertainment are very much related to gender and age.

The significance of student major is supported by both survey data and findings from the qualitative interviews. From student interviews, a picture emerged of student technology use driven by the demands of the major and the classes that students take. Seniors reported spending more time overall on a computer than do freshmen, and they reported greater use of a computer at a place of employment. Seniors spent more hours on the computer each week in support of their educational activities and also more time on more advanced applications—spreadsheets, presentations, and graphics.

Men, and especially the youngest men in our sample, were more likely to spend more hours playing computer games, surfing the Net, and downloading music. Women spend more time communicating. Confirming what parents suspect, students with the lowest grade point averages (GPAs) spend significantly more time playing computer games; students with the highest GPAs spend more hours weekly using the computer in support of classroom activities. At the University of Minnesota, Crookston, students spent the most hours on the computer in support of classroom activities. This likely reflects the deliberate design of the curriculum to use a laptop extensively. In summary, the curriculum's technology requirements are major motivators for students to learn to use specialized software.

Level of Skill

Undergraduate students need to develop two types of skills: information literacy or fluency and the technical skills needed to use the tools. Defining technology skills is difficult because of rapid changes in software that require new and different skills. Recognizing this dynamic, the National Research Council in 1999 defined technology fluency,[4] and our research is premised upon their definition.

When asked about the level of skill they felt they had attained for each application, students rated themselves highly skilled in the use of communications, word processing, and the Internet (see Table 2). On a scale where 4 = very skilled, 3 = skilled, 2 = unskilled, and 1 = very unskilled, the means for e-mail, instant messenger, word processing, and Web surfing were all greater than 3.0. They

Table 2. Levels of Skills Attained

Application	Mean*
E-mail	3.60
Instant messenger	3.54
Word processing	3.53
Web surfing	3.47
Presentation software (PowerPoint)	2.90
Online library resources	2.88
Spreadsheets (Excel)	2.86
Course management systems	2.83
Graphics (Photoshop, Flash)	2.45
Creating Web pages (Dreamweaver, FrontPage)	2.17
Creating and editing video/audio (Director, iMovie)	2.07

Scale: 1 = very unskilled to 4 = very skilled

rated themselves least skilled on graphics (mean = 2.45), creating Web pages (mean = 2.17), and creating and editing audio and video (mean = 2.07). Seniors tended to rank themselves higher than freshmen with tools such as PowerPoint and spreadsheets. The student's major had a significant influence, with the highest skills reported by business, engineering, and life science students. While the quantitative data indicate that students say they have the skills they need, in the qualitative interviews student skills seemed more problematic. The interviews indicated that students are skilled with basic office suite applications but tend to know just enough technology functionality to accomplish their work; they have less in-depth application knowledge or problem solving skills.

Sharon Fass McEuen's study of student technology skills at Southwestern University in Georgetown, Texas, noted similar patterns.[5] Skill levels were highest in the use of word processing, use of the Internet, and communications. They were significantly lower for specialized applications such as spreadsheets and presentation software. She also found much lower levels of skill in the maintenance of computers. According to McEuen, student technology skills can be likened to writing skills: Students come to college knowing how to write, but they are not developed writers. The analogy holds true for information technology, and McEuen suggested that colleges and universities approach information technology in the same way they approach writing.[6]

As noted earlier, the highest levels of self-reported computer and application skills were among business students, engineering students, and life science students. But when we looked at graphics skills, having a fine arts or engineering major was associated with higher self-reported skills. What this suggests is that the major requires the development of higher-level skill sets with particular applications. Business students are more likely to use presentation applications and spreadsheets; arts students are more likely to use graphics applications. At the University of Minnesota, Crookston, all students are required to use PowerPoint to present their work. Not surprisingly, we found that Crookston students had the highest reported level of skills in PowerPoint.

There is virtually no difference in reported skills by GPA, and differences among the 13 institutions in our study were minimal for every application when controlling for majors. One explanation may be that students rate themselves vis-à-vis their peers, so the variation in skill levels may not appear in our study. Conversely, using these applications might be like riding a bicycle for these students. Everyone can do it. Or it may confirm Garrison Keillor's observation about the upper Midwest—"everyone is above average."

Our quantitative data show that, in general, students say they have the skills they need. The qualitative data suggest a slightly different picture. Students have very basic office suite skills as well as e-mail and basic Web surfing skills. Moving beyond basic activities is problematic. It appears that they do not recognize the enhanced functionality of the applications they own and use.

The comparative literature on student IT skill self-assessment suggests that students overrate their skills; freshmen overrate their skills more than seniors, and men overrate their skills more than women.[7] Our data supports these conclusions. Judy Doherty, director of the Student Technologies Resource Group at Colgate University, remarked on student skill assessment, "Students state in their job applications that they are good if not very good, but when tested their skills are average to poor, and they need a lot of training."[8]

Professor Larry Rudnick of the University of Minnesota, Twin Cities, noted that one danger of the computer, especially for those students who expect the computer to give them an instant answer, is that it always comes up with an answer, even if that answer is wrong.[9] Mary Jane Smetanka of the Minneapolis–St. Paul *Star Tribune* reported that some students are so conditioned by punch-a-button problem solving on computers that they approach problems with a scattershot impulsiveness instead of methodically working them through. In turn, this leads to problem-solving difficulties.[10]

A student technology service worker at the University of Wisconsin–Milwaukee observed that students "mystify" technology and some are "afraid to putz." The aversion to experimentation seems driven by a fear of doing damage to their machines and applications. One Colgate student stated, "I know that I am clueless. I am so afraid. I am petrified that I am going to do something wrong." This student described how he was trying to get rid of some of the viruses on his computer and somehow deleted the driver for his sound card. No one had been able to get it back for him.

In short, institutions need to provide ample opportunity for training of students. It cannot be assumed that they come to college prepared to use advanced software applications.

Information Technology in the Classroom

We expected to find that the Net Generation student prefers classes that use technology. What we found instead is a bell curve with a preference for a moderate use of technology in the classroom (see Figure 1). The mean (3.07), median (3.00), and mode (3) were squarely at the moderate level of preference for technology use on a scale of 1 to 5, with 1 being "I do not prefer the use of technology" to 5 being "I prefer taking courses that are taken totally online." We found that 30.8 percent of the students preferred taking courses that use extensive levels of technology. Least preferred (2.2 percent) were courses that are delivered entirely online. Nevertheless, 25.6 percent of the students preferred limited or no use of technology in the classroom.

One student captured the respondents' mixed opinions on technology in the classroom, noting, "Information technology is just a tool. Like all tools, if used properly it can be an asset. If it is used improperly, it can become an obstacle to achieving its intended purpose. Never is it a panacea." Another commented, "I think universities should ease up on pushing information technology. I have an associate's degree in computer science, and, yes, I am a Luddite." Conversely, one enthusiastic student commented, "I love information technology. It has helped me to grow tremendously academically this year and it strengthened my relationships

Figure 1. Student Preference for Use of IT in Classes (*N*=4,363)

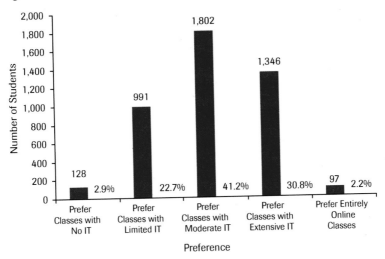

with teachers, classmates, and friends." Another noted that technology made the faculty member seem more detached.

For many, Luddite or not, information technology in the classroom is problematic in that it undermines face-to-face contact and has little impact on their learning. "I feel like I have lost part of the vital student-teacher connection."

The following factors were considered in evaluating students' preferences:

▶ Previous experience with the use of technology in the classroom
▶ Faculty skill using technology
▶ Hours students use technology
▶ Perceived levels of skill using computers by the respondents
▶ Institution
▶ Major
▶ GPA
▶ Demographics

A student's previous positive experiences in the classroom had a beneficial impact on the preference for classroom technology. It is not surprising that if technology is used well by the instructor, students will come to appreciate its benefits. This may explain why seniors had a higher preference level for the use of technology in the classroom than did freshmen.

Table 3. Preferences for Technology by Major			
Discipline	**Prefer No Technology**	**Prefer Limited Technology**	**Prefer Extensive Technology**
Engineering	4.8%	24.4%	67.8%
Business	1.3%	28.2%	64.3%
Life sciences	4.8%	35.3%	56.3%
Physical sciences	5.7%	40.9%	51.8%
Social sciences	7.9%	44.4%	44.2%
Education	3.5%	47.9%	42.9%
Humanities	7.7%	47.9%	40.2%
Fine arts	9.0%	46.9%	39.3%

A student's major was also an important predictor of preferences for technology in the classroom (see Table 3), with engineering students having the highest preference for technology in the classroom (67.8 percent), followed by business students (64.3 percent).

We also found minor gender differences in preference for the use of technology in the classroom (see Figure 2).

When analyzing students' preferences for classes using technology, a student's GPA was not a significant factor. Students with lower GPAs preferred classes using technology equally with those students with higher GPAs, with the exception of students with the highest grade point averages (3.51–4.00), who modestly preferred less technology in the classroom.

Students were asked how technology affected various classroom activities. The highest scoring affect was "helped me to better communicate with the instructor," with a mean of 3.85 (Table 4).[11] Other responses with a mean over 3.60 included "resulted in prompt feedback from the instructor," "helped me communicate and collaborate with my classmates," and "I primarily use information technology in courses to improve the presentation of my work." The highest scores were given to improved communications, followed by factors related to the management of classroom activities. Lower impact activities had to do with comprehension of classroom materials (complex concepts). Time-on-task and grading outcomes

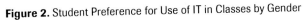

Figure 2. Student Preference for Use of IT in Classes by Gender

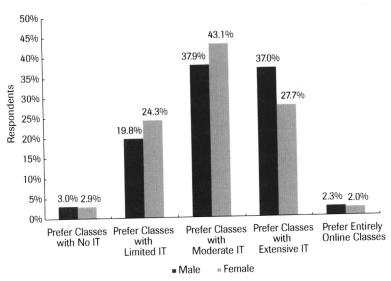

were shown to be more neutral from the perspective of the respondents, with means as low as 3.04.

Engineering and business majors indicated that classroom technology did better their understanding of complex concepts and provided more opportunities for practice and reinforcement. Seniors provided overall higher scores than freshmen.

Interestingly, students do not feel that use of information technology in classes greatly increases the amount of time engaged with course activities (3.22 mean).[12] This is in direct contrast to faculty perceptions reported in an earlier study, where 65 percent of faculty reported they perceived that students spend more time engaged with course materials.[13]

Perceived Benefits

We asked students about the perceived benefits of using technology in the classroom (see Figure 3). The most cited benefit was convenience (48.5 percent). In the survey's open-ended comments, 134 students voluntarily identified convenience as one of the primary benefits of using information technology in classes. When

Table 4. Effect of IT on Class Activities (*N*=4,374)

Activity	Mean*
The use of information technology in classes has helped me to better communicate with the instructor.	3.85
The use of information technology in courses has resulted in prompt feedback from the instructor.	3.84
The use of information technology in courses has helped me communicate and collaborate with my classmates.	3.64
I primarily use information technology in courses to improve the presentation of my work.	3.61
The use of information technology in courses provides more opportunities for practice and reinforcement.	3.58
The use of technology in my classes met my expectations.	3.54
Classes that use information technology allow me to take greater control of my class activities.	3.45
The use of information technology in classes has helped me better understand complex or abstract concepts.	3.38
The instructors' use of technology in my classes has increased my interest in the subject matter.	3.25
Classes that use information technology are more likely to focus on real-world tasks and examples.	3.23
I spend more time engaged in course activities in those courses that require me to use technology.	3.22
I get better grades in courses that use information technology.	3.19
Faculty members need to give us more in-class training for information technology used in the class.	3.04

*Scale: 1 = strongly disagree to 5 = strongly agree

convenience was combined with saving time, the percentage increased to 64.6 percent. Only 12.7 percent said the most valuable benefit was improved learning; 3.7 percent perceived no benefit whatsoever. Note that students could only select one response, so more than 12.7 percent may have felt learning was improved, but

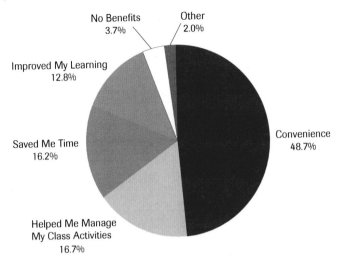

it was not ranked highest. These findings compare favorably with a study done by Douglas Havelka at the University of Miami in Oxford, Ohio, who identified the top six benefits of the current implementation of IT as

▶ improving work efficiency,
▶ affecting the way people behave,
▶ improving communications,
▶ making life more convenient,
▶ saving time, and
▶ improving learning ability.[14]

Colleges and universities have significant investments in technology. Students see these investments as contributing primarily to convenience and facilitating communications. We have made life much easier for students in the administrative area. The jury is out on its impact on learning and the learning experience.

Many students acknowledge that technology has improved learning; we suspect this occurs where there is a deliberate institutional or faculty strategy to improve the learning experience. Software applications such as PowerPoint and Excel are tools, as is a classroom management system. But by themselves they do not contribute to an improved learning experience. It is incumbent upon the faculty member to understand the promise and performance of these tools in support of improved learning and to use them accordingly. Our data suggest that we are at best at the cusp of technologies being employed to improve learning.

Course Management Systems

The percentage of students who have used a course management system has increased dramatically since they were first introduced. More than 83 percent of the students reported having used a course management system. Seniors (90.1 percent) were more likely to have taken a class that used a course management system than freshmen (78.5 percent).

Overall Experience with Course Management Systems

Of the students who had used a course management system, 76.1 percent were positive or very positive; 17.3 percent were neutral; and only 6.6 percent were negative or very negative (see Figure 4). Females (mean of 3.93) liked course management systems slightly better than males (mean of 3.74).[15]

Course Management System Features Used

Course management systems offer a number of features in support of learning and course administration. See Table 5.

Impact of Course Management System Use

Students were asked whether they perceived that a particular tool within a course management system improved learning, whether it improved class management, or whether it improved both learning and class management. Students were also given the option of reporting whether a tool had no effect on either learning or class management, or whether it had a negative effect. Classroom management (convenience) scored highest, followed by improved learning. Negative perceptions were minimal.

The interactive features least used by faculty were the features that students indicated contributed the most to their learning. The students were especially positive about sharing materials with students (38.5 percent), faculty feedback on assignments (32 percent), and online readings (24.9 percent).

Features considered to improve class management included track grades (45.7 percent), online quizzes (38.5 percent), online readings (29.1 percent), and sample exams online (21.2 percent). All other features received less than a 20 percent response.

Figure 4. Students' Overall Experience Using a Course Management System

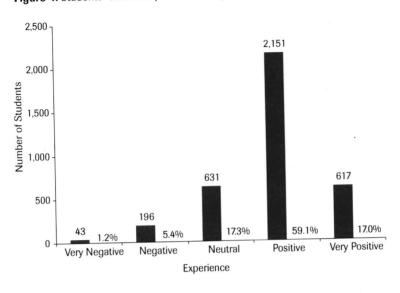

Table 5. Student Use of Course Management System Features	
Use of Features	**Percentage**
Use a syllabus feature	95.0%
Read online	94.8%
Track grades	89.4%
Take sample exams	88.8%
Submit assignments	78.5%
Discuss online	74.2%
Share materials with students	73.4%
Obtain faculty feedback	71.8%
Take online quizzes	70.0%

When combining the percentage of students who said that the course management system improved both learning and class management, sharing materials with students was ranked highest (52.8 percent); tracking grades was second (47.9 percent). Fully 80.3 percent said that tracking grades improved their ability to manage their classroom activities as well, when combining the percentage of students who said that the course management system improved class management and both improved class management and learning.

Course Management System Improvement Needed

In the qualitative interviews, students indicated a need for a more consistent approach to course management system use. Also, students and faculty commented on the need for training. In a separate study, 12 percent of the faculty indicated that they would increase their use of the course management system if more training were made available.[16] A University of Minnesota, Twin Cities, student recommended, "With so many courses now using a course management system, there is a need to have an introductory class on using a course management system at the freshmen or sophomore level." Some students, however, noted in interviews that such training was unnecessary.

Potential of Course Management Systems

Course management systems and their implementation are a work in progress. They promise to significantly reduce the restrictions of time and space on learning for students and faculty, in much the same way their predecessor enterprise administrative systems did for student administrative services. Used properly, they have the potential to greatly improve student access to information and to communicate with their instructors, enhance the quality of learning, and increase learning productivity.

Course management systems can enhance learning quality by enabling instructors to convey information more effectively, helping instructors meet the needs of students with varied learning styles, as well as enriching the interactions students have with each other and with their instructors. That is the promise. However, the students in this study called our attention to performance by noting an uneven diffusion of innovation using this technology. This may be due, in part, to faculty or student skill. It may also be due to a lack of institutional recognition of innovation, especially as the successful use of course management systems affects or does not affect faculty tenure, promotion, and merit decisions.

From Convenience to Learning Revolution

We expected to find that Net Generation students would demand greater use of technology in teaching and learning in the classroom. They did not. What we found was a moderate preference for technology.

We expected that it would be increasingly necessary for faculty to use technology in order to appeal to this generation of students. Ironically, we found that many of the students most skilled in the use of technology had mixed feelings about technology in the classroom.

We expected students to already possess good IT skills in support of learning. What we found was that many necessary skills had to be learned at the college or university and that the motivation for doing so was very much tied to the requirements of the curriculum. Similarly, the students in our survey had not gained the necessary skills to use technology in support of academic work outside the classroom. We found a significant need for further training in the use of information technology in support of learning and problem-solving skills.

Course management systems were used most by both faculty and students for communication of information and administrative activities and much less in support of learning.

The consequences of these findings are significant. Some complacency may have occurred because of the belief that Net Gen students require less training with technology. Student and faculty use of instructional technology is more limited than is often portrayed. Students appear to be slower developing adequate skills in using information technology in support of their academic activities, which limits technology's current value to the institution. Higher education's investment in learning technology may be paying less than optimal returns because students and faculty often lack the appropriate skills or motivation to use it effectively. Colleges and universities appear not to be reaching enough students and faculty with technology education and training.

Our findings are much like an audit—a snapshot in time or an early picture of a process that has great potential to support learning and is most promising. We were both surprised and disappointed by what we learned. We attribute much of what we saw to growing pains.[17] We saw enough good practice and favorable, if not enthusiastic, commentary from the students to know that the potential of technology in the classroom is enormous.

In 1997, Michael Hooker proclaimed, "higher education is on the brink of a revolution." Hooker went on to note that two of the greatest challenges our institutions face are those of "harnessing the power of digital technology and responding to the information revolution."[18] Hooker and many others, however, did not anticipate the likelihood that higher education's learning revolution would be a journey of a thousand miles rather than a discrete event. Indeed, a study of learning's last great revolution—the invention of moveable type—reveals, too, a revolution conducted over centuries leading to the emergence of a publishing industry, intellectual property rights law, the augmentation of customized lectures with textbooks, and so forth.

In the eight years since Hooker's proclamation, information technology has continued its inexorable penetration into myriad aspects of work, education, and recreation, including activities that our students and faculty hold dear. During this time, the videogame industry surpassed the motion picture industry in revenues, the University of Phoenix opened the University of Phoenix Online, many notable virtual university efforts came and went, and course management systems became a common element of higher education's base of enterprise applications. Also, the use of information technologies in classrooms and dormitories became widespread, and the research persuaded us that there were no significant differences in the learning outcomes from courses mediated by information technologies and those that were not. Finally, student access to computing and narrowband networking has become nearly ubiquitous, and access to broadband networking and online information resources is increasingly commonplace.

Both the ECAR study on faculty use of course management systems and this study of student experiences with information technology concluded that, while information technology is indeed making important inroads into classroom and learning activities, to date the effects are largely in the convenience of postsecondary teaching and learning and do not yet constitute a "learning revolution." This should not surprise us. The invention of moveable type enhanced, nearly immediately, access to published information and reduced the time needed to produce new publications. This invention did not itself change literacy levels, teaching styles, learning styles, or other key markers of a learning revolution. These changes, while catalyzed by the new technology, depended on slower social changes to institutions. I believe that is what we are witnessing in higher education today.

Acknowledgments

This article is a summary of work by Robert B. Kvavik, ECAR Senior Fellow and Associate Vice President at the University of Minnesota, Twin Cities; Glenda Morgan, Director of Academic Technology Initiatives at the California State University Chancellor's Office; and Judith B. Caruso, ECAR Fellow and Director of Policy, Security, and Planning at the University of Wisconsin–Madison.

Endnotes

1. (a) Marc Prensky, "Digital Natives, Digital Immigrants, Part I," *On the Horizon*, vol. 9, no. 5 (October 2001), p. 1; available from <http://www.marcprensky.com/writing/>. See also (b) Diana Oblinger, "Boomers, Gen-Xers, and Millennials: Understanding the 'New Students,'" *EDUCAUSE Review*, vol. 38, no. 4 (July/August 2003), pp. 37–47, <http://www.educause.edu/apps/er/erm03/erm034.asp>.

2. Jason Frand, "The Information-Age Mindset: Changes in Students and Implications for Higher Education," *EDUCAUSE Review*, vol. 35, no. 5 (September/October 2000), pp. 17, <http://www.educause.edu/apps/er/erm00/articles005/erm0051.pdf>.

3. Paul Hagner, "Interesting Practices and Best Systems in Faculty Engagement and Support," final report to the National Learning Infrastructure Initiative (January 25, 2001), p. 1, <http://www.educause.edu/ir/library/pdf/NLI0017.pdf>.

4. National Research Council, *Being Fluent with Information Technology* (Washington, D.C.: National Academies Press, 1999), <http://www.nap.edu/catalog/6482.html>.

5. Sharon Fass McEuen, "How Fluent with Information Technology (FIT) Are Our Students?" *EDUCAUSE Quarterly*, vol. 24, no. 4 (2001), pp. 8–17, <http://www.educause.edu/ir/library/pdf/EQM0140.pdf>.

6. Ibid., p. 9.

7. A. C. K. Lee, "Undergraduate Students' Gender Differences in IT Skills and Attitudes," *Journal of Computer Assisted Learning*, vol. 19, no. 4 (December 2003), p. 488.

8. Robert B. Kvavik, Judith B. Caruso, and Glenda Morgan, *ECAR Study of Students and Information Technology, 2004: Convenience, Connection, and Control* (Boulder, Colo.: EDUCAUSE Center for Applied Research, research study, vol. 5, 2004), p. 43, <http://www.educause.edu/ers0405/>.

9. Ibid., p. 30.

10. Mary Jane Smetanka, "Millennial Students," Minneapolis–St. Paul *Star Tribune*, May 7, 2004, p. A19.

11. The scale for this question was 1 = strongly disagree, 2 = disagree, 3 = neutral, 4 = agree, and 5 = strongly agree.

12. The scale for this question was 1 = strongly disagree, 2 = disagree, 3 = neutral, 4 = agree, and 5 = strongly agree.

13. Glenda Morgan, *Faculty Use of Course Management Systems* (Boulder, Colo.: EDUCAUSE Center for Applied Research, research study, vol. 2, 2003), p. 53, <http://www.educause.edu/ers0302/>.

14. Douglas Havelka, "Students Beliefs and Attitudes Toward Information Technology," *Information Systems Education Journal*, vol. 1, no. 40 (2003), p. 3, <http://isedj.org/isecon/2003/2434/ISECON.2003.Havelka.pdf>.

15. The scale for this question was 1 = very negative, 2 = negative, 3 = neutral, 4 = positive, 5 = very positive.

16. Glenda Morgan, op. cit., p. 53.

17. Robert Zemsky and William F. Massy, *Thwarted Innovation: What Happened to E-Learning and Why* (West Chester, Penn.: The Learning Alliance at the University of Pennsylvania, 2004), <http://www.thelearningalliance.info/Docs/Jun2004/ThwartedInnovation.pdf>.

18. Michael Hooker, "The Transformation of Higher Education," in *The Learning Revolution: The Challenge of Information and the Academy*, Diana G. Oblinger and Sean C. Rush, eds. (Bolton, Mass.: Anker Publishing, 1997), p. 20.

About the Author

Robert B. Kvavik is an EDUCAUSE Center for Applied Research (ECAR) senior fellow and professor of political science and associate vice president at the University of Minnesota. He has held visiting teaching positions at Columbia University, the University of Oslo, and the University of Ibadan in Nigeria and has written extensively on European government and politics. As the principal architect of the University of Minnesota's Initiative for Excellence in Undergraduate Education, Kvavik was responsible for enterprise systems planning and implementation and business process redesign, especially in the area of student services. He has shared his vision for educational technology as a featured speaker at numerous national and international meetings. Kvavik received his doctorate from Stanford University in 1971.

CHAPTER 8

The Real Versus the Possible: Closing the Gaps in Engagement and Learning

Judith Ramaley
University of Maine

Lee Zia
National Science Foundation

The Next Generation of Learners

It is natural to assume that each generation can be described easily, and we often use labels such as Generation X or the Net Generation to describe generational differences. In thinking about educating the next generation, it is helpful to realize that not everyone is a member of the Net Generation—not because of age but because of access to technology. Many students, both in K–12 and in postsecondary education, have only limited access to advanced instructional technologies or to the Web. Although technology-enabled interactive instruction may be highly engaging, many students, teachers, and faculty have no experience with it. One study found that in spite of the fact that 99 percent of K–12 schools have Internet access, as do most classrooms (87 percent), these resources are rarely used effectively.[1]

While high-speed classroom connectivity is good, most actual Internet usage takes place in media centers or computer labs. This suggests that Internet resources are not yet fully integrated into the day-to-day classroom routine. In fact, 56 percent of respondents to the study identified integrating technology into the classroom or learning experience as their top technology challenge. The same percentage (56 percent) named teacher professional development as their top challenge, a finding consistent with an earlier Pew study.[2] Through 14 national, diverse focus groups, students reported a substantial disconnect between how they use the Internet for school and how they use it during the school day and under teacher direction. Fundamental changes in school organization, time management, and teacher preparation will be needed to generate the most value from this massive investment in technology. These changes will affect what students and teachers do in the classroom.

The experience of students in the introduction and use of instructional technologies in school varies widely. The 2004 National Research Council report on fostering high school students' motivation to learn argued that motivation is a key factor in the success or failure of education and that "by the time many students enter high school, disengagement from course work and serious study is common."[3] The consequences of this disengagement are often much more serious for young people from disadvantaged backgrounds because they do not usually get a second chance; students from more privileged backgrounds frequently do. The primary ingredients that foster involvement and motivation to learn are "competence and control, beliefs about the value of education, and a sense of belonging."[4] These personal factors work within a complex convergence of other more visible things such as curriculum, instruction, the organization and management of the schools, and the conditions in the community surrounding the schools.

The Board on Children, Youth, and Families, which produced the 2004 National Research Council report, offered a research-based set of recommendations for what we can do to keep young people in school, make high school meaningful, and keep students engaged and motivated. The ideas include

▶ forming a good connection between a learner and the social context in which learning will take place; and

▶ making "the curriculum and instruction relevant to adolescents' experiences, cultures, and long-term goals, so that students see some value in the high school curriculum."[5]

These recommendations will serve as an interesting starting point for exploring the role and impact of interactive instructional technologies in education, both in K–12 and in postsecondary education.

Similar conditions exist in K–12 and higher education. Connectivity investments, particularly wireless, are growing (81.1 percent of the campuses participating in the 2004 Campus Computing Survey reported wireless LANs, up from 77.2 percent in 2003, 67.9 percent in 2002, and 29.6 percent in 2000).[6] Internet usage is very high among 18–29-year-olds in the general population (78 percent) and among those with some college experience (75 percent), or those with at least four years of college (88 percent).[7] Only 38 percent of college students, however, reported using the Internet for work in classes. Instead, the Internet is used primarily to communicate.

While undergraduates reported a positive impact of the Internet on their academic experience, a closer read of the data reveals that IT usage beyond e-mail remains relatively low. For example, only 6 percent of students reported taking an online course for credit, and only half of the students in this group reported that the course was worthwhile. Moreover, while students and faculty are communicating by e-mail, it appears that the communication is primarily about procedural matters: absences, homework assignment questions, grades, review session schedules, and the like. Students did report, however, that e-mail permits them to communicate ideas to faculty they otherwise might not have expressed face-to-face.

Approximately 25 percent of the students enrolled in postsecondary education are traditional students pursuing traditional pathways and traditional goals. Traditional students enter college immediately after graduation from high school, attend full time, usually work only part time, and are financially dependent on their families. Nontraditional students may differ on a number of characteristics, such as entering postsecondary education as an adult student, attending part time, working full time while enrolled, or being financially independent. Approximately 28 percent of postsecondary students are single parents or have not graduated from high school, having instead completed a GED. Nontraditional students are less likely than traditional ones to complete a degree and are more likely to begin their postsecondary education in a community college or a private for-profit institution. Their pathway to a degree is complex, and the yield of successful bachelor's graduates is low compared to traditional or nontraditional students who begin their postsecondary education at a four-year institution. What kinds of educational experience will engage these students? How might interactive technologies enrich their education, maintain their commitment to learning, and help them succeed? Beyond nontraditional learners, what about the significant proportion of "traditional" undergraduates who fail to complete a degree? Might interactive instruction help them to experience competence and control, develop an appreciation for the value of an education, and feel a part of a learning community?

As we think about what all high school students and undergraduates should learn and how interactive technologies might contribute to effective education, it is helpful to keep two larger issues in mind:

- At the most basic level, educational technologies are a means to a good education. If we lose sight of what it will mean to be educated in the 21st century, we will not be able to connect our new technological capabilities to the underlying purposes for which they should be used.
- We need to think about interactive technologies in the context of what we know about how to promote learning.

Learning and Technology

The emergence of new technology challenges our assumptions about the nature and locus of learning. In turn, advances in the learning sciences reveal new possibilities for the application of technology in support of educational goals centered on the engaged learner.

What We Know About Learning

Although we know a lot about learning[8] and continue to learn more, there is a gap between what the education research community and the learning sciences have discovered about learning and what most of our faculty know or practice. Because faculty develop and implement most of the content and teaching practices, this gap impacts

- the development of materials for interactive technology,
- what faculty incorporate into their teaching, and
- the design of the curriculum.

We need to find creative ways to close that gap by encouraging our faculty and their graduate students to take educational issues seriously. We must also approach the development of interactive technologies and programming with the same rigor, discipline, and habits of inquiry that faculty bring to their own research agendas.

Goals of Education

All fields have their own vocabulary, ways of talking about ideas, standards of proof, and methodologies. Undergraduates should become acquainted with these "ways of knowing," not just because they are a necessary part of becoming a professional but because they may offer insights into other disciplines. Students should not be asked to abandon scientific thinking when they study humanities, for example. Science and math are important components of the liberal arts. A major in science or math should not only prepare students to pursue a career in their field but also foster the desired qualities of a liberally educated person, regardless of discipline. We must prepare all young people for lives of creativity, citizenship, and social responsibility as well as success in a workplace increasingly shaped by science and technology. This requires us to think about the meaning of literacy and the way we "read" the world around us. Interactive instruction can offer an especially engaging way to learn this skill. In addition to learning the habits of mind, forms of expression, and inquiry of a discipline, students should be expected to demonstrate the qualities of a person prepared to live a productive, creative, and responsible life.

There are many approaches to articulating the purposes of a college education. All involve bringing together intellectual engagement and cognitive development with emotional maturity and social responsibility. A college graduate should be informed, open-minded, and empathetic. These qualities are not engendered solely by general education in the first two years of college. Academic departments must build these expectations into their conception of the work of the major as well. It is helpful to think of an undergraduate education as a continuum of increasingly complex intellectual challenges, accompanied by increasingly complex applications, with consequences of increasing significance for the learner and others. A special emphasis should be placed on preparing our technical workforce to communicate with the general public and with policymakers. Interactive instruction must build in both cognitive and affective domains in order to give students experience with responsible learning and practice.

The Promise and Limitations of Technology

Since the introduction of the World Wide Web, we have seen dramatic advances in the communication capabilities of the Internet. Continued improvements in the underlying hardware and software infrastructure have stimulated growth in the number of access points, bandwidth, and new transmission technologies (DSL, cable modems, satellite), with no end to this growth in sight. Emergent wireless technologies, from Wi-Fi to WiMax,[9] promise to "untether" users, enabling unforeseen applications of the Internet that challenge our assumptions about user behavior and information needs.

Concurrently, the commodification of computation has lowered the financial barriers to Internet access for individuals. Low-cost fixed and mobile computers are more available, as are a variety of even lower-cost devices that blur the lines between cell phones and personal digital assistants. Tremendous increases in computational power have also enabled the development of rich multimedia capabilities that offer greater levels of interactivity for the user's experience via modeling, animations, simulations, voice, and other audio applications.

Finally, new applications are changing the nature of the Web and the way in which users—and learners—can interact. Individuals may now more easily express themselves, contribute their commentary, provide expertise, and otherwise participate in potentially wide-ranging conversations. Ubiquitous, one-to-one computing places greater control "at the edge" of the network. Thus, instant messaging and other variants of peer-to-peer communication, along with blogging and other self-publishing models, are enabling content, commentary, and community to commingle at an unprecedented scale.

In his essay on technological revolutions that he has known, Edward Ayers made clear that the real impact of new technologies only becomes manifest when the "machine as a separate box needing elaborate maintenance and full attention"[10] fades into the background. At that point the new capabilities can be effectively integrated into teaching and learning. As Ayers put it, "It is not until we find ways to integrate electronic teaching (and learning) into our established rhythms, strategies, and purposes that the very real potential of the new media will begin to be realized."[11] IT will not replace older forms of learning or teaching because each type of interaction between instructors and students accomplishes a unique goal. However, it will open up new and engaging ways to learn. So what is that very real potential?

Ayers argued that we need a balance of individual and active learning, along with collaborative learning and passive learning, which occurs in groups and through lectures. A live lecture has its place. It is a way for a dedicated and passionate scholar to dramatize and embody the intellectual content of a subject and demonstrate the appeal and importance of the material. It is important for students to see not only *what* they need to know, but also *why* it is important. Reading also has its place. Reading "is the most individualized, active, and reflective intellectual activity and as such is the measure for intellectual work in general."[12] Of course, reading can also be deadly and boring when the reader is trapped in a technical frame that is unfamiliar in content, structure, vocabulary, or forms of expression. The important insight that will guide our exploration of the value of interactive technologies is that a user of digital information is certainly being asked to be active, but is probably not being asked to be reflective. "The computer, unlike a text, is built for action; it sits there humming, waiting, demanding that you punch some key or click some button. It is distracting, perpetually promising something more interesting than your own unfocused thoughts or the words currently before you on the screen."[13]

As we explore the newer forms of interactive technologies, whether live ones on the Web or multimedia presentations on DVDs, we must keep in mind that these are not meant to replace traditional forms of learning. Rather, they enrich traditional forms of learning and serve as links between active and passive, individual and group, and transmission and generation of knowledge. The criteria we apply when assessing the *quality* of the material we offer will, at one level, resemble the standards that the academy has set for any intellectual work: originality and importance, thorough grounding in the field, clarity of goals and expression, effective use of materials, and ethical handling of material and ethical approach to the user.[14] However, The standards for *presentation* in these new media and formats will be different. We must be clear about when an interactive instructional strategy is appropriate and when it is not. In most cases, experience with an interactive program branches and adapts to the user. It does not encourage a "linear argument or narrative nearly as well as a book"[15] or convey, as a live performance or a group discussion can, the passion and personality of an engaged learner and scholar.

Interaction

The Net Generation has been described as experiential, engaged, and constantly connected, with a strong need for immediacy. For all learners, research points to the importance of learning environments which are active, social, and learner-centered. These environments might be described as interactive. Information technology supports at least four major categories of interactivity.

People to People

People to people interactions may be synchronous or asynchronous; they can take place in the same place or at a distance. In education, there can be one-to-many communication (for example, between faculty and students); however, information technology's power rests in its ability to enable this traditional communication mode to take on a bidirectional character. Many-to-many communication (students to students, faculty to faculty, or students to faculty) may occur in a vertical learning community. In addition, one-to-one peer mentoring is facilitated by IT. The work of the Math Forum (http://www.mathforum.org/) provides a good example of how the process of communication about content (in this particular case, mathematics) can exhibit symmetric (same level of preparation and background) and asymmetric (novice with expert) modes. In addition, the online setting permits subtle renegotiation of roles within the conversation and introduces a balancing effect among participants.

People and Tools

A second category involves interaction between *people and tools*. An example is a distributed computing environment that can involve a single user making use of distributed computational resources, or multiple users who are at a distance making use of a computing resource, whether centralized or distributed. Another example is provided by what might be termed a distributed observational environment, which can feature one-to-many or many-to-one modes. Through the Sloan Digital Sky Survey project (http://www.sdss.org/), a vast network of professional and amateur astronomers can interact at any time with the same vast data storehouse of information rather than wait sequentially for an opportunity to use a single telescope. And the data in the survey comes from a distributed network of observational platforms. A similar example is the One Sky, Many Voices project (http://groundhog.sprl.umich.edu/) that engages school children in distributed data collection and analysis. Students can submit their results to a larger community for scrutiny and use, ensuring that novice learners feel ownership of their intellectual activity. These examples illustrate the Internet's ability to provide access to data, either derived (from models) or directly observed. They also illustrate how instrumentation may be remotely accessed.

People with Concepts

The interaction of *people with concepts* is a third category in which an information technology device, rather than being a tool itself, is the vehicle by which concepts are presented or rendered. For example, image databases such as two-dimensional slices of objects (both animate and inanimate) illustrate the complex geometry and physical relationships of constituent parts. More abstractly, interrelationships among concepts and/or numerical data can be represented visually.[16a,b] Simulations and animations also fall into this category. They are often "steerable" or controllable through a graphical user interface. The underlying data that is represented visually can be manipulated in varying ways, often revealing patterns and relationships not immediately visible in the standard tabular or serial formats of the original data.

Virtual reality environments fall into this category; they permit the learner to work with concepts and their representations in a dynamic, interactive manner.

People with Contexts

The fourth category involves the interaction of *people with contexts.* Various forms of rich-media communication enable people to interact with each other. Collaboration enhanced by interaction with tools and organized around interaction with concepts fosters the development of community. This larger context situates learning. Norms of interaction and contribution grow from within the community and include processes by which a collective understanding develops about a core amount of definable knowledge that "everyone should know." This leads to several questions, however. How should the learner come to know this core? How is this demonstrated? How is it certified? Can learners demonstrate their competence individually? How do members of the community attain authority or otherwise receive certification of competence?

Examples

Examples from K–12 and higher education illustrate how education can be made more interactive, resulting in better engagement for the Net Generation and other learners.

Animation

Simple animations, even with relatively limited interaction, can promote conceptual learning. A particularly compelling example depicts three standard sorting algorithms.[17] It animates the effect of the algorithms on the task of ordering (from shortest to longest) a random set of different length line segments. Not only can users see the way each algorithm makes its choices, but they can also compare the relative speeds of each by determining when to start each demo so that they will all finish their respective sort at the same time.

Concept Inventories

Since David Hestenes's pioneering work on the development of the Force Concept Inventory (http://modeling.la.asu.edu/R&E/FCI.PDF), numerous other disciplines and subdisciplines such as mechanical engineering and civil engineering have developed similar "diagnostic tests" to help faculty ascertain student conceptual understanding.[18] Typically, concept inventories are used in large-enrollment courses. A hallmark of these inventories is their interactive implementation. The faculty member poses questions, and short student responses are recorded and aggregated. Information technology has enabled the rapid recording, analysis, and representation of the results, making the technique particularly attractive in large-enrollment settings. A notable practitioner of this technique is Harvard physics professor, Eric Mazur.[19]

It is worth noting that an information technology overlay is not necessary for useful implementation of the approach; however, the development of low-cost wireless interactive response systems[20] and accompanying receiving stations allows the concept test approach to be implemented at reasonable cost. At the most rudimentary level, interactive response systems are used as polling devices. The interaction is mostly one way; however, the real-time snapshot of a group's understanding contributes directly to the faculty member's understanding of what conceptual emphases are needed based on the class's progress.

WeBWorK

An example of a distributed system for providing feedback on student work for the sake of building conceptual understanding is WeBWorK (http://webwork.math.rochester.edu/). WeBWorK, developed by mathematics faculty, begins with the assumption that doing homework is still important, especially problems that provide "practice" in certain basic levels of rote computation. But faculty believed that this should not be the sole learning assessment in a course. Therefore, they created an automated homework grading system that places the responsibility for homework exercises on students while providing interactive feedback along the way. This frees up significant time, both in and out of class, enabling faculty and graduate teaching assistants to deal with conceptual learning. This goal has been achieved. The number of installations of WeBWorK at other mathematics departments has grown steadily. Moreover, departments outside mathematics are beginning to use the system.

AskNSDL

AskNSDL (http://www.nsdl.org/asknsdl/) is the electronic reference service of the National Science Digital Library. This service illustrates interactive engagement between novice learners (question posers) and experts (providers of responses) that occurs both at a distance and asynchronously. As such, it is a many-to-many and people-to-people form of interaction. A notable feature of the service is that it harnesses expertise that is widely distributed in both a geographic and a disciplinary sense. AskNSDL is currently considering the engendering of virtual communities of experts that would exist for a concentrated period of time (for example, during National Chemistry Week or other similar celebrations).

The Molecular Workbench

More complex simulation environments such as the Molecular Workbench developed by the Concord Consortium (http://workbench.concord.org/) offer what is essentially an entire virtual environment in which to carry out experimentation, observation, and analysis. Model comparisons are possible; moreover, the user can control parameters that affect both the choice of models and parameters within any given model. This particular environment also has 3-D representations that can be manipulated. At one level, this is a very rich interactive environment in the *people and tools* category, but it also supports both *people with concepts* and *people with contexts* interaction if it is used intentionally by a group of learners with guidance from an "expert." Such an expert might start out as the teacher or faculty member, but could build in expectations for students to become peer mentors and thus improve their own learning by teaching others.

BugScope

A final example of interactive learning enabled by information technology is the use of remote instrumentation. For instance, the BugScope project (http://bugscope.beckman.uiuc.edu) at the University of Illinois makes a scanning electron microscope available to users worldwide. Such use affords a number of advantages. An expensive item of equipment that an institution cannot afford, for example, can be made accessible to its students via the Web. Moreover, such equipment can be made accessible on a 24 x 7 basis, thereby decreasing its unit cost per user. This suggests that "buying cooperatives" can be organized to distribute costs across multiple sites.

Skeptics argue that the tactile "feel" of operating such equipment is an important part of the learning experience—that it is important to gain a sense of how to properly manipulate devices. Haptic feedback, however, can be incorporated into such devices and transmitted across the Internet; some experiments are already being conducted with this technology. Perhaps the most important aspect of this type of work is that it affords students chances to collect, generate, and analyze their own data. Learner-constructed, sense-making experiences consistently are found to be key to improved learning. This example also illustrates how environments initially constructed for one level (university students) may find use at other levels (middle and secondary school students).

The Emerging Cyberinfrastructure and New Experiments

The examples above illustrate how an emergent cyberinfrastructure is already benefiting education. When fully developed, cyberinfrastructure will provide a suite of enabling tools essential to the study of complex systems and to the modeling of real-world behaviors of these systems for learning purposes. It will include software to support collaboratories, visualization tools, data-mining capacity, and data management techniques, as well as support for geographically distributed sensing systems and observation sites that generate enormous amounts of data. This data can be assimilated and interpreted using knowledge representation and manipulation software—for research or instruction.

Furthermore, cyberinfrastructure will permit the "instrumenting" of the learning environment that will enable us to "see" into the classroom and to examine the pathways by which students explore ideas and acquire mastery of material—individually and collectively. The educational context opens up new challenges and new areas of research for the designers of cyberinfrastructure and other cybertools; these tools, in turn, can generate new research questions. Cyberinfrastructure also permits investigators to deal with the enormous data sets created by multimedia observations of classrooms, individual student learning, and scientific observations. Below are some early-stage examples that offer great promise.

Participatory Simulations

A number of education research groups are exploring participatory simulations—the use of low-cost mobile devices in secondary and middle school settings. For example, Lee McKnight and colleagues[21] are working with the Boston Museum of Science and local high schools in Everett and Malden, Massachusetts, to assess the impact of equipping students with networked wireless devices through which they can engage in simulation experiments. Similar, more extended efforts have been launched at the Concord Consortium under the direction of Bob Tinker[22] and at the University of Michigan under the direction of Elliot Soloway and his research group.[23]

In these projects, the electronic clickers described earlier can be replaced by more sophisticated devices such as handheld computers. These offer inter-active, two-way communication. For example, not only can data be gathered through the devices, but, after it is analyzed and manipulated centrally, it can be published back out to the learners for local synthesis (along with further distributed analysis).

Distributed Data Collection

Another instance of distributed data collection is in various 311 call center con-solidation experiments such as that taking place in New York City.[24] New York City consolidated 40 call centers and 14 pages of phone numbers into a 311 center that handles more than 30,000 calls each day. The information from calls to the central 311 line serves to provide feedback from the community. For example, question-answer pairs are stored in a database; analysis of their patterns reveals citizen concerns. Moreover, collective citizen knowledge of local conditions of the public civil infrastructure helps inform municipal government of priorities. On the scale of a college or university campus, a similar system could be built to support learning.

3-D Digital Printing

Although 3-D digital printing[25] is still quite expensive, it presents the opportunity to print physical artifacts from high-resolution data files that represent the complete internal geometry and exterior surfaces of objects. As this technology becomes more affordable, access issues can be addressed either by interacting with virtual reconstructions of objects via the Web or by printing out 3-D replicas of objects after downloading the appropriate data files.

Immersive Virtual Reality Experiments

Finally, immersive virtual reality experiments that can support telecollaboration and telepresence are under way. Applications exist in telemedicine, for example. Working examples in this area exist, but they are still quite costly. For example, Brown University researchers are developing interactive diffusion tensor MRI brain visualizations as part of the work being conducted by the National Science Foundation–funded Graphics and Visualization Center.[26] Similar environments that support virtual field experiences are under development.

Significant Research Challenges

As the examples illustrate, cyberinfrastructure can help us teach difficult and important material that requires more sophisticated modeling, simulations, and visualization. It allows us to examine and interact simultaneously with multiple, heterogeneous, dynamic, and nonlinear processes that may also exhibit stochastic and irregular behavior. But many challenges remain.[27]

▶ Often sophisticated mathematics or other science concepts are buried beneath virtual simulations or animations; for example, approximation algorithms are hidden. If these are not "certified" to be numerically stable and well implemented, then the output of the simulations might be incorrectly calculated and mislead the viewer. Thus even though visually striking learning environments can be rendered, vital implementation issues need attention. Moreover this suggests that the incorporation of "visual counterexamples" might be used to create effective learning opportunities. What are the conditions under which such approaches can be used?

▶ How is experimental error "faithfully" reproduced? What about artificial error that results from an incorrect choice of an approximation algorithm?

▶ What is the relationship of virtual or otherwise Web-enabled laboratory environments to the traditional "lab bench" or "wet lab" experience? How can hybrid models be created that marry the best of both worlds? What *is* the "best" of each world?

▶ What does *effective* mean in the phrase "effective learning environments"? How do we instrument these environments to measure effectiveness? Moreover, what are the conditions for effective use? Are there any generalizable conditions? Learner behavior in the laboratory—physical and virtual—can be tracked and observed with much greater detail (for example, via electronic "footprints") thanks to cyberinfrastructure. How can these data trails be analyzed, and what understanding do they provide?

▶ Even in virtual or Web-enabled learning environments, there is still a need to create a "wrapper" around the images/animations, the framework of inquiry around the simulation, or the experimental process around the remote manipulation of instrumentation. How will this major faculty development effort be addressed?

▶ What is the (new) role of the instructor within the learner-centered environment? How is the professional role of the teacher/professor changing? How must pre- and in-service teacher preparation programs change? What are the implications for faculty development?

▶ Informal learning settings are also being changed, raising the question, where is the locus (or loci) of learning?

▶ How does the educational system respond to changing behavioral patterns and technical skills of students who are increasingly more comfortable with IT than teachers? What is the impact on the actual development of new materials, resources, products, and processes? What are the new continuing professional development needs for teachers and faculty?

▶ Is there a proper "mix" of the analog and digital? If so, what are its features? As more and more senses are recruited to represent phenomena, what cognitive issues come into play when dealing with the interaction of these different inputs in the process of sense making? Is there an optimal use of haptic feedback?

What Will It Take to Succeed?[28]

Significant changes in teaching and learning are possible, particularly when interactive technologies are involved. These changes promise to better engage the Net Generation and the adult learner. But, what will it take to turn the promise into success?

Revisit Your Assumptions

The deep reflection required to convert a course or elements of a course into cyberspace forces a fresh consideration of students' experiences in typical classroom settings. Many faculty shy away from this reexamination. Those who do, however, report that cyberspace or the introduction of technology into their site-based classes can be a transformational and refreshing experience in which they rediscover the source of their original attraction to the academy and renew that commitment in exciting new ways.

As one faculty member put it, "Technology is a giant mirror reflecting back to you your own deepest issues. It challenges you to clarify what you value, to rediscover why you went into teaching in the first place, and to be honest about whether your original hopes have been realized. It also sheds light on how we interact with our students and how they respond to our courses, and [it] forces us to think about the real meaning of community and what it is that a group of people assembled in a single physical space experience and how that compares to what a group of people in cyberspace might experience." This same faculty member went on to say that the real power of technology resides in its ability to help us reassert our basic purposes and values as we seek to translate these fundamental purposes into new media and forms of interaction.

Deeply held values and assumptions that we have not examined for a long time must be revisited—and either affirmed or amended—before we can approach the use of different media for communication and exchange.

Engage Learners

Everyone can and will participate in cyberspace; the ideas will generate ongoing discussion long after the class is over. The very thought process that leads to discovery and understanding in a particular field can be exposed and modeled for students, who can then have an authentic experience within the discipline.

How many teachers take time to assure themselves that every student has truly participated in a classroom setting and that the exchange is meaningful? How often is the exchange simply a set of questions raised by students—sometimes in the form of "Will this be on the exam?"—that are answered by the instructor in the form of a monologue?

Relax Control

While reexamining instruction is good, it can be exhausting and unsettling to faculty who have grown up with a traditional view of faculty roles. Online students may interact with the material or each other at any time day or night. This means that the instructor's time is equally unbounded. In cyberspace, the whole thought process is laid open in the building of understanding through much richer conversation. Students can find material that challenges the faculty member's worldview and expertise; they can uncover stories and research results that the faculty member has never heard about. It can be uncomfortable when the instructor no longer controls the subject matter the students will use.

Return to Core Values

In electronic exchanges, faculty members are free to be experts (for example, a physicist, a biologist, or an historian) and to draw their students into the ways of thinking, examinations of ideas, and forms of proof that are the intellectual basis of a field. In addition, original documents and fresh research data are readily accessible on the Web.

In simple terms, students can *do* history, not just hear someone talk about history; they can do biology, not just talk about other people doing biology. In cyberspace, the instructor has unbounded access to electronic images and texts that open up the full range of historical inquiry, analysis, and interpretation, as well as access to contemporary material.

The instructor can model intellectual work, exposing through electronic means thought processes and realities—the blind alleys and sudden bursts of clarity—that we all experience in our search for understanding. For many, this is unnerving; control is lost over both the interaction and the material. For others, it is a true liberation. For everyone, however, it can provide a much more immediate and authentic experience of inquiry than most classroom interactions can offer.

Reflect on the True Meaning of Learning

We face vexing questions today as we try to define the meaning and purpose of an undergraduate education, the nature and goals of graduate education, and the nature of faculty work.

▶ What do we need to know and be able to do with what we know?

▶ Is the very nature of the production of knowledge changing? How can we be sure that we are basing our actions on valid understanding?

▶ If the university and the disciplines are no longer the sole source of discovery, interpretation, and validation, how will we know "truth," and who will have the authority to declare that a particular form of knowledge is valid?

▶ What do we learn alone without interactions with others? Is this self-study different from what we learn as members of a community? Does it matter whether that community is bounded by a specific location or sense of place or placed in cyberspace?

▶ Will electronically facilitated interactions—in the absence of personal experience and knowledge of each other—promote a new kind of "unconnected" learning? If so, what difference will this make in the development of practitioners, citizens, and scholars?

The most important gift of liberal learning is the nurturing of a prepared mind, a deep sense of social responsibility, and a commitment to the importance of citizenship in a community of others. Can this kind of "virtuous learning" occur through virtual encounters in cyberspace? Are there other ways to accomplish the same integration of cognitive, social, and emotional development that occur now in face-to-face encounters with others? In cyberspace, can we foster some of the fundamental qualities of a prepared mind, such as

▶ the ability to learn, not just to memorize the rules of a particular task but to be able to discern or discover what the rules are or should be from a study of situations that are unfamiliar to us;

▶ the ability to recognize when we do know something and when we don't;

▶ the capacity to make sense out of an infinite world of images, assertions, words, and "facts," as well as act responsibly and wisely on that knowledge; and

▶ the ability to apply knowledge resourcefully and ethically.

Model the Highest Standards

In our direct and recorded electronic interactions with students, as educators we must be mindful of our duty to set good examples of what it means to be truly educated, to be responsible learners, to reflect in our ideas and our interactions with others the values of a liberal education, and to be models of integrity. Whether we like it or not, the record of our exchanges in cyberspace reveal a great deal about us. In many ways, technology can both deepen and clarify our educational aims and help us further them. Technology, appropriately used to enhance and expand the scope of educational experience, can enrich our intellectual lives and offer our students an authentic route to discovery.

The most powerful effect of cyberexperience may not manifest in the things people do on the Web or with broadband communication, but rather in how they think and in what they expect from education. People who innovate and create in cyberspace likely will not sit still for a lecture.

Endnotes

1. Consortium for School Networking (CSN), *Digital Divide Leadership* (Washington, D.C.: Consortium for School Networking, 2004), <http://www.cosn.org/resources/grunwald/digital_leadership_divide.pdf>.

2. Douglas Levin and Sousan Arafeh, "The Digital Disconnect: The Widening Gap Between Internet-Savvy Students and Their Schools" (Washington, D.C.: Pew Internet & American Life Project, August 14, 2002), <http://www.pewinternet.org/report_display.asp?r=67>.

3. National Research Council, Institute of Medicine, *Engaging Schools: Fostering High School Students' Motivation to Learn* (Washington, D.C.: National Academies Press, 2004), p. ix, <http://books.nap.edu/catalog/10421.html>.

4. Ibid., p. 2.

5. Ibid., p. 3.

6. Kenneth C. Green, *2004 Campus Computing Survey* (Encinco, Calif.: Campus Computing Project, 2004), <http://www.campuscomputing.net/>.

7. Steve Jones at el., "The Internet Goes to College: How Students Are Living in the Future with Today's Technology" (Washington, D.C.: Pew Internet & American Life Project, September 15, 2002), <http://www.pewinternet.org/reports/toc.asp?Report=71>.

8. National Research Council, *How People Learn: Brain, Mind, Experience, and School: Expanded Edition*, John D. Bransford, Ann L. Brown, and Rodney R. Cocking, eds. (Washington, D.C.: National Academies Press, 2000), <http://www.nap.edu/catalog/9853.html>.

9. WiMAX Forum, <http://www.wimaxforum.org/>.

10. Edward L. Ayers, "Technological Revolutions I Have Known," in *Computing in the Social Sciences and Humanities,* Orville Vernon Burton, ed. (Urbana, Ill.: University of Illinois Press, 2002), p. 24.

11. Ibid., p. 24.

12. Ibid., p. 24.

13. Ibid., p. 25.

14. For a discussion of the assessment of scholarship, see Charles E. Glassick, Mary Taylor Huber, and Gene I. Maeroff, *Scholarship Assessed: Evaluation of the Professoriate* (San Francisco: Jossey-Bass, 1997).

15. Ayers, op. cit., p. 27.

16. See (a) <http://www.smartmoney.com/marketmap/?nav=hp_marketmap> for an interesting nonacademic example of an image database; and (b) <http://www.nsdl.org/collection/ataglance/browseBySubject.html> to view a digital library's collection holdings by content domains.

17. See <http://java.sun.com/applets/jdk/1.1/demo/SortDemo/index.html>.

18. See <http://www.foundationcoalition.org/home/keycomponents/concept/introduction.html>.

19. See <http://mazur-www.harvard.edu/news.php?area=8>.

20. See <http://www.einstruction.com/>.

21. See <http://www.wirelessgrids.net/>.

22. See <http://www.concord.org/research/handhelds.html>.

23. See <http://www.techworthy.com/Laptop/January2004/Handhelds-With-Class.htm?Page=1>.

24. See <http://www.govtech.net/?pg=magazine/story&id=91038&issue=8:2004>.

25. See <http://kmoddl.library.cornell.edu/about6.php>.

26. See <http://graphics.cs.brown.edu/research/sciviz/brain/brain.html>.

27. Funding of course remains a constant challenge. It is necessary to support not only the building out of the physical information technology infrastructure (especially in the face of continued evolution of technology), but also critical faculty development needs. This condition has been reported on in greater depth elsewhere, along with calls for a corresponding shift in culture that rewards efforts and innovation in the scholarship of bringing innovative educational technologies to bear on the classroom. It should be noted, however, that not all solutions are necessarily expensive ones (for example, the use of low-cost electronic clickers described above), and access and equity issues remain.

28. Material adapted from Judith A. Ramaley, "Technology as a Mirror," *Liberal Education,* vol. 87, no. 3 (summer 2001), pp. 46–53.

About the Authors

Judith A. Ramaley holds a presidential professorship in biomedical sciences at the University of Maine and is a fellow of the Margaret Chase Smith Center for Public Policy. She is also a visiting senior scientist at the National Academy of Sciences. From 2001 to 2004, she was assistant director, Education and Human Resources Directorate, at the National Science Foundation (NSF). Prior to joining the NSF, Ramaley was president of the University of Vermont (UVM) and professor of biology from 1997 to 2001. Before coming to UVM, she was president and professor of biology at Portland State University in Portland, Oregon, for seven years. Ramaley has a special interest in higher education reform and has helped design regional alliances to promote educational cooperation. She has also contributed to a national exploration of the changing nature of work and the workforce and the role of higher education in the school-to-work agenda. Ramaley has played a national role in the exploration of civic responsibility and partnerships between higher education and society.

Lee Zia is the lead program director for the National Science Foundation (NSF) National Science, Mathematics, Engineering, and Technology Education Digital Library (NSDL) program. He served as a "rotator" in the NSF Division of Undergraduate Education during calendar years 1995 and 1996 while on leave from the Department of Mathematics at the University of New Hampshire. Zia rejoined the NSF as a permanent staff member in the fall of 1999 and was named the lead program director for NSDL in late 2000. He earned his bachelor's in mathematics from the University of North Carolina, where he was a Morehead Scholar and graduated Phi Beta Kappa. Zia holds a master's in mathematics from the University of Michigan and a doctorate in applied mathematics from Brown University.

CHAPTER 9

Curricula Designed to Meet 21st-Century Expectations

Alma R. Clayton-Pedersen with Nancy O'Neill
Association of American Colleges and Universities

Introduction

When I first began working in higher education, most of the traditional-aged students in the class of 2005 had just been born. I remember my excitement when a departing colleague gave me her PC. I confess that I've never used my computer as more than a glorified typewriter; however, I can also say that colleagues and I have done groundbreaking work that used many cutting-edge technologies in the service of learning. This chapter focuses on how higher education can use technologies to implement curricula designed to meet 21st-century expectations for students' learning.

Recently, a new college graduate said to me that, in her experience, professors' use of technology had largely consisted of converting their teaching notes into PowerPoint slides. Where students had once called a large number of their classes "death by lecture," she noted they were now calling them "death by PowerPoint." Why did this student have such a cynical view of the use of technology for learning? Prior to college, most students have used a wide variety of technologies in their everyday lives, ranging from audio book cassettes as very young nonreaders, to sophisticated handheld games as adolescents, to instant messaging programs to "talk to" their friends—at home or abroad—anytime, anywhere via the Internet as young adults.

Yet too often, students' use of technology in higher education settings has been relegated to searching the Internet, accessing an online course, or word-processing. In some pockets of campus, faculty have used technological applications to disseminate information or to help students expedite problem solving. Some typical examples include

- graphing calculators for complex mathematical computations and displaying trigonometric functions;
- graphics programs for displaying phenomena in the natural and earth sciences;
- statistical software packages that can manipulate large data sets in the social sciences; and
- design software for developing architectural and engineering models.

With such specific applications of technology and the limited use of other forms (for example, multimedia), students' low expectations for the use of technology in the curriculum is not surprising. Such constrained use of technology by the faculty in the curriculum and low student expectations may serve to limit innovation and creativity as well as the faculty's capacity to engage students more deeply in their subject matter. Like all organizations, colleges and universities respond to the demands placed upon them. Students' and institutions' low expectations for the use of technology for learning provide insufficient impetus for faculties to change their behavior and make broader, more innovative use of these tools in the service of learning.

Students' personal experience with technology is typically broad and in many cases very deep. Moreover, their extensive use of technology continues throughout their college experience—that is, except fully integrated into the curriculum.

Implications

- Faculty's understanding of the teaching and learning power of technology needs to be increased.
- Increasing the use of technology will increase demands for technological tools to be effectively integrated into the curriculum to enhance student learning.
- Tools need to be developed to help faculty integrate technology into the curriculum.

21st-Century Expectations

Changes in the larger society over the last 100 years—various social movements, the advent of telecommunications, the movement from industrial-based to knowledge-based work, struggles over political boundaries, modern technology and science breakthroughs employed in both the most positive and most negative of circumstances—have in some form or another impacted the ways colleges and universities "do" higher education. Colleges and universities in the 21st century educate a much larger, more diverse population of students, foster scholarship countless new areas of inquiry, and offer opportunities in many new settings and formats, including online. Yet many facets of higher education have remained relatively untouched by time, at times to the detriment of our functioning in this new era. To better meet individual and societal needs of the 21st century, numerous leaders—inside and outside higher education—recognized at the end of the 20th century that college and university missions and practices needed to be reinvigorated. Within such a process, perhaps consensus could be reached about the new expectations we needed for students, for curricula, and given its infusion into society, for technology.

For Students

Since 2000, the Association of American Colleges and Universities (AAC&U) has engaged colleges and universities across the nation in such a process, through a multiyear, multilayered initiative called Greater Expectations. For the first two years of the initiative, AAC&U senior staff convened a national panel of experts who were charged with identifying the hallmarks of a 21st-century college graduate. With input from a consortium of leadership campuses engaged in innovative practices to realize high achievement levels for their students, the national panel recommended new emphasis be placed on educating students to be purposeful and self-directed in multiple ways—on becoming intentional learners. The report issued from their work, *Greater Expectations: A New Vision for Learning as a Nation Goes to College,* states:

> Becoming such an intentional learner means developing self-awareness about the reason for study, the learning process itself, and how education is used. Intentional learners are integrative thinkers who can see connections in seemingly disparate information and draw on a wide range of knowledge to make decisions. They adapt the skills learned in one situation to new problems encountered in another—in a classroom, the workplace, their communities, and their personal lives. As a result, intentional learners succeed even when instability is the only constant.[1]

The report also notes:

> The intentional learner is empowered through intellectual and practical skills; *informed* by knowledge and ways of knowing; and responsible for personal actions and civic values... Mastery of a

range of abilities and capacities empowers intentional learners as they maneuver in and shape a world in flux.... Intentional learners possess a core of knowledge, both broad and deep, derived from many fields.... Through discussion, critical analysis, and introspection, intentional learners come to understand their roles in society and accept active participation.[2]

In short, students are expected to draw on various knowledge bases, integrate them, conduct increasingly more sophisticated analyses as they progress through college, and use their integrated knowledge to solve complex problems.

In 2004, AAC&U commissioned a series of focus groups to determine students' views of liberal education. Data obtained from these sessions with high school and college seniors in Indiana, Oregon, and Virginia revealed that both groups of students have individualized and material interests in mind in wanting to obtain a four-year college degree.[3] Greater Expectations—and by extension, many institutions of higher education—has broader goals for Net Generation student learning than do students themselves. In other words, each group has a very different view of higher education's purpose. In addition to articulating the larger purposes of higher education and aligning students' and institutions' expectations, increased attention must be paid to how technology can be used for both these purposes.

Implications

▶ Better alignment is needed between higher education's communication of its purposes and what K–12 education, parents, and the community perceive as its purpose.

▶ Communication needs to include better uses of technology to assess[4] high-quality educational environments.

For the Curriculum

Low-level technologies such as overhead projectors, televisions, and videocassette recorders have been used for some time to focus college students on specific subject matter. The use of technologies typically included text, equations, graphics, and pictures to enhance learning through models and content-rich stories. Early work in learning technology focused on combining what we knew about visual learning and low-end technologies to create multimedia tools to enhance student learning.

Examples of products of this early work by the Cognition and Technology Group at Vanderbilt University (CTGV) included the Adventures of Jasper Woodbury Series and Scientist in Action.[5] Today, these tools still provide middle school teachers with vehicles to enlarge their students' learning. Math and science problem sets are embedded in authentic stories that students understand because the stories reflect their everyday experiences. These authentic problem-solving exercises not only engage students in their learning but also stimulate them to want to learn more.

From the beginning, however, a problem arose in that those middle school students went on to high schools and later to colleges that did not (and do not) provide this type of rich learning experience—a learning experience that can best be achieved when technology is used in the service of learning. If we are to adequately prepare students for an era of change, information, and knowledge explosion in the 21st century, we must alter this scenario. Schools, colleges, and universities must draw on a variety of technologies and use them as resources to deepen students' learning. When we simply ensure that students have access to the latest, most powerful computers, we make technology an end unto itself instead of the powerful teaching and learning tool that it can be.

Implications

▶ Much of the learning technology innovation in higher education has been focused on K–12 teacher preparation and development. More focus needs to be placed on preparing existing faculty for the future Net Generation students who will populate the 21st-century classroom.

▶ To the extent that colleges and universities involve interested faculty and students in working together to develop tools that truly engage them both, the more fruitful their efforts are likely to be for the larger higher education community.

For Technology

Over the past 20 years, most colleges and universities have moved technology from being a one-time budget expenditure to being a hard budget line to support the purchase, maintenance, and, in many cases, use of technology on campus. Less attention has been given to how to help students achieve the desired learning outcomes through technology. While significant financial resources have been devoted to building the technical infrastructure at colleges and universities, much less has been devoted to ensuring that this investment is used to its maximum.

For example, at present, new residence halls are almost never built without considering the choice of hardwired or wireless high-speed Internet access. The question is not if, but how, to make technology more accessible for students. Colleges also increase students' access to technology by establishing computer labs in various locations on campus, defining laptop requirements, and offering computer loan programs. Yet, comparatively little support has been devoted to helping faculty use computers and other technologies in creative and innovative ways to deepen student learning. Worse yet, institutional structures and practices to resolve technical problems that faculty invariably encounter are very limited or are not the type of aid needed. Such lack of support limits the amount of time faculty can spend on what they do best—building a compelling curriculum and integrating technology for more powerful learning.

College and university faculty must effectively tap students' existing familiarity with technology to engage them in constructing an integrated knowledge base and developing habits of the mind that will enable them to become lifelong learners. Technology can then become a tool used in the service of learning rather than an end itself.

Implications

▶ Institutions need to establish greater expectations for maximizing their investment in technology by exploring and assessing the best use of technology for learning.

▶ Greater investments may be needed in faculty professional development in the effective use of technology for learning.

▶ Faculty's effort to infuse technology into the curriculum requires support in developing strategies and in resolving technical difficulties. This means more than the technical help desk. What is needed is assistance for using technology to achieve the teaching and learning outcomes we desire.

Technology and the Curriculum

What is the current role of technology in the college curriculum? To develop intentional learners, the curriculum must go beyond helping students gain knowledge for knowledge's sake to engaging students in the construction of knowledge for the sake of addressing the challenges faced by a complex, global society.

According to the Greater Expectations National Panel, the curriculum and the cocurriculum should provide numerous paths by which students can achieve broad liberal education outcomes alongside specialized knowledge of one or more disciplines. If students have achieved these outcomes, they will excel at

▶ communicating well in diverse settings and groups, using written, oral, and visual means;
▶ employing both quantitative and qualitative analysis to describe and solve problems; and
▶ working well in teams, including those of diverse composition, and building consensus.[6]

These outcomes can be achieved through strategies such as writing assignments (expository, creative, and personal writing); required and critiqued oral presentations; and problem-based learning.

Students need mastery in areas that include knowledge of human imagination and expression, global and cross-cultural communities, and modeling the natural world. This mastery can be obtained thorough

▶ undergraduate research;
▶ inquiry-based science labs;
▶ planned and supervised experiences in teamwork, both in class and in off-campus settings;
▶ interdisciplinary and integrated courses on creativity through the ages;
▶ drawing on students' diverse experiences to enrich classroom discussion;
▶ integrating study abroad into courses back on the home campus;
▶ teaching courses worldwide through videoconferencing; and
▶ student team-designed lab experiments to answer questions.[7]

Students can be expected to be responsible for active participation as citizens of a diverse democracy, understanding themselves and their multiple identities by engaging in

▶ service learning;
▶ debate on proposed solutions to current social problems; and
▶ personal writing that requires self-reflection on a wide variety of subjects and that situates the self in relation to others.[8]

Use of Technology

In what ways might technology enhance each of these innovations and help students achieve desired learning outcomes? At the most basic level, effectively using computer technology is itself a skill that we want students to develop. Using computer applications such as Access and Excel makes managing and manipulating data much more efficient.

While it's clear that such applications have great utility in business administration courses such as accounting, these programs are often used for other purposes and in other subjects. These applications can be designed to sort a variety of types of information, such as to sort information obtained from qualitative interviews or to sort by predetermined criteria a number of funding possibilities for a service-learning project. The mere act of setting up small text databases and linking them to equations for analysis gives students practice in managing knowledge, as well as allowing them to easily transfer text to charts and displaying information in a variety of ways. Knowing how to use all the functions of these and other programs such as PowerPoint enables learners to efficiently edit text and include graphics in the final products they submit to demonstrate their learning. These uses of technology can be applied to undergraduate research and can contribute to students making reasoned linkages among seemingly discreet pieces of information, therefore integrating knowledge for deeper learning.

Multiple Media

By using multimedia, faculty and students can demonstrate an enriched teaching and learning enterprise that goes well beyond more traditional "cubicle-based" computer use. Consider this scenario: A sociology professor forms student teams to explore the presence of various racial and ethnic populations in the United States over time, with a focus on groups that are underrepresented in higher education today. Technology is to be used to facilitate team cohesion, as well as to demonstrate outcomes of the research. The professor first has the class discuss the process of working in teams, both in person and virtually, with one outcome of the project being for students to learn to work in diverse groups.[9] The professor then explains that the project will require a traditional literature review and written analysis, but teams are encouraged to make the text Web-based and combine it with graphics and video to provide comparative analysis and illustration of, for example, voluntary immigration to the United States among new African populations versus patterns of involuntary enslavement of Africans over a specifiedperiod of time. The use of multimedia allows this particular team to incorporate video clips of descendents of slaves from library archives and their own interviews with new immigrants alongside third-person historical accounts and newspaper articles. At the end of the project, the professor asks the teams to include video clips of a reflection session where the group considers what benefits might have been accrued from working in a diverse team that would not have been gained by tackling the project individually. By opening up both the process and the content to multimedia, the professor encouraged more powerful learning than would have occurred with simply assigning independent term papers.

The use of multimedia enables students to demonstrate learning beyond a specific topic under study. The example above specifically focuses on comparisons of voluntary and involuntary immigration; however, working in teams and using multiple technological forms facilitates the introduction of other topics such as social justice, ethics, and economic systems more easily. Group work where students can match their talents and interests to specific technological tasks enables each student to pursue an aspect of the assignment that appeals to the way she or he learns best.

Add Flexibility
Because we know that different students learn best when they are challenged to learn in different ways, technology allows teachers to add flexibility to how they present new information and provide feedback to students. For example, both skills and content will be enhanced when students are asked to demonstrate their learning through multimedia presentations to the rest of the class. Virtual discussions allow instructors to help the class develop their analytical judgment.

Real-Time Engagement
The course assignment cited above can also help students explore the circumstances surrounding each immigrant group's departure from its homeland, the route or routes taken to arrive in the United States, where they arrived, and why. The assignment could take on a deeper dimension by using videoconferencing and e-mail to link teams to students living in the countries of origin of the groups being studied. Integrating real-time global experiences into the classroom can provide a new, first-person information source and engender debate about the validity of various sources of information used in conducting research. These technologies make it easier for courses to depart from chronological, linear formats.

Undergraduate Research

Undergraduate research can provide students with an opportunity to learn problem-solving and discovery techniques and to apply what they've learned to real-life, unscripted problems. With the infusion of technology, students can learn not only new techniques for discovery but also techniques for demonstrating the results of discovery. For example, as part of a Fund for the Improvement of Postsecondary Education grant, several colleagues and I at Vanderbilt University embedded student research in a course designed to develop a multimedia Diversity Opportunity Tool (DOT). The tool was designed to help students, faculty, and staff develop the skills needed to productively respond to acts of discrimination and to make decisions about when they need to act, depending on the situation. The team-taught course required students to conduct a literature review on U.S. race relations historically and currently, the psychology of discriminatory behavior, and racial-attitude development. Students also conducted interviews with peers and analyzed the data in light of specific topics they would cover in their final projects. They then developed scripts that told compelling stories centered on discrimination, connected to the findings of their original and archival research. Students integrated their learning through a demonstration video that served as a companion piece to their final written work.

Our goal was to combine students' research with video stories to shape vignettes that would make up this educational tool. In developing the scenarios, scripts, video, pilot testing, and final products related to DOT, graduate and undergraduate students were engaged in filming, acting, and producing the tool. Undergraduate research, combined with technology, became a vehicle to bring research into practice in a tangible way and to contribute to the fields of educational and antidiscrimination training.

Repositories over Time

These illustrations focus on course-level learning, but technology can support learning in broader, cumulative ways as well. For example, students can use multimedia e-portfolios as repositories for culminating classroom assignments, for demonstrations of learning in the major and in general education, and for a senior-year capstone project. Additionally, e-portfolios can be used to demonstrate leadership and learning outcomes gained through cocurricular and work experiences, and they can follow a student if she or he transfers from one institution to another.

Blended Instruction

As faculty become more comfortable with assigning multimedia projects—and students with completing them—there will likely be growth in interdisciplinary multimedia assignments and projects. These assignments not only serve the student developing the project but also can be used as a resource for users' learning. Tools such as the Adventures of Jasper Woodbury, Scientists in Action, and DOT illustrate this potential. Each had elements of its development tied to graduate and undergraduate research and coursework. Such tools can enable users to engage in self-paced movement through activities or can be blended into traditional group training.

The examples given above integrate multiple learning objectives and introduce students to many of the learning strategies outlined in the *Greater Expectations* report, such as

▶ practice in team building;
▶ writing that is both expository and creative;
▶ multiple forms of communication;
▶ informed judgment about sources of information; and
▶ reflection that situates the self in relation to others and provides an opportunity for individuals to come to a deeper understanding of differences, commonalities, and systemic inequities.

Technology alone does not make this happen. Each of these strategies is facilitated through the intentional use of a variety of tools—both traditional and cutting edge—by individual faculty and campus-wide curriculum planners.

Some faculty have expressed concern that expanding the use of technology in and out of the classroom will both undermine the role of faculty and overburden them with additional responsibilities. With the expansion of online courses, cyberdiscussion groups, the increasing ubiquity of communication technologies, and faculty already feeling the pressure of added responsibilities, these concerns are not surprising. Faculty concerns perhaps center less on being "replaceable" and more on worrying that the teaching and learning enterprise will be reduced to students gathering information that can be easily downloaded, causing them to rely too heavily on technology instead of intellect.

The *Greater Expectations* report recognizes new demands on the faculty at all educational levels. Yet there are at least two reasons why technology concerns should be allayed. First, traditional age students overwhelmingly prefer face-to-face contact with faculty to mediated communication. Second, technology used in the service of learning will require more—not less—sophistication on the part of students as they engage in processes of integration, translation, audience analysis, and critical judgment. The learning outcomes of a 21st-century education will enable us to meet new challenges here and abroad, ranging from information "overload" to persistent inequality and pressing social issues. These challenges require educators who can think in interdisciplinary, multimedia ways to construct the 21st-century curriculum. Faculty with expertise in one or more subjects, who have been exposed to what we know about how people learn, can determine how to enhance this learning through the use of technology. But simply understanding how to use technology will not provide the integration needed to reach the desired learning outcomes.

When thinking about integrating technology into the curriculum, Chickering and Gamson's seven principles of good practice continue to be sound:

▶ Encourage contact between students and faculty.
▶ Develop reciprocity and cooperation among students.
▶ Encourage active learning.
▶ Give prompt feedback.
▶ Emphasize time on task.
▶ Communicate high expectations.
▶ Respect diverse talents and ways of learning.[10]

Implications

▶ There is a need for integrating technology that is in the service of learning throughout the curriculum.
▶ More intentional use of technology to capture what students know and are able to integrate in their learning is needed.

Assessment

As we increase the use of multiple technologies in the service of learning, we will need to assess its impact. Students tend to be more technology savvy than faculty. Faculty are still much more knowledgeable about the subject matter at the heart of what students should learn. As such, concerns that students choose form over substance are probably unwarranted—content will triumph over glitz when it is delivered in rich, engaging, purposeful, and practical ways, as can be done with multilayered teaching strategies and tools.

In light of this, higher education will need to assess the elements of technology that work best to facilitate students' learning—not just generically but under specific circumstances. This requires that an initial baseline of students' prior use of technology be established (including the kinds of technology used) and the contexts in which they have used technology. Faculty, as architects of the curriculum, must then articulate learning outcomes for the different levels of curriculum (course, sequence, major, general education, and entire collegiate curriculum). Those faculty members interested in the intersection of teaching, technology, and learning must identify the elements critical to learner success as well as those that can impede success. But we must also listen to our learners. Too often we engage in curricular design and assessment without benefit of feedback from students.[11]

Implications

▶ Students' learning of the subject matter and the role of technology in their learning will need to be assessed.
▶ The extent to which technology is a tool for learning and a tool for assessment of learning will facilitate faculty's increasing comfort in integrating technology into the curriculum.

Conclusion

Future careers will require higher levels of education than in the past. That education must enable individuals to discover what they need to know rather than just having static knowledge. Society will need college graduates with mental agility and adaptability.

If this is the goal of education, colleges and universities must reexamine how that goal is achieved. The Net Generation and the current capabilities of information technology make it possible to support learning activities that will enable graduates to be mentally agile and adaptable. However, beyond technical infrastructure, the use of technology in the service of learning is limited.

The *Greater Expectations* report calls for a focus on developing intentional learners; it also calls for developing intentional institutions. Colleges and universities are connecting silos of administrative work with relational databases so that, for example, financial aid structures can interface with human resources and accounting, ensuring students can work for the institution and maintain simultaneous student and staff categorizations. Eight years ago this was not easy, but today no one thinks it should be any other way. Clearly, technology can facilitate the achievement of the operational goals of the institution. But achieving one of its most important goals—improving the learning of all students—through technology will require conversations at all levels—department, college, institution, and state. With calls for greater accountability for increased spending and for assessment of student learning, we can ask for no less than the effective and coherent integration of technology into an enriched curriculum that meets both student and societal expectations.

Endnotes

1. Association of American Colleges and Universities (AAC&U) *Greater Expectations National Panel, Greater Expectations: A New Vision for Learning as a Nation Goes to College* (Washington, D.C.: Association of American Colleges and Universities, 2002), <http://www.greaterexpectations.org/>, pp. 21–22.

2. Ibid., pp. 22–23.

3. AAC&U, unpublished research.

4. The Education Trust will be releasing a database of information that provides every college and university's graduation rates disaggregated by race and ethnicity. This database will enable parents and communities to begin to make comparative analysis of their college choice based on one criterion—graduation rates. This will not indicate quality, but it is a start in demonstrating comparatively the outcomes of colleges. As such databases become easier to develop and make accessible, I envision the inclusion of more compelling criteria that gets directly at the learning outcomes defined in the Greater Expectations initiative.

5. A description of the Adventures of Jasper Woodbury Series can be found at <http://www.enc.org/about/partners/donors/0,2134,86356,00.shtm>. New copies of the series are unavailable, as efforts are focused on converting the video materials into a CD-ROM problem-solving format. Contact the Department of Teaching and Learning at Peabody College, Vanderbilt University (http://peabody.vanderbilt.edu/tl/index.htm) for more information.

6. AAC&U Greater Expectations National Panel, op. cit., p. 22.

7. Ibid., p. 33.

8. Ibid., p. 33.

9. For more on structuring groups to accrue the educational benefits of students' compositional diversity, see Jeffrey F. Milem, Mitchell J. Chang, and Anthony L. Antonio, *Making Diversity Work on Campus: A Research-Based Perspective* (Washington, D.C.: AAC&U, 2004); available January 2005 at <http://www.aacu.org/>.

10. See Arthur W. Chickering and Zelda F. Gamson, "Seven Principles for Good Practice in Undergraduate Education," *AAHE Bulletin*, vol. 39, no. 7 (March 1987), pp. 3–7, <http://aahebulletin.com/public/archive/sevenprinciples1987.asp>.

11. Beyond classroom and programmatic assessment, it is important to consider how research on technology and learning can be fostered on our campuses and used to inform our institutional functioning. For more information on the scholarship of teaching and learning, visit the Web sites of The Carnegie Foundation for the Advancement of Teaching (http://www.carnegiefoundation.org/CASTL/index.htm) and the American Association for Higher Education (http://www.aahe.org/projects/campus_program/index.html). A simple Google search on the scholarship of teaching and learning and technology will reveal many campus efforts devoted to this work, such as Penn State's Teaching and Learning with Technology (http://tlt.its.psu.edu/).

Further Reading

J. D. Bransford et al., "Anchored Instruction: Why We Need It and How Technology Can Help," in Don Nix, R. J. Spiro, and Rand Sprio, eds., *Cognition, Education, and Multimedia* (Hillsdale, N.J.: Erlbaum Associates, 1990).

Arthur W. Chickering and Stephen C. Ehrmann, "Implementing the Seven Principles: Technology as Lever," *AAHE Bulletin*, vol. 49, no. 2 (October 1996), pp. 3–6; available with updated information at <http://www.tltgroup.org/programs/seven.html>.

Cognition and Technology Group at Vanderbilt, "Anchored Instruction and Its Relationship to Situated Cognition," *Educational Researcher*, vol. 19, no. 6 (1990), pp. 2–10.

Cognition and Technology Group at Vanderbilt, "Anchored Instruction and Situated Cognition Revisited," *Educational Technology*, vol. 33, no. 3 (1993), pp. 52–70.

About the Authors

Alma R. Clayton-Pedersen is a vice president at the Association of American Colleges and Universities (AAC&U). She codirects the Network for Academic Renewal, a series of four annual meetings that addresses institutional leadership topics including technology and learning. As part of the Greater Expectations initiative, Clayton-Pedersen directs a summer institute designed for campus teams of administrators and faculty to explore institutional change strategies. While at Vanderbilt University (1984–1999), she and her colleagues developed the Diversity Opportunity Tool (DOT), an interactive multimedia product. There she was also an investigator on the project Building on Strengths: Accelerated, Integrated Curriculum and Its Effects on Children, Teachers, and Parents, which combined technology-based middle school curriculum in science, math, and language arts for more integrated learning. She completed her undergraduate degree at the University of Wisconsin–Milwaukee and her MEd and PhD degrees at Vanderbilt University.

Nancy O'Neill is director of programs for the Office of Education and Institutional Renewal at AAC&U, where she works with the Pathways to College Network, BellSouth Foundation's College-Going Minorities initiative, and the new Inclusive Excellence initiative. At the University of Maryland (UMD), she served as the Arts and Humanities liaison at the Career Center, directed the Sexual Harassment Prevention Program, and launched First Year Focus, designed to support students outside honors and enrichment programs. O'Neill earned her bachelor's from State University of New York–Buffalo. She holds an MA in American Studies and an MEd in College Student Personnel from UMD. Her interests include student development, academic affairs/student affairs partnerships, diversity, women's studies, and pedagogical reform.

CHAPTER 10

Support Services for the Net Generation

J. James Wager

The Pennsylvania State University

Introduction

Traditional-age first-year freshmen entering college in the fall of 2005 were most likely born in 1987 when the information age was well under way. These students, known as the Net Generation, have grown up in an environment significantly different from the one most higher education faculty, staff, and administrators experienced during their developmental years. Many characteristics of the Net Generation have been described in other chapters of this book.

One of the most striking generational differences is that access to and use of technology is simply assumed by today's learners. Technology is invisible and intuitive; students don't "learn technology," nor do they think of it as separate from the activities it enables. For the Net Generation, just as television sets have "always" been in color with a remote control and a cable or satellite connection, the delivery of services has "always" been available on the Web or other relevant technology. Because of their background, the Net Generation has adopted a different set of premises and expectations that call for new—and sometimes challenging—responses from the academy.

Some have described changing colleges and universities as akin to turning an aircraft carrier. Unlike a small pleasure boat that can maneuver quickly and change course rapidly, the aircraft carrier requires a carefully planned maneuver and a large berth to complete its turn. While information technology has had a significant impact on the Net Generation, practices and expectations within the academy remain relatively unchanged. Classes continue to be taught by instructors in classrooms. Students are expected to navigate complex administrative processes. In many ways, the academy continues to be staff centric. Although some colleges and universities have demonstrated measurable progress in moving toward a student-centered philosophy, many have not. Their administrative structure, information systems, and approach to the delivery of student services continue to represent the traditional hierarchy experienced by previous generations of students.

Nevertheless, the academy is changing. In addition to the Net Generation, external forces are influencing higher education.

▶ Tuition increases are exceeding standard measures of inflation due to the escalating fixed costs of health insurance for employees, utility costs for buildings, and competitive salaries.

▶ The growing belief that the cost of a college education should be paid for by students, not taxpayers, has shifted the balance and delivery of federal student aid programs.

▶ A recent Supreme Court decision in a case involving admissions at the University of Michigan prompted a national examination of both admission and financial aid practices.

▶ The Y2K phenomenon resulted in great angst among system administrators, often driving the replacement of administrative information systems.

▶ The rise of for-profit educational institutions has begun to change the delivery of both online and on-campus courses, as well as associated services.

▶ The rise of personal identity theft has forced colleges and universities to rethink their use of the Social Security number as the primary record identifier.

Such environmental changes have caused the academy to examine its policies, practices, and more importantly, the application of information systems to create more efficient operations and more effective student services.

Students as Consumers

The Net Generation expects good customer service. To many in higher education, using the term *customer* or *consumer* in the same sentence as *student* is akin to blasphemy. Yet, the Net Generation was raised in a customer-service culture. Today's students often exhibit less altruistic goals compared to past generations—they're primarily concerned with how their degree will affect lifelong salary potential and quality of life. In a very practical way, students want to see a relationship between the cost of their education and the delivery of quality services. For example, many institutions impose a required fee for information technology (IT) services. Students ask whether they are receiving the service for which they are required to pay—a reasonable question from the perspective of a consumer.

The Net Generation brings a special flavor of consumerism to basic student services. Three generations ago, the model for registering students was to conduct an "arena registration." Most, if not all, academic administrators packed their offices and moved to the campus convocation hall, invited each student to report to the registration site at a designated time, and proceeded to match the student with courses. While some have argued that this approach was reasonably efficient, few have asserted that it was an effective mode of delivering this critically important student service. The introduction of voice-response touch-tone telephone technology in the mid-1980s and the emergence of Web-based registration services in the early 1990s have typically replaced the arena-registration approach. It would be an interesting social experiment to require Net Geners to leave the convenience of anytime, anyplace registration to return to the arena-style registration.

Crossing Organizational Boundaries

The Net Generation expects their problems to be solved—quickly and easily. Students are not intimidated by titles such as registrar and bursar. The actual process of registering for courses extends over many campus offices—academic advising, student aid, registration, student accounts, and often ancillary units that handle items such as student ID cards or health services. The process of applying for and receiving student aid is complex, involving federal and state regulations as well as a myriad of grant and loan programs. The student's ability to succeed academically and graduate involves working with numerous offices, faculty, staff, policies, and procedures. While employees often know the institution's administrative structure, students generally do not.

During the arena-registration era, these services were typically integrated through a predetermined set of signatures on student-processing forms. The intention was for students to meet with the appropriate student services personnel to ensure they would be properly advised and guided. When seen from the student perspective, more often than not this approach was an exercise in collecting a sufficient number of signatures from departmental assistants. A staff member in some obscure office would complete the requested transaction.

In the past decade, colleges and universities have improved the integration of student services through a "one stop" model. Common characteristics of this interorganizational approach are the physical construction of a student services center that houses all appropriate student services offices and staff, as well as a student services desk staffed by trained student services personnel. In spirit, such a response is an improvement over the approach used during the arena-registration era; however, in practice this approach has serious limitations that stand in the way of true integration. It is expensive to build new buildings or to renovate existing buildings to physically establish a student service center. Complete integration of all students services into a single job description is not realistic—there is simply too much to learn, and such positions are generally delegated to the most junior staff.

Rather than this brick-and-mortar approach to improving and integrating the delivery of student services, a more robust approach is to capitalize on the power of information technology. Creating a seamless virtual organization specifically commissioned to exceeding the expectations of today's Net Generation students is a reachable objective.

It's Not About Technology

The Net Generation cares about the activity technology enables, not the technology, per se. The use of technology to improve student services will be critical to the academy. Yet, it's not about technology. Technology is a tool—it represents the means, not the desired outcome. Students will use technology; in fact, they will expect services delivered through technology. But before focusing on technology, student service professionals must articulate a clear and unambiguous vision that provides the framework for the technology. IT staff are important contributors to the desired outcome and must be part of the process; however, the leadership for improved student services should not be expected to come from within the technology ranks. Rather, it must come from those charged with advising and registering students, administering student aid, admitting students, collecting tuition and fees, and so on.

IT Supports Rather than Leads

Since every college and university is uniquely structured, specific student service offices vary in title and function. At the University of Kansas, the student affairs organization is called Student Success. During the past decade, offices or divisions of enrollment management have become common titles. Traditionally, titles such as registrar, admissions, student aid, student accounts, student affairs, and housing all identify units responsible for the delivery of specific student services. The availability and adoption of technology-driven applications does not change the focus or responsibility of these business units.

The units responsible for student services will not change, but their staffing levels, knowledge, and approach to the delivery of services will. Even though senior administrators anticipate staff reductions because of technology, in practice this is rarely the outcome. While administrative positions may decrease, typically the number of IT positions increases. In many cases, the growth of IT positions occurs in both the central IT support office and the business units. IT becomes part of almost everyone's position; the remaining business unit nontechnical staff need to understand the new technological solutions and acquire new skills.

The institution's business units are faced with new issues as technology-based services grow. For example, properly developed Web applications should enable users to contact a business specialist if they encounter problems or have questions. Such questions are often e-mailed to a business unit drop box. It becomes imperative that the business unit has a plan to receive, read, and reply to this steady stream of incoming e-mail messages. Net Gen students are more inclined to e-mail requests than to ask for advice in person. In many cases, the business unit must reorganize its staff to shift from receiving walk-in traffic to replying to e-mail.

Another common change to staffing patterns within the business unit is to en-sure the ability to "see what the student sees." Given the typical design architecture of secure Web services, only the designated individual (student) may access and modify his or her personal record. The staff member within the business unit may have the organizational authority to access and modify the student's record, but the technology may prevent staff access.

As student services are developed, they must continue to be the responsibility of the business unit. It can be tempting to rely on the IT staff when problems arise or when a student challenges the process or results. Similarly, technologists might want to assume responsibility for the business process because they "own" the hardware that stores the data and the business logic. Both of these approaches are inappropriate: the business unit must retain primary ownership of the process and the delivery of its set of student services, and the IT department should focus on infrastructure support issues such as networking, security, database manage-ment, backup and recovery, and other global issues.

For Both the Net Generation and Nontraditional Learners

Students want customized and personalized services, not a one-size-fits-all approach. There is little question that the Net Generation has expectations that are more encompassing, and perhaps more demanding, than those of previous generations. At the same time, the landscape of higher education is changing in other ways. For example, the number of adult learners continues to increase at many colleges and universities.

Adult learners have a different set of support needs compared to Net Geners. Beyond the obvious difference of age and time away from the classroom, adult learners may not have the same comfort level or familiarity with technology—and they may be the least advised on how to use it.

The difference in populations places a challenge on service developers to ensure that all students have equal access to services, which may require extended support to adult learners in order for them to gain a working knowledge of the systems and supporting tools (campus IT account, classroom management systems, Web services, e-commerce). Serving adult learners might also require that student services continue to be delivered in an in-person, synchronous manner. The simple caution is that when it comes to the deployment of technology-based solutions to students, a one-size-fits-all solution may not be appropriate.

Technology as a Transformational Tool

For the Net Generation, quality of service matters. This requires more than automation; it requires transformation. Perhaps the single most interesting challenge to college and university administrators responsible for delivering student support services is the role technology plays in transforming the delivery of these services. While it is not about technology, it is about a symbiotic relationship between a basic need and the technology that delivers a response to that need.

A prime example of how technology has transformed basic student services is the National Student Clearinghouse. A decade ago, there was a three-way exchange of paper documents between an enrolled student, the institution, and the financial lender. The lender required proof of enrollment for the student to retain a nonrepayment status on the loan. The student would receive a document from the lender for completion by the institution; the school would receive the document from the student, complete it, and return it to either the student or the lender. This process was inconvenient for the student, time-consuming for the institution, and difficult to schedule for the lender.

Technology enabled a transformation that is much better suited to Net Geners—or any busy student, regardless of age. Through the establishment of a central repository, colleges and universities can transfer the pertinent data to the clearinghouse; the lending institutions now make their enrollment status inquiries against this repository. The clearinghouse increased effectiveness for students and improved efficiencies for both lenders and institutions.

In this example, the goal—validation of student enrollment to ensure continuance of student aid borrower status—did not change. What changed significantly were the processes employed to achieve this outcome. Shifting from a manual to an automated system established new research capabilities and eliminated lost or misplaced documents and resulting delays or duplicate effort.

Pennsylvania State University's recent modification of placement testing for new students offers another example of using technology to transform processes. The purpose of administering a placement test (for example, in English, chemistry, or mathematics) is to ensure that students start these courses at the proper level. Some students are academically prepared for college-level work, some need remediation, and others are ready for more advanced levels.

Traditionally, students were invited to campus during the summer before their first year of study. The placement test was administered; the student was notified of the result. Traveling to campus to take the placement test was often an inconvenience (or impossibility). Participation was lower than desired, and timely feedback was impossible due to test grading. The process did not meet the Net Generation's need for convenience, customization, and immediate feedback. Thanks to technology, these placement tests are now administered through secure Web applications. Students can take these tests at their convenience and at their location. Although these are placement-level tests, not exams for academic credit, student cheating on these examinations was nevertheless a concern; however, the examination of placement recommendations compared to actual performance in the enrolled course of both pre- and post-Web populations indicates that cheating has not occurred. The unexpected, but positive, student response has been a feeling of trust. Many students have commented on their genuine appreciation that the university demonstrated trust early by allowing them to take these placement tests unmonitored.

Technology can also transform business processes by enabling them to become more efficient, effective, and student focused. Consider the process of informing students and their advisers of the courses that will be available for registration the upcoming semester. Traditionally, Penn State printed a booklet each semester containing timetables of course offerings, course descriptions, registration instructions, and other pertinent enrollment information. These booklets were prepared well in advance of the semester, and subsequent course changes were either unpublicized or a supplement was printed.

Through technology, this process changed in ways that are responsive to the Net Generation. The information is published on the Web rather than on paper. Rather than a one-time publication, the schedule is updated and republished in real time. The Web allows for the inclusion of additional information that was impossible in the paper format. Faculty can link to their course syllabus, the registrar can link to characteristics of the classroom and the course, and academic departments can link to descriptions that exceed the typical 30-word limit for course catalogs. In short, technology has enabled institutions to respond to student expectations in ways that were impossible before.

Interrelationship of Service and Technology

The Net Gen expects convenient, safe, reliable, and flexible access. While the development of student services is not about technology, the support of today's extended and accessible services would be impossible without the presence of a robust technology infrastructure. Conceptually, there is a clear distinction between application development and the "system" that allows these services to be delivered. In reality, the two issues are tightly coupled.

The constant and rapidly changing nature of technology requires those developing support services for the Net Generation to be aware of both the current technology boundaries and the emerging promises. The following examples illustrate this important interconnectedness between the service and the technology used to deliver it.

▶ **Occasionally lateral steps that do not improve the nature of the service are required due to the shifting technology at the core of the process.** The half-life of software and hardware continues to decline; the period of time from acquisition to obsolescence keeps getting shorter. The latest laptop, desktop, or midtier server purchased today will likely be improved by the manufacturer within a year. The resulting machine will be less expensive (all other attributes held constant) with greater performance capabilities. While this does not necessarily make the original purchase an inappropriate decision, it does provide a warning that within a few years hardware or software may need to be replaced. Constant, escalating change has a direct impact on student services.

▶ **Inappropriate uses of technology require that developers take a defensive posture to ensure the integrity and stability of their services.** Unfortunately, these preventive steps are expensive and represent a diversion of time and money from the business at hand—supporting our constituencies. As the adoption of Web-based services continues to expand, we are also experiencing the dark side of innovation—using technology to promote fraudulent services or disrupt legitimate services. The number and severity of Internet-spread viruses are on the rise, as are instances of fraudulent services that result in identity theft or credit card fraud. In direct response, many colleges and universities are expending huge resources to migrate away from using the Social Security number as the primary identifier for students, faculty, and staff. Within the higher education sector, the number of diploma-mill operations is on the rise.

▶ **A reliable, fast, and secure network—both wired and wireless—is necessary to deliver the developed support services.** Another critical infrastructure issue is networking. During the past decade, colleges and universities spent enormous sums of money wiring their campuses. The goal was to connect every residence hall room, classroom, and faculty office to the Internet. With much of this accomplished, these same institutions are now investing heavily in wireless networks. Although needed, these expenditures divert investment from new support services. In addition, they represent an ongoing commitment to maintenance and necessary upgrades.

▶ **The preferred solution, from a number of perspectives, is integrated and full-service support services.** As the number and extent of support services continue to grow, students want the university to provide a complete, full-service approach. Those who pay fees, as students do, expect services and convenience. These expectations result in the need to provide the infrastructure for e-commerce applications, for example.

▶ **Support services must be reliable, consistent, and available.** Mistakes happen and hardware fails; as a result, data recovery and system recovery are important. Files or databases may be accidentally destroyed. A virus may penetrate the security perimeter and cause damage. A failed hard drive might result in the inability to access a file. Whatever the root cause, there must be a data backup service so that critical information is not lost permanently. Institutions also need to consider their ability to recover from a larger disaster—fire, hurricane, earthquake, terrorist attack, and so on. Disaster recovery represents yet another necessary diversion of resources from support service development. Without a robust and reliable technology infrastructure, however, the services cannot be delivered.

So, while not about technology, higher education cannot ignore technology support issues; they are critical as strategic services are developed for our constituents.

Integration, Opportunity, and Service

The Net Generation wants integrated and convenient services. Technology has the power to integrate the delivery of support services, create new opportunities, and deliver world-class levels of service. Many colleges and universities now use the Web to organize, present, and deliver support services. The University of Michigan provides services through Wolverine Access. At the University of Texas, students access UT Direct. The University of Minnesota delivers services through One Stop, and the University of Maryland uses Testudo. At Penn State, students faculty, and academic advisers use eLion (https://elion.oas.psu.edu/).

Overview of the Penn State eLion System

In the early 1990s, Penn State received an increasing number of student complaints that the academic advising system was lacking. Students felt they were not receiving good advice; many were not assigned an adviser, and assigned advisers were not available when needed. Students claimed that rather than seeking assistance from their advisers, they would turn to other students, friends, or parents for academic advice. The administration responded to these complaints by committing to improve the quality and accessibility of academic advising.

A cross-functional team was formed with representatives from key offices—academic advising, the registrar, and several colleges. Their charge was to develop an expert-based, empirically grounded advising and information system, delivered by the latest technologies, to supplement the student-adviser relationship and engage students in inquiry for informed educational planning.

This charge was not about technology. It was about the development of a set of services that would improve student success. Technology would simply be the delivery vehicle. As the work of the team progressed, the following developmental principles emerged:

▶ **Expert interactive advising—**Use the knowledge base of the university's best academic advisers to develop an expert system to extend this knowledge to the full array of students seeking advice.

- **Direct service to consumers—**Use of the services would not require an administrative staff member's involvement.
- **Personalized to the student—**The services would be student specific, based on the student's academic record and affiliations. The system would not use generalities to convey information and advice.
- **Secure Web-based delivery—**Accessibility would not be limited by place or time. Any student with access to the Web would have access to these services at any time.
- **Multiple development teams—**To grow the system as rapidly as possible, concurrent development teams were established to design, test, and implement specific services. These teams were sponsored by the primary business units (registrar, student aid, bursar, and academic advising) responsible for the support services.
- **Standards based—**By necessity, a multiple development team environment required both presentation and technical standards to ensure the end user experienced a seamless set of services.

Eliminating the Stovepipe Approach to Student Services

This developmental approach dramatically changed Penn State's overall design of support services both for eLion and more general services. While each application is owned by a business unit, all applications are branded eLion (see Figure 1); there is no attribution to the specific office that developed the application. From a student perspective, application ownership does not matter; what matters is that the service is fulfilling a need.

The early internal challenge, and to some extent a continuing one, was for the developers to think about a service from the student perspective rather than their own internal administrative perspective. For example, a student might not have been able to complete registration due to a delayed scholarship. This same student may be living in a residence hall and involved with a student organization. From the student's perspective, one issue cut across several administrative offices. One of the intended outcomes was for the developmental staff to think in a more horizontal mode—as a student would solve a problem—and not in a vertical, stovepipe mode. The approach has worked. When enrolled students were asked about their use of technology, they responded that their most often used application was e-mail; a very close second was eLion. The popularity of eLion is due to the services it provides—services students need.

Figure 1. Screen Shot of the eLion Interface

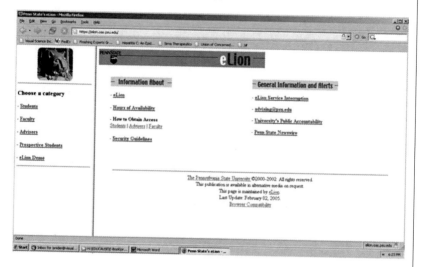

Leadership and Vision

The development of the Penn State eLion system did not follow a traditional development pattern; the development efforts were intentionally decentralized across many offices, and the project leadership was highly integrated through the use of collaborative teams. The system was not the result of incremental planning or change but of a strategic decision. The evolution of systems within colleges and universities is often driven by external forces. The articulated need at Penn State was to improve academic advising services; however, there was no specific vision of how to accomplish this. Through the creative and collaborative efforts of staff in leadership roles, the early model and design of eLion emerged.

The first models were virtual prototypes that described the intended function and result. The models were presented to senior university administrators who allocated development funds ($50,000) to pursue the creation of a prototype. These funds were used to provide training for existing staff and to purchase specialized software. Following a successful proof-of-concept demonstration, several teams were organized. One was responsible for the design of application standards and presentation techniques. Two additional teams were tasked with the development of the first student service applications. A fourth team focused on technical architecture requirements.

For the first three years, progress was slow. During this time, Penn State leadership remained committed to the original vision and provided the fiscal and emotional support needed to keep the project moving forward. Today's system would not have been possible without this strong, top-down support and without a clear vision from the project team itself.

Disciplined Development

An important part of the vision was to provide a set of services that would quickly scale to a very large (100,000+) population of users, which required that the system be standards based, uniform, self-documenting, and reliable. Further, users needed to be able to offer comments and suggestions and receive personalized help.

A standards document (see https://elion.oas.psu.edu/governance/eLionGov_9.pdf) was developed to provide guidance to all eLion developers. This document includes information on how to create a new application or modify an existing one, Web standards, and technical standards, as well as general information about the structure and governance of the eLion initiative.

Each eLion application has internal help documentation for users. Because the system is secure, a demonstration service provides a nonauthenticated view of typical applications. A statement in the standard footer of each page indicates that the page is maintained by eLion. Behind this link is a page-specific e-mail address that routes questions or inquiries to the appropriate developer.

Applications are also designed to be self-documenting. This is a difficult challenge, since every user is unique (personal background, Web familiarity, comfort level with technology). Nevertheless, the goal has been to design all applications so that specialized training, documentation manuals, and staff involvement are not required.

Politics, Tradition, and Turf

The Net Generation's expectation is for immediacy; they don't understand why colleges are slow to change. Perhaps the most challenging issue in developing enhanced student support services has to do with the campus administrative climate. Ideally, there would be unanimous agreement regarding the services that are needed, how they should be deployed, and the support plan necessary to keep them robust and relevant. In reality, multiple issues and perspectives on campus do not converge into a single vision. One colleague described this effort as attempting to herd cats. Another described this management issue as akin to managing a cemetery—a lot of people are involved, but there's not much move-ment. Whatever the analogy, an administrative climate must be established that provides an enabling environment, focused on the academic support that fosters student success. Students do not attend an institution because it has the best registration system or the most complete self-service Web system. Rather, they attend because of the quality of academic programs, the reputation of faculty, and the perceived value of their degrees. While registration systems and other administrative applications are essential, they are secondary compared to the fundamental academic objective.

As stated earlier, establishing this climate is not about technology. More likely, it is about the on-campus political environment, institutional tradition, and the perception of whose turf is being violated. The decision to develop technology-delivered student services should be both a top-down and bottom-up decision. The initiative must be supported by the institution's leadership to move in this direction. Fiscal support will also be needed to keep this initiative alive, as well as support, at times, to defend fundamental change. Many campus organizations will likely be involved, so establishing and promoting cross-functional project teams becomes critical.

Similarly, the initiative must have bottom-up support. What specific services or array of services will improve student satisfaction, academic retention, and administrative efficiency? The project objectives must be complementary and lead to a seamless, logical, and integrated set of services.

Beyond the campus political climate, tradition is an important factor in the de-velopment of student services. A classic argument is that if registration procedures are automated, the computer will replace the adviser, the quality of the advising system will decline, and students will make uninformed choices. Developing eLion challenged this traditional hierarchy. Does the adviser's signature on a student action form represent permission or consultation? Is it reasonable to conclude that all faculty advisers are fully aware of institutional policies and procedures? Do students know the name of their academic adviser? Is the adviser available for consultation? These questions must be addressed because they challenge traditional processes and assumptions.

Integration Depends on the Organization

During the past decade, higher education has sought to become more student centered. One of the manifestations has been the establishment of one-stop student service centers that combine the front desks of multiple offices. The intention behind such centers has been to reduce the hassle for students and provide one comprehensive service center. This approach has met with varying degrees of success. In most cases it has required the construction—or extensive remodeling—of physical space, administrative reorganization, cross-training of staff, and a cultural change. Penn State and others have bypassed this physical approach and have concentrated instead on a virtual student service center. The virtual approach, exemplified by eLion, provides a richer opportunity to integrate services and allows greater extensibility by time and distance. This approach, however, requires a strong IT infrastructure.

Where does the institutional decision regarding support service reside, and what are the implications of implementation? Should the top-down approach prevail to ensure an integrated and systematic enterprise-wide approach to the development of student services? Should this initiative be championed by the chief academic officer, the IT director, student affairs, enrollment management, business services, or another senior executive? What role should the current IT organization play? Should existing campus information systems be retooled, should the mainframe be unplugged, or should an enterprise system be installed? Or, should the entire IT operation be outsourced to an independent third party? These questions require a careful and open analysis. The answer will depend on the institution and a series of factors.

One of the leading factors will be the institution's ability to attract and retain a qualified IT workforce. In recent years, the supply and demand for IT professionals has become more balanced, but in many areas it remains difficult to retain IT staff due to the compressed salary structures of colleges and universities. Further, recent graduates are unfamiliar with legacy programming languages. To close this gap of technical needs and available talent, some institutions have established internal development programs to ensure a steady supply of interested and trained IT professionals. Others have purchased packaged systems and rely on external consultants to lead implementation efforts.

Matching institutional practice with technical features is another decision point; most likely there will be a mismatch. Should institutional practice match the capabilities of the IT system, or should custom IT solutions be developed to meet the service needs? With the former, changing the institutional culture is at best difficult, and at worst divisive. With the latter, the institution loses the leverage of maximizing future system growth and enhancements unless corresponding modifications are made to custom software modifications. There are more than 3,600 colleges and universities in the United States. Even if grouped by similar size, mission, and objectives, perspectives on the delivery of student systems are diverse. Individual institutions differ on student expectations, learning environments, academic and administrative policies, academic advising, and the role of faculty governance. The combination results in a high degree of uniqueness among institutions. Well-designed vendor-supplied student services recognize these variables and make some provisions for flexibility. Yet, there are practical limitations on the flexibility of any software.

Another decision involves the current IT infrastructure, including databases, enterprise-wide servers, midtier servers, authentication and authorization services, e-commerce support, Web development, data warehouse capabilities, and help desk availability. Are the multiple campus systems interfaced to greater or lesser degrees? Does the institution have common or varied business practices for admission, financial aid disbursement, and grade reporting? These business process and IT components combine to provide a launch point for the future development of student services.

Success Depends on People and Culture

Nearly a decade ago, Penn State began moving toward a new way of processing applications for admission. The traditional glossy view-book and multipage paper application were replaced with electronic versions. This effort initially involved technologies that are now obsolete. As the Web emerged, the development process quickly migrated to its current technology base.

When this initiative began in the mid-1990s, the goal was to receive at least 80 percent of all applications electronically before the year 2000. Although not reached by 2000, the goal has since been surpassed. The goal may have been too aggressive, but not from a technology perspective. Adequate technology was available, and the new application process was far superior to the traditional paper-based one. The reason the goal was not reached had little to do with technology, but it had a lot to do with people. When a Penn State prospect sought advice from a high school counselor, the counselor would advise the prospect to contact Penn State and request a copy of the admission application. When the prospect asked for parental advice, the response was to complete a traditional paper application. If an interested prospect called the admissions office and asked for an application, the response was that an application would be mailed. These responses reflected tradition. It took a concerted effort to change the culture away from a paper-based mentality, enabling the goal to be reached.

Technology provides the ability to dramatically improve the delivery of student services, yet it can be intimidating—a source of fear, uncertainty, resistance, and avoidance. Such emotions and responses cannot be ignored. To realize the effectiveness and efficiencies of technological change, attention must be focused on the larger context of these services and the constituents involved with the change. After all, it's not about technology!

Conclusion

The need to provide improved student support services has never been greater. In recent years, the cost of higher education has continued to increase, often outpacing other economic indicators. As tuition increases, external pressures from students, parents, legislators, and alumni to contain costs mount. At the same time, Net Generation students expect improved and comprehensive services from the academy.

The availability of technological solutions for student services has never been greater. The plethora of enterprise-wide solutions, outsourcing opportunities, and on-campus development tools provide a wide range of options for the design and deployment of responsive student services.

Although the delivery of student services is not about technology, it is about using technology wisely. The use of technology requires a strong partnership between service providers and technologists. The Net Generation's expectations for student services are high and rising. The opportunities for us to respond to—and even exceed—these expectations are equally boundless.

About the Author

J. James Wager currently serves as assistant vice provost for enrollment management and university registrar at The Pennsylvania State University. He provides oversight for all academic records and associated activities for the university's 80,000-plus student enrollment at 24 campuses across the Commonwealth of Pennsylvania, leadership on enrollment management, and deployment of student system applications. Wager also spends time in the classroom teaching management courses and is a member of the university's faculty senate. He has been an active member of the American Association of Collegiate Registrars and Admissions Officers (AACRAO), presenting numerous papers at annual and regional meetings and serving on various committees. Wager serves as a board chairman of the Registrars of the Association of American Universities (AAU) and was the program coordinator of its Summer Institute in Aspen. He has been an advocate for the delivery of student services using technology. Wager holds a bachelor's in management with a minor in information systems and an MPA in public administration.

CHAPTER 11

Faculty Development for the Net Generation

Anne H. Moore, John F. Moore, and Shelli B. Fowler
Virginia Polytechnic Institute and State University

Introduction

In the past 10 years, many colleges and universities have actively engaged in integrating technology in teaching and learning. Approaches to this integration are as varied as the institutions' missions and the clarity of their aims for technology-assisted instruction. Regardless of the approach, institutions must make the necessary human and financial investments. Faculty development for existing and future faculty is a pivotal investment for integrating technology in higher education; it can catalyze innovations in learning across generations.

Today's students are described as busy instant messaging, blogging, downloading music and videos, and playing video games with an international network of friends and acquaintances. The technological engagement and interaction related to students' formal learning activities are not so widespread, however. Surveys of Net Generation students suggest that their learning experiences reflect mixed technology usage at best, and at worst they may experience ineffective or inappropriate uses of technology in their academic programs.[1] Faculty report that students are asking for more online activities.[2] A growing range of pilot programs and emerging practices document improvements in learning.[3] But, when will such models be systematically adopted by institutions, resulting in widespread gains in student learning? That answer may be closely tied to faculty development.

Defining what constitutes faculty development is an important first step. Expertise should be developed, not just in how to use technology or in pedagogical practice but also in how to understand learners and how they perceive technology.

Jason Frand[4] reinforced the need for faculty to work thoughtfully and creatively with Net Generation students' changing mindsets. Today's multitasking, Nintendo-born-and-bred students do not view computers as technology. They have a range of attributes that distinguish them from older generations. Baby Boomers and Gen-Xers populate higher education's existing faculty ranks; they have different mindsets. In order for higher education to ensure that productive teaching and learning exchanges occur across generations of learners, these different mindsets may need to be reconciled. As we've designed faculty development at Virginia Tech, the following characteristics of the Net Generation have influenced our programs.

▶ **Life online.** For several decades, a growing body of research points to the ways in which computers and related technologies influence the ways we live and work—indeed, the way we think.[5] Sherry Turkle[6] has also studied the effects of computers on children and adolescents, describing the manner in which online environments offer spaces for identity, play, and expressing multiple aspects of the self. The so-called loner or silent student who might have never spoken in a face-to-face learning environment today may have online companions and also may interact more readily in online learning activities.

▶ **Rapid communication.** Turkle's research suggests that word processing has made thinking with our hands commonplace, for it allows people to quickly display their thoughts—good and bad, organized or chaotic—on a page. The resulting communications, public and private, often demonstrate wide variations in quality of thought and writing style; current experience in online education bears this out as well.

▶ **Social networking.** The Net Generation uses technology to enliven and extend their social networks. Reports of Weblog use in higher education indicate that blogs are "helping students across the country meet their dorm mates, form study groups, and make friends before they set foot on … campus."[7a,b]

▶ **Games and simulations.** Net Generation students cut their teeth on computer games and simulations. This may have profound effects for learning. Fortunately for educators, games and simulations can be used to provide beneficial insights on simple or complex phenomena. Yet, life tends not to play out solely through the logic or binary rules of games and simulations; students' learning today needs to be more than simulacra.

▶ **Digital literacy.** Just as word processing makes it physically easier for students to express themselves, computers make it possible to use many applications, from spreadsheets to databases, without knowing how the hardware or software works. Turkle claimed that today's college students are so used to thinking about things at "interface" value, clicking on icons to accomplish their work and play, that all they require is *seeing* how something works rather than *knowing* how it works. Although the Net Generation is considered digitally literate, they might not possess the full complement of the knowledge and skills they need to use technology wisely and well. The same may be true for faculty.

Fluency in Information Technology

The National Research Council concluded that fluency with information technology is imperative today. This state of mind is called FIT, for fluency in information technology.[8a,b] FITness requires three kinds of knowledge:

▶ **Contemporary skills**—the ability to use today's computer applications, enabling people to apply information technology immediately. Skills are an essential component of job readiness. Most importantly, skills provide a store of practical experience on which to build new competence.

▶ **Foundational concepts**—the basic principles and ideas of computers, networks, and information that underpin the technology. Concepts explain the how and why of information technology, and they give insight into its opportunities and limitations. Concepts are the raw material for understanding IT as it evolves.

▶ **Intellectual capabilities**—the ability to apply information technology in complex situations, encapsulating higher-level thinking in the context of IT. These capabilities empower people to manipulate the medium to their advantage and to handle unintended and unexpected problems when they arise. Intellectual capabilities foster more abstract thinking about information and its manipulation.

To help students gain the knowledge necessary for FITness, an institution's strategic plan and teaching and learning activities should contain appropriate goals for becoming FIT. Faculty and staff who do not have the requisite knowledge and skills to work toward fluency in information technology may need professional development programs that help them achieve FITness in their teaching and research. To bridge the gap between faculty expertise and student needs, institutions must address awareness, enablement, and integration:

▶ Awareness of students' approaches to meeting their learning needs and of what technologies are available to them

▶ Enablement through professional development so they have the skills needed to implement systemic change

▶ Integration, or the ability to bring together the disparate pieces needed—pedagogy, learning space design, technology, support, policies—to enable successful learning

Because technology, pedagogy, and practice change so rapidly, faculty professional development may need to be ongoing. When IT is involved, institutions also need to provide easy and convenient support for technology-integrated learning. To leverage the creativity of faculty and staff—to turn their intellectual and social imaginations to the task—institutions need to provide systematic encouragement and assistance through comprehensive faculty development programs.

The remainder of this chapter will describe two programs at Virginia Polytechnic Institute and State University that focus on professional development: for faculty, the Faculty Development Institute (FDI); and for graduate students, the Graduate Education Development Institute (GEDI). Both programs are grappling with ways to engage Net Generation students to benefit their learning.

The Faculty Development Institute

Virginia Tech's Faculty Development Institute helps faculty acquire teaching strategies that leverage instructional technologies to improve student learning (http://www.fdi.vt.edu/). FDI is the cornerstone of a large-scale, continuing strategy to systematically promote innovative, informed uses of technology in daily practice for faculty and students. FDI also represents one institution's attempt to focus on the knowledge and skills development required for a FIT faculty in order to meet today's students' needs for fluency in using information technology, or FITness. Begun in 1993, FDI

▶ offers a recurring four-year cycle of faculty development workshops,
▶ links professional development to replacing faculty computers every four years,
▶ supports course development initiatives,
▶ promotes student digital literacy, and
▶ outfits classrooms with appropriate technology.

As a result, Net Generation students today are likely to find that a majority of their courses involve blended face-to-face and online learning activities, online discussions, archived learning materials, and discipline-specific software and Web-accessed resources—aspects of learning they claim to fully appreciate. And as these Net Gen students clamor for more, faculty report that their repeated FDI participation has made them likely to use technology more effectively across the spectrum of their professional lives, including teaching, research, and service roles.

Early FDI programs focused more on lowering faculty anxieties related to using new technologies in teaching. In the early 1990s, students were not always comfortable with changes in teaching or learning practices that technology introduced. Some students and faculty questioned whether the new technologies were just passing fads. But after the successes of the first full FDI cycle and with growing technology use plainly evident across a spectrum of institutional life, the university's 1996 strategic plan established the faculty development process as a strategic objective. Acknowledging that institutional leadership at the highest levels was necessary to sustain widespread technology integration, the 1996 plan and one in 2002 outlined aims for FITness. With strategic objectives and the requisite support structures in place, the university sought not only to provide for grassroots experimentation and innovation but also to nurture the seeds of change for faculty and students, regardless of generational affiliation.

Repeated participation of virtually all faculty (96 percent) and all department heads over more than a decade of FDI programs has helped build a wider familiarity and understanding of the complex issues involved in adopting and successfully integrating technology in traditional and hybrid courses. Awareness of the challenges raised in fully online distance-learning programs has increased as well. In addition, the evolving expectations of successive generations of students (of which Net Generation students are the latest and perhaps most vocal about technology's place in their lives) surface in faculty narratives shared in FDI workshops about successful strategies and practices. In turn, informal peer-mentoring activities have proven particularly productive in helping faculty address specific concerns. An especially effective feature of FDI is the series of presentations by faculty demonstrating how and why they have changed their approaches to teaching. These presentations provide credible responses to questions about the effects of technology use on student learning and attitude, productivity, student-faculty communication, instructional development time, and more.

Since its inception FDI has sought to involve faculty as workshop presenters on as many topics as feasible. Not surprisingly, the credibility and practicality evaluations of these presenters are high. Faculty selected to present to their peers are able to clearly describe successes and failures of early adoption strategies with emerging technologies in the context of their personal interaction with students. For example, presenters might illuminate how the use of instant messaging within a course fits with current expectations, habits, and practices of Net Generation students, as well as how it might benefit learning. FDI extends this approach to helping faculty understand changing norms and expectations in their use of course management systems, collaboration and conferencing tools, e-portfolios, digital library resources, and similar learning assets.

Further, faculty indicate that they find equal or greater value in systematic assistance from their peers. Such assistance includes sorting out ways in which new techniques or procedures relate to possible changes in course goals and outcomes, the incorporation of interdisciplinary agendas, and the introduction of gaming and simulation strategies to stretch and deepen learning. Faculty presentations, case studies, and Webcasts provide examples and personal narratives about successful (and problematic) implementations of emerging strategies to interested workshop participants.

FDI encourages interaction among presenters and other faculty. Resources and contact information are provided for each program track on its Web site.[9] Modeled much like an online course, these faculty-to-faculty queries and conversations can be extended after workshops through online forums or e-mail with presenters. If developing course materials outside scheduled workshops is necessary, FDI provides production resources for digitizing content (for example, slides, audio, video) or limited quantities of graphic or animation developed through its partnership with the university's New Media Center (http://www.nmc.vt.edu).

As mentioned earlier, evaluation of the workshops by faculty attendees is positive. During a workshop, evaluations are conducted every 90 minutes using a Web-based form, providing rapid reports to workshop facilitators who, in turn, make changes expeditiously. Faculty clearly value the opportunity to explore instructional issues with their colleagues and to discover the potential of technology for enhancing their teaching; and they have indicated that FDI resources are critical if they are to adapt to the needs of their students. Indeed, faculty cite increased pressure from Net Generation students for more sophisticated uses of current and emerging technologies; these students say there is more to innovative teaching than PowerPoint and Excel.

Over a dozen years, FDI programs have evolved in several important ways. The content of FDI workshops changes each year as new technologies emerge and faculty demonstrate improved approaches to using technology in instruction. Early programs focused more on the basics of using technology and software. Current programming places more emphasis on

▶ Shifts in faculty perceptions of students' expectations
▶ Students' use of technologies such as instant messaging and blogs

- Teaching strategies that can successfully address such behavioral shifts
- Ways to design for active learning
- The appropriate means for dealing with a range of privacy and security issues

Many workshops have also featured strategic, discipline-specific software with which faculty have requested assistance, such as MATLAB (math software used in engineering, science, and business), AutoCAD (design software used in architecture and engineering), ESRI Geographic Information Systems (GIS software used in agriculture, engineering, science, and social science), LabVIEW (instrumentation software used in agriculture, engineering, and science), and others. All workshops include open lab time designed to give faculty opportunities to apply what they learn to their courses. FDI staff also encourage faculty to bring their graduate assistants to workshops to facilitate the incorporation of new methodologies and technologies into the future professoriate's teaching practices.

Other changes in programming include immersing faculty in more online activities that might lead to creating learning environments similar to their students' personal communication environments. A workshop might include an online tutorial, a short streaming video segment, and an online chat or discussion. The overall context emphasizes how technology-based resources may be useful to students in the learning; in the background, the hands-on use of software and Web-based tools such as course management systems or e-portfolios provides opportunities to practice.

A third shift has involved recognizing that FDI, while beginning as a teaching/learning enhancement program, should enlarge its scope to directly address how information technologies can be useful in all aspects of faculty life. Indeed, FDI staff work hard to maintain programming relevance and value. The identification of new topics and issues often comes directly from faculty through program evaluations, internal grant proposals, consultations, and direct suggestions. In addition, staff hold periodic program-planning briefings with each college to gather feedback on current offerings and to gain faculty input on topics that should be addressed in the future. Examples of new topics introduced based on faculty suggestions include Creating Learning-Centered Instruction, Parallel Programming for Supercomputing, and Using LabVIEW to Enhance Laboratory Learning. Other workshops and support for technology-assisted or enhanced research collaboration, grant writing, and presentation of research findings also resulted directly from faculty requests.

Another aspect of maintaining FDI relevance and value involves providing just-in-time, need-to-know access to information. FDI provides several Web-based information resources. An instructional design portal provides in-depth information, examples, and Web references covering instructional design models, pedagogy and learning theories, teaching strategies, media selection methodologies, and guidance on evaluation and assessment.[10] For those with immediate questions concerning software functions and operations, FDI licenses online tutorials from Element K and Atomic Learning.[11a,b] Because the tutorial is well indexed, it is also easy to search when looking for specific information, such as how to insert graphs into documents. Thus the tutorial can also serve as an on-demand reference or help tool.

While faculty may refer to these resources for their own use, they also frequently treat the tutorials as supplements or references for students. Some faculty assign tutorials to be used outside class, saving valuable face-to-face time for other topics. Hundreds of tutorials are available and marketed alongside face-to-face workshops to emphasize continual availability. Faculty and students expect such immediate access—a characteristic of the Net Generation.

Carefully coordinated faculty development programs are a critical component of teaching and learning improvement. But these efforts are not stand-alone initiatives; they must be linked to infrastructure and services. For example, holistic planning is a necessity when curricular changes occur that require long-term planning for upgrades of discipline-specific computer classrooms and development of new courseware by faculty. Likewise, planning for workshops related to effective uses of wireless Internet access in classrooms should be coordinated with campus network planning efforts so that faculty are ready to leverage such an asset as soon as it is operational.

Virginia Tech, like many institutions, offers an array of services on behalf of technology-assisted learning that are closely aligned with the supporting infrastructure. Presenting a comprehensive, cohesive view of the breadth and depth of development services and programs is useful; old-fashioned marketing helps. Strategies aimed at better cohesion and communication include coordinating institutional offerings, cosponsoring and cobranding presentations, workshops, and lecture series, as well as internal grant programs and course development assets. Because different development programs and agencies within an institution often attract different segments of university faculty and staff, joint marketing and sponsorship can broaden the awareness and impact of each unit's work while simultaneously amplifying communication of institutional aims. In addition, Virginia Tech constructed Torgersen Hall, a building designed to showcase university activities for integrating technology in teaching and research as well as to provide spaces where such efforts might come together more spontaneously. Torgersen Hall also provides a home for FDI, the New Media Center, the digital library research, and more.

In summary, the FDI aims to help faculty construct a personal linkage between their professional needs in teaching and research as well as with the Net Generation and emerging technologies. Such development programs should emphasize teaching, learning, curriculum, discovery, and the needs of faculty and students; they should not focus on technology for its own sake. This focus underlies FDI's long-term, strategic value to the faculty and the university, which faculty and students have confirmed in surveys. Survey respondents indicate that active learning is integrated into instruction; greater student collaboration is taking place; and communication between faculty and students is enhanced. More important, perhaps, the surveys suggest that students feel they have a better understanding of course materials. Plus, they believe that they are provided opportunities to develop skills—such as problem-solving and critical thinking—that transcend individual subjects.

The Graduate Education Development Institute

Building on the success of the Faculty Development Institute, Virginia Tech launched a pilot project in 2003. Working in collaboration with the Graduate School, Learning Technologies (the division of Information Technology at Virginia Tech that also houses FDI) created the Graduate Education Development Institute (GEDI) to engage future faculty in teaching, learning, and technology issues as an integral part of their graduate student professional development. According to the EDUCAUSE Current Issues Committee, the "rapid introduction of new technologies and the constant enhancements and upgrades to existing technologies" indicates that faculty development models that focus on continuous learning and that take a systemic approach are increasingly necessary.[12] With the creation of GEDI, Virginia Tech is moving toward a systemic approach that addresses current faculty (in FDI) and that engages our future faculty (in GEDI). While we encourage faculty-to-graduate-student mentoring, GEDI also recognizes the importance of peer mentoring in the process of learning to teach effectively. To that end, GEDI serves as a multidisciplinary site where graduate students can explore the integration of teaching, learning, and technology that meets the needs of Net Generation learners and their own professional needs for FITness.

GEDI invites future faculty, at the beginning of their teaching careers, to begin thinking about how they can best communicate with Net Generation students. In doing so, GEDI staff hope to facilitate the development of a reflective teaching practice that better enables 21st-century faculty to recognize the importance of continuous learning for themselves as well as their students.

In many ways, professional development issues are as old as academe itself. Yet the future professoriate is facing a new academy, one which asks them to envision "new structures and funding models, new professionals, new relationships, new accountability, and new leadership roles."[13a,b] For graduate students who plan to remain in academe, the 21st-century university is an exciting place. Even as novice teachers and scholars, many are eager to critically analyze the kinds of teaching and mentoring practices that have—and have not—worked well. The majority of graduate students in GEDI are a mix of late Baby Boomers and Generation Xers; almost all of these young professionals are technologically savvy in ways that their senior professors are not. As such, GEDI participants are curious about how the Net Generation's learning processes may differ from their own; they are intent on becoming teachers with skills that engage Net Generation learners.

Still in a pilot phase, the primary focus of GEDI is a semester-long, for-credit, multidisciplinary seminar, "Pedagogical Practices in Contemporary Contexts." This course asks participants to explore (and begin to develop) the kinds of reflective pedagogical practices that stimulate 21st-century lifelong learning and engagement within the Net Generation. (The course is also part of a recently approved Future Professoriate graduate certificate that students may choose to earn.) The intent of the GEDI pilot project is to move beyond the unavoidable limitations of short-term, workshop-based training. GEDI staff work to create an interactive community over the span of a semester. This community crosses disciplinary lines, offering the potential for multidisciplinary collaboration and opportunities to "think outside the box" of discipline-specific perspectives. This process begins by discussing the importance of having pedagogical practices informed by pedagogical theory. In many disciplines there is little organized discussion of teaching methods, and rarely is there assigned reading in any pedagogical theory that might inform practice. (Colleges and schools of education, as well as some disciplines within the humanities, are notable exceptions.)

In the first part of the GEDI course, students look at the potential usefulness of a critical pedagogical praxis. In particular, participants examine ways in which critical pedagogy may inform teaching practices with the goal of helping students think about their own learning processes. For example, seminar participants read selected works and discuss ways in which theory and practice might be reinvented and reframed for their own discipline. GEDI participants are encouraged to read other pedagogical theory as well. Emphasis is placed on thinking about pedagogical practices in terms of the learning objectives each instructor is trying to achieve, not on a specific theoretical approach. This process is increasingly important as participants learn to recognize the ways in which Net Generation students differ from their predecessors and the ways in which learning to be FIT might successfully occur.

Regardless of the domain knowledge being taught, traditional teaching methods are often viewed as less effective with Net Generation students. With attention to what Jason Frand called the attributes of the "information-age mindset,"[14] GEDI participants discuss ways to use technologies that the Net Generation views as normative (rather than as technology) to challenge these learners to think creatively and critically. As Frand suggested, moving from "interacting on the Net" to "critical thinking" is not necessarily a simple or easy leap. Yet it is a necessary one. Helping students understand that finding information via Google is not synonymous with the critical evaluation of information is one of the tasks of contemporary higher education. As Net Generation students leave college and enter the broader society, "the ability to deal with complex and often ambiguous information will be more important than simply knowing a lot of facts or having an accumulation of knowledge."[15]

For some faculty, many of whom have been teaching for several decades, the learning processes of Net Generation students are viewed within a negative framework. Differences in learning processes are perceived as shortcomings—the desire for ubiquitous connectivity, the preference for multitasking and "channel-surfing attention spans," and less tolerance for delays, for example—when compared with previous generations of learners. In GEDI, participants avoid judgmental evaluations of different learning processes and focus instead on creating problem-based, active-learning environments that prepare Net Generation students for the complex 21st-century context in which they live and work.

GEDI participants, across a wide range of disciplines, are interested in discovering how current technologies might further students' intellectual movement from simplistic "absolute knowers" to more sophisticated "contextual knowers."[16] The GEDI seminar conversations also focus on issues of diversity: recognizing diverse curricular goals, diverse learning styles, and the increasingly diverse demographics that exist both inside and outside 21st-century classrooms. GEDI's primary emphasis, though, is on developing curricular approaches and pedagogical practices that facilitate Net Generation learners' abilities to problem solve in complex contexts—a process that requires the contemporary skills, foundational concepts, and intellectual capabilities that go with a FIT mindset.

Within the GEDI seminar, participants from fields as diverse as engineering, political science, chemistry, and English examine various problem-based learning case studies. Participants decide how and why a particular case study does (or does not) work and how to improve it. They explore whether the case study involves problem-based learning that encourages students to problem solve while simultaneously using domain knowledge, skill sets, and tools particular to that discipline. Participants assess whether a strategy inadvertently has a closed-ended answer, or whether it provides opportunities for students to suggest alternative solutions. They focus on how Net Gen students' technology skills and learning processes are engaged. In addition, emphasis is placed on case studies requiring students to address complex domestic and/or global contexts in finding possible solutions. These conversations take place with attention to different teaching and learning environments—from small labs and discussion-based classrooms to large lecture halls, hybrid/blended situations, and fully online courses. Following the collective cross-disciplinary discussions about what makes a successful case study, participants work individually or in teams to develop a sample problem-based learning module or case study for use in a course. Part of the task includes providing audience- and site-specific learning objectives for the case study and rationales for how and why various technologies are integrated.

In seminar dialogues, participants talk about active learning that recognizes and develops undergraduate students' sense of agency as FIT critical thinkers; they are also fostering their own sense of agency—as future faculty—about their teaching. For example, GEDI facilitators prefer not to overemphasize "how to" prescriptions about various teaching and learning technologies; instead, they encourage graduate students to explore how they might shape the technology to fit their pedagogy rather than vice versa. Likewise, since a critically engaged, self-reflective teaching praxis is what GEDI participants are encouraged to develop, the seminar and assignments are designed to foster a reflective practice. As part of this process,

GEDI participants explore the use of Virginia Tech's e-portfolio software as both a teaching tool and a professional development tool. To understand some of the ways they might incorporate the use of an e-portfolio into their teaching and how they might engage Net Generation learners in critical reflection via the tool, they simulate and use the e-portfolio with each other in much the same way that they might ask their own students to use it. GEDI participants also use the e-portfolio to begin the process of building a teaching portfolio. The creation of a teaching philosophy, syllabi, and digital video clips of their teaching can be "housed" in the e-portfolio along with reflections about their teaching and learning praxis.

It is important that we develop teaching and learning practices that encourage the Net Generation to develop critically engaged lifelong learning skills—with the emphasis on critically engaged. Technology should not be used to allow students to become passive recipients of information, as some traditional teaching methods do. Integrative approaches to teaching, learning, and technology should not render our students passive learners, however unintentional. Tony Bates has argued that students should be provided opportunities to interact with their instructors and with other learners, whether minutes, miles, or continents apart and, most important, that Net Generation learners "need to be able to challenge and question what they are being taught."[17] Higher education needs to foster active learners with the complex critical thinking and problem-solving skills required for this new century. At Virginia Tech, the GEDI project engages future faculty—those who will be responsible for teaching the Net Generation—in developing "best practices" in technology-enriched teaching and learning.

Conclusion

Current and future faculty are expanding their understanding of the Net Generation, technology, and pedagogy in an effort to improve teaching and learning. For this to occur, Baby Boomer and Gen-X faculty, as well as graduate students, need systematic support to develop and maintain their own fluency in information technology—to be FIT. Net Generation students assume a technology-enabled context in much of their lives and work; they exhibit a degree of digital literacy not necessarily shared by faculty; and they too need the full complement of knowledge and skills to be FIT. A first step is to focus on what students should know and be able to do. A next step is to understand what technology means to students. Programs such as FDI and GEDI illustrate how to support faculty in their efforts to engage the Net Generation.

Endnotes

1. Robert B. Kvavik, Judith B. Caruso, and Glenda Morgan, *ECAR Study of Students and Information Technology, 2004: Convenience, Connection, and Control* (Boulder, Colo.: EDUCAUSE Center for Applied Research, research study, vol. 5, 2004), <http://www.educause.edu/ers0405/>.

2. I. Elaine Allen and Jeff Seaman, *Sizing the Opportunity: The Quality and Extent of Online Education in the United States, 2002 and 2003* (Needham, Mass.: Sloan-C, September 2003), <http://www.sloan-c.org/resources/sizing_opportunity.pdf>.

3. Browse the Web sites at the Center for Academic Transformation <http://www.center.rpi.edu>, the Sloan Consortium <http://www.sloan-c.org>, WCET <http://www.wcet.info>, and the EDUCAUSE Center for Applied Research (ECAR) <http://www.educause.edu/ecar/> for numerous resources, from case studies to program analyses of pilot initiatives and emerging practices.

4. Jason Frand, "The Information-Age Mindset: Changes in Students and Implications for Higher Education," *EDUCAUSE Review*, vol. 35, no. 5 (September/October 2000), pp. 15–24, <http://www.educause.edu/apps/er/erm00/articles005/erm0051.pdf>.

5. Sherry Turkle, "How Computers Change the Way We Think," *Chronicle Review*, vol. 50, no. 21 (January 30, 2004), p. B26; available by subscription at <http://chronicle.com/weekly/v50/i21/21b02601.htm>.

6. Sherry Turkle, *Life on the Screen: Identity in the Age of the Internet* (New York: Touch-stone, 1995).

7. (a) Brock Read, "Back-to-School Blogging: Web Logs Help Students Prepare for Campus Life," *Chronicle of Higher Education*, September 3, 2004; available by subscription at <http://chronicle.com/prm/weekly/v51/i02/02a03501.htm>. For more information about educational blogging and student behavior, see also (b) Stephen Downes, "Educational Blogging," *EDUCAUSE Review*, vol. 39, no. 5 (September/October 2004), pp. 14–26, <http://www.educause.edu/pub/er/erm04/erm0450.asp>.

8. (a) National Research Council, *Being Fluent with Information Technology* (Washington, D.C.: National Academies, 1999), <http://www.nap.edu/catalog/6482.html>; (b) browse further at the host site <http://www.nap.edu/> for numerous other resources on related topics.

9. Browse Virginia Tech's Faculty Development Institute Web site <http://www.fdi.vt.edu/summer/2004/TrackC.html> for more information about faculty training programs.

10. Browse Virginia Tech's Educational Technology Web site <http://www.edtech.vt.edu/edtech/id/index.html> for more information on instructional design and other teaching resources.

11. See (a) Element K <http://www.elementk.com> and (b) Atomic Learning <http://www.atomiclearning.com>.

12. Donald Z. Spicer, Peter B. DeBlois, and the EDUCAUSE Current Issues Committee, "Current IT Issues: 2004," *EDUCAUSE Review,* vol. 39, no. 3 (May/June 2004), pp. 12–26, <http://www.educause.edu/pub/er/erm04/erm0430.asp>.

13. See (a) Carole A. Barone, "The Changing Landscape and the New Academy," *EDUCAUSE Review,* vol. 38, no. 5 (September/October 2003), pp. 40–47, <http://www.educause.edu/ir/library/pdf/erm0353.pdf>; and (b) Susan Walsh Veronikas and Michael F. Shaughnessy, "Teaching and Learning in a Hybrid World: An Interview with Carol Twigg," *EDUCAUSE Review,* vol. 39, no. 4 (July/August 2004), pp. 50–62, <http://www.educause.edu/pub/er/erm04/erm0443.asp>.

14. Frand, op. cit.

15. Ibid.

16. Marcia B. Baxter Magolda, *Making Their Own Way: Narratives for Transforming Higher Education to Promote Self-Development* (Sterling, Va.: Stylus Pub, 2001), pp. 27–36.

17. Tony Bates, "Teaching, Learning, and the Impact of Multimedia Technologies," *EDUCAUSE Review,* vol. 35, no. 5 (September/October 2000), pp.38–43, <http://www.educause.edu/pub/er/erm00/articles005/erm0053.pdf>.

About the Authors

Anne H. Moore is associate vice president for learning technologies at Virginia Tech, where she coordinates such programs as the Faculty Development Institute and the Graduate Education Development Institute. In addition to teaching in urban affairs and planning, she assists underserved rural and urban communities with integrating technology in learning activities. Moore is founding chair of the Electronic Campus of Virginia. She has served as staff director for two reports on the future of Virginia higher education and sits on several advisory boards. Moore holds three degrees from the College of William and Mary and has authored numerous articles, book chapters, and policy papers.

John F. Moore is director of educational technologies at Virginia Tech's Faculty Development Institute, recognized for its best practices in a national benchmarking study sponsored by the State Higher Education Executive Officers Association. Moore leads initiatives in e-portfolios, online learning systems, and faculty development. He also heads Virginia Tech's planning and implementation of e-portfolios. Moore codirected the Sloan Foundation–funded ACCESS project to study the effects of asynchronous learning courses on students and faculty, as well as several National Cancer Institute-funded consumer health intervention projects using interactive kiosks. Moore holds bachelor's and master's degrees from Ohio University and a doctorate in instructional systems from Virginia Tech.

Shelli B. Fowler is director of the Graduate Education Development Institute in Learning Technologies at Virginia Tech and associate professor of English. Her research areas include critical pedagogy and the integration of teaching and technologies, and she is the coeditor of *Included in English Studies: Learning Climates That Cultivate Racial and Ethnic Diversity.* She is the recipient of several department, college, and university teaching awards. Fowler earned her doctorate from The University of Texas at Austin.

CHAPTER 12

Learning Spaces

Malcolm Brown
Dartmouth College

New ideas about learning spaces represent a significant opportunity for higher education to make learners—and learning—more successful. Through the application of information technology, today's learning spaces have the potential to serve the new learning paradigm and at the same time meet the needs and expectations of the most recent generation of students: the Net Generation. Since education is the core mission of higher education, learning and the space in which it takes place are of the utmost importance. In order to best serve the educational enterprise, we must design leaning spaces that optimize the convergence of the Net Generation, current learning theory, and information technology.

This chapter establishes the links between Net Gen students, learning theory, and IT, showing their relevance to the concept of learning spaces. The definition of learning space has become broader and much more inclusive over the past decade. Learning theory will be discussed, as well as its implications for both Net Gen students and learning space design. The ties between this new conception of learning spaces and the habits and characteristics of Net Gen students will be established. Finally, scenarios will illustrate what these new spaces might look like.

What Are Learning Spaces?

What does the term *learning space* mean? Why not use *classroom* instead? As recently as a decade ago, classrooms were the primary locus for learning in higher education. Other spaces included the library, the faculty office (for individual mentoring), and perhaps the café in town. But classrooms were by far the single most important space for learning.

Since then, a great deal has changed. The World Wide Web has emerged as the primary way most people use the Internet. The Web has spawned a wealth of new, network-based applications, from digital music stores to new venues for scholarly publishing. Indeed, the availability of network access, in one form or another, is today almost taken for granted. Handheld devices have acquired a growing set of functions, providing a telephone, a digital camera, and an operating system running a variety of applications. Laptop prices have declined while increasing in functionality—to the point that their use exceeds that of desktops for most students.

In parallel with these developments in IT, an entire generation of learners has grown up using computers and other networked devices. While for previous generations IT was a kind of exotic overlay or an optional tool, for the Net Generation student IT is essential. It is clear that IT and Net Gen students have had a mutually influential—almost symbiotic—relationship. The characteristics of Net Gen students mesh very closely with IT and IT's increasing mobility, its 24 x 7 availability, and its increasing value as a communications tool. Net Gen students are social and team oriented, comfortable with multitasking, and generally positive in their outlook, and have a hands-on, "let's build it" approach—all encouraged by the IT resources at their disposal. Net Gen students have embraced IT, using it in ways both intended and unforeseen by programmers. Their rapid and enthusiastic adoption of IT has in turn influenced its development, particularly with respect to Web-based services.

The New Classroom

These developments impact the locus of learning in higher education. The notion of the classroom has both expanded and evolved; virtual space has taken its place alongside physical space.

Over the past decade, higher education has invested millions of dollars in classroom technology. The addition of document cameras, DVD players, Internet access, and projectors (to name a few) has added new functionality to the classroom. It is now possible to bring much more diverse materials to the classroom, to present them in a variety of ways, and to devise new classroom activities for students. As a result, the concept of the classroom has expanded to include this set of new functions.

These new classroom capabilities have, in turn, sparked interest in new pedagogical approaches. Wireless networking, for example, makes real-time or synchronous interaction (such as real-time polling) among all class participants a very real (and increasingly practical) possibility. Videoconferencing makes it feasible for an invited expert from a remote institution to join a class session. Discussions, notes, and other in-classroom events can be captured and disseminated for further study. It is important to note that these approaches mesh well with the habits of Net Gen students, such as their enjoyment of social interaction, their preference for experiential learning activities, and their use of technology. In these and other ways, technology acts as the lever that makes it possible to develop new and more effective pedagogies. Hence the classroom and the activities associated with it are evolving.

The resources used in higher education are increasingly digital and delivered via the network. In addition, network connectivity is increasingly portable. These two developments make it possible for learning to happen informally, in areas outside the traditional classroom, library, and faculty office. Student project teams can meet outside on the green, in a lounge, in any campus café—and they can meet almost any time of day. With wireless networking, numerous digital devices, and longer battery life, we are closer than ever to realizing the goal of fully ubiquitous access. This means that learning, too, can occur any time and anywhere.

Net Gen students, using a variety of digital devices, can turn almost any space outside the classroom into an informal learning space. Similar to the traditional classroom, educators have an important opportunity to rethink and redesign these non-classroom spaces to support, encourage, and extend students' learning environment.

Virtual Space

These changes catalyzed by technology make it clear that the term classroom, at least in its traditional sense, can no longer encompass where learning takes place. Equally obvious is that the space in which learning takes place is no longer just physical; it is virtual as well. The virtual space is an entirely new environment. *Virtual space* is any location where people can meet using networked digital devices. We should understand virtual space in its widest sense, referring not just to synchronous, highly interactive functions (such as chat, blogs, and wikis) but also to asynchronous functions such as e-mail and discussion threads.

Unlike physical spaces, virtual spaces come and go. They can be spontaneous as well as deliberate, synchronous or asynchronous. Participants and their relationships in the virtual learning space can shift rapidly. Participants can also multitask, "inhabiting" more than one virtual space at a time. As networking technology matures and costs for devices such as laptops and handhelds decline, these virtual spaces play an increasingly larger role in all aspects of higher education.

Again an IT-based function—virtual space—meshes closely with Net Gen characteristics. Net Gen students are mobile, as is virtual space. Net Gen students are facile at multitasking and moving back and forth (sometimes rapidly) between real and virtual spaces. Net Gen students are comfortable with the fast tempo that this kind of multitasking implies. In short, virtual space is tailor-made for the work habits of Net Gen students.

It is clear that the virtual space is taking its place along side the classroom and other physical locations as a locus for learning. The result is that we are compelled to expand our concept of where learning occurs. Learning spaces encompass the full range of places in which learning occurs, from real to virtual, from classroom to chat room.

Learning Theory

A shift in the teaching and learning paradigm is well under way, moving away from a transmission paradigm to a constructivist paradigm. In 1900, basic literacy skills included reading, writing, and calculation. *Knowing* meant being able to remember and repeat, which was appropriate to an industrial age in which practices changed slowly (at least by today's standards). Workers anticipated having a single profession for the duration of their working lives. Education was based on a factory-like, "one size fits all" model. Talent was developed by weeding out those who could not do well in a monochromatic learning environment.

The postindustrial age is characterized by rapid change. Literary skills now include critical thought, persuasive expression, and the ability to solve complex scientific and organizational problems. Knowing now means using a well-organized set of facts to find new information and to solve novel problems. In 1900, learning consisted largely of memorization; today it relies chiefly on understanding.

This shift has come about partly due the emergence of a constructivist theory of learning. Stated simply, this theory holds that learners construct knowledge by understanding new information building on their current understanding and expertise. Constructivism contradicts the idea that learning is the transmission of content to a passive receiver. Instead, it views learning as an active process, always based on the learner's current understanding or intellectual paradigm. Knowledge is constructed by assimilating new information into the learner's knowledge paradigm. A learner does not come to a classroom or a course Web site with a mind that is a tabula rasa, a blank slate. Each learner arrives at a learning "site" with some preexisting level of understanding.

Knowledge exists at multiple levels, ranging from novice to expert. It is the sophistication and depth of this understanding that differentiates experts from novices. Experts have a deep and rich set of well-organized facts, as well as the capacity to use that understanding to solve problems in their fields of expertise. Novices lack that depth and, as a result, have a much harder time solving problems.

The constructivist theory has important implications. The theory implies that learning is best served when it is:

▶ **Contextual**—taking into account the student's understanding
▶ **Active**—engaging students in learning activities that use analysis, debate, and criticism (as opposed to simply memorization) to receive and test information
▶ **Social**—using discussions, direct interaction with experts and peers, and team-based projects

Problem-based learning, which encourages learners to construct knowledge based on the experience of solving problems, is significantly different from methods such as recall and repetition. This is but one of many ways the older, traditional teaching paradigm contrasts with the learning paradigm. Table 1 summarizes some (though by no means all) other important ways these two paradigms differ.

Learning science research also highlights the importance of learner engagement, or as the American Psychological Association describes it, *intentional learning*.[1] This means that learners must have a "metaperspective" from which to view and assess their own learning, which is often referred to as *metacognition*.[2] An active learning environment provides the opportunity to assess one's own learning, enabling learners to make decisions about the course, as well as reflect on and assess their progress. In the past, the measure of learning was the final grade (a summative measure). But a final grade is merely a measure of the student's performance on tests. It does not measure the learning that did—or did not—take place. To encourage learning, summative testing or assessments must be combined with formative assessments. Formative assessment is not directly associated with the final grade; it helps learners understand their learning and make decisions about next steps based on that understanding.

Net Generation and Learning Theory

As with IT, there are overlaps between the working characteristics of Net Gen students and practices that research has shown encourage and strengthen learning. For example, the Net Generation is social. They like to stay in touch with peers (and even parents!). They have a preference for group activity and working in teams. This dovetails with research indicating that learning is encouraged when

Table 1. Differences in the Teaching and Learning Paradigms

Traditional Paradigm "Teaching"	Constructivist Paradigm "Learning"
Memorization	Understanding
Recall	Discovery
One size fits all	Tailored; option rich
Talent via weeding out	Talent cultivated and sought out
Repetition	Transfer and construction
Acquisition of facts	Facts + conceptual framework
Isolated facts	Organized conceptual schemas
Transmission	Construction
Teacher = master and commander	Teacher = expert and mentor
Fixed roles	Mobile roles
Fixed classrooms	Mobile, convertible classrooms
Single location	Plurality of locations and space types
Summative assessment	Summative and formative assessment

it includes social components such as debate or direct engagement with peers and experts. Learning is strengthened through social interactions, interpersonal relations, and communication with others.

Net Generation students are achievement and goal oriented. Their question is not "What does it mean?" or "How does it work?" (as previous generations were inclined to ask), but rather "How do I build it?" This predilection maps to learning theory's emphasis on active learning. Discovery, exploration, experimentation, criticism, analysis—all represent active learning, a style that suits the Net Gen well.

A pedagogy that emphasizes active learning has additional "targets of opportunity" among the Net Gen characteristics. Net Gen students are experiential, tending toward learning by doing rather than listening. Research indicates that learners need to be active with respect to their own learning process and assessment. Net Gen students' goal and achievement orientation comes into play here: that achievement focus can be directed toward quizzes and exercises that assist learners in evaluating their progress toward learning goals.

Obviously not all forms of learning must be social or team-based. In a variety of learning contexts, individual work is important. It may well be that Net Gen students' strengths are also their weaknesses. The expectation for fast-paced, rapidly shifting interaction coupled with a relatively short attention span may be counterproductive in many learning contexts. Repetition and steady, patient practice—key to some forms of mastery—may prove difficult for Net Gen students. Designing courses for them necessitates balancing these strengths and weaknesses.

Learning Space Implications

There are a number of implications of learning theory and the Net Generation for learning spaces. The convergence of the learning paradigm, IT, and the Net Gen is occurring now at colleges and universities. Current and future planning must encompass and encourage this convergence by thinking of learning spaces (classroom, informal, virtual) as a single, integrated environment. We should not neglect the informal for the formal, or assume that Net Gen students somehow will figure out the virtual space on their own. We should connect what happens in the classroom with what happens in informal and virtual spaces.

This implies that institutions may need to rethink their vision for learning and the spaces in which it occurs. Creating a vision for learning and learning spaces is a powerful leverage point; it informs almost all other decisions about learning space design. A vision also allows us to effectively articulate to all constituents what we are trying to accomplish. The vision helps organize all participants in the design and implementation of these spaces as well as the activities they support. Simply installing wireless access points and fresh carpeting isn't enough if done in isolation; such improvements pay real dividends only if they are in concert with the institution's overall teaching and learning objectives. It is the vision that generates the design principles that will, in turn, be used to make key decisions about how learning spaces are configured.

One important implication is that the vocabulary we use to describe what learners do in these spaces must become active. We must go beyond describing ways to help the instructor to be active; we must include students as well. The vision and design principles should emphasize the options students have as active participants in the learning process. Design principles should include terms such as *analyze, create, criticize, debate, present,* and *classify*—all directed at what the space enables the students to do. For example, students should be able to present materials to the class. Outside class, they should have access to applications and materials that directly support analysis of data, text, and other media. Forums for discussion and critical debate, both real and virtual, are key to encouraging learning and will be looked for by Net Gen students.

Learning spaces should accommodate the use of as many kinds of materials as possible and enable the display of and access to those materials by all participants. Learning space needs to provide the participants—instructors and students alike—with interactive tools that enable exploration, probing, and examination. This might include a robust set of applications installed on the computer that controls the room's displays, as well as a set of communication tools. Since the process of examination and debate leads to discovery and the construction of new knowledge, it could be important to equip spaces with devices that can capture classroom discussion and debate, which can be distributed to all participants for future reference and study.

Learning does not stop once the instructor has left the classroom. Instead, the end of the class meeting marks a transition from one learning mode to another. As a result, institutions must address real and virtual spaces outside the classroom to ensure that they, too, encourage learning. For example, there should be access to class materials (which are increasingly digital) so that the active and social work of learning can continue outside the formal classroom. The design of "neutral" spaces, such as hallways and corridors, could be rethought and re-equipped to promote learning. Some institutions provide small discussion spaces in corridors so that discussion begun in class can continue when class ends. As for the virtual space, institutions should consider well-integrated work environments that support collaborative projects and resource sharing.

Informal learning spaces—those outside the classrooms—present particularly intriguing opportunities for pioneering and cultivating new teaching and learning practices. These spaces, while informal, are key areas for student academic work. Students spend far more time in these spaces than they do in formal classrooms. Research, Web browsing, writing, statistical analysis, and compiling lab reports all take place in the library, study hall, media center, dorm room, and learning commons. Because of their enthusiasm for IT and their experiential, hands-on approach to learning tasks, Net Gen students will easily "tune into" the virtual aspects of informal spaces. Well-designed and integrated physical layouts and IT "tool sets" will find a ready audience with Net Gen students.

Scenarios

If we could implement this new vision of how learning occurs by buying the right kind of chair, purchasing projectors with sufficient lumens, or installing digital whiteboards, learning space design would be simple. Obviously it is much more complex—the task of designing and implementing learning environments that encourage good learning practice and accommodate the Net Gen learning style is a challenging one.

A starting point is to try to imagine what these new spaces might look like and how students would function in them. Creating scenarios helps define functions, usage practices, and design goals. Consider the following three scenarios as examples.

Scenario 1: The New Lecture Hall

Sandra, a junior, is heading to her psychology class, which meets at 10:00 a.m. It's a relatively large class for her liberal arts college, with some 150 students, so it meets in a lecture hall. As she arrives, she sees that the professor has, as usual, both projection screens lowered, one showing course material, the other displaying the familiar "voting" screen. Sandra finds a seat among some friends and begins "moving in" to her space. This lecture hall is of relatively recent vintage; its seats and paired tables make it much easier to deploy and use her "tools," which include printouts of the day's reading, as well as a small laptop computer. Her fel-

Figure 1. Technology-Supported Lecture Hall

Photo: Joe Mehling, Dartmouth College

low students are doing likewise. Each of them is using some device to access the course's Web site—some with laptops, others with tablet computers, still others with handheld computers. Using wireless connections, they all access the course's Web site and navigate to the site's "voting" page.

The professor commences her lecture. In one of the older lecture halls, she might have been tied to the lectern so that she could click through her PowerPoint slides. Or she might have abandoned her slides in order to write on the blackboard while her students scribbled notes in their notebooks. But in this newly renovated lecture hall, she and her students have many more options. She has what the campus technology office calls a "magic wand," a radio-frequency controller that enables her to operate her computer—as well as many of the classroom's functions—wirelessly, from any point in the room. She can capture anything she writes on the blackboard and make it available to her students on the course Web site. Freed from needing to take extensive notes, the students are able to participate more fully in the class discussion. Finally, the professor is carrying a small recorder that captures her lecture, digitizes the audio, and uploads it to the course Web site for the students to review when they prepare for finals.

Today she begins class by circulating through the room, using aisles that create paths through the students' seats. As she roams, she calls on students to share reactions to the readings. She encourages other students to offer additional comments. Soon there is some debate about the reading, which is facilitated by

Figure 2. PDA/Handheld Computer

Photo: Joe Mehling, Dartmouth College

the room's rows of paired tables and swivel chairs, making it possible to maintain eye contact with nearly everyone in the room.

At one point in the discussion, Sandra sketches a diagram on her laptop that she feels helps explain the concepts being discussed. She asks the professor if she could show it to the class. The professor agrees, and Sandra launches the classroom's screen sharing application. Within a few seconds, her computer's screen is projected on the room's main screen. The class discussion focuses on this diagram, and the professor, using a virtual pencil, is able to make notes on the diagram. The diagram and notes are captured and placed on the class Web site for review.

Soon the debate gets stuck; the students can't resolve the issue. The professor goes to the podium, types briefly, and then asks the students to go to a URL to see a question and to choose the answer they feel is correct. The students access the Web page from laptops, handhelds, or wireless IP-based phones. In two minutes they have completed the poll and submitted their responses. The results are quickly tabulated and displayed. The wide diversity of opinion surprises everyone. The professor reframes the issue, without giving the answer, and the students continue to discuss it. She repeats the poll; this time there is more agreement among the students, enabling her to move the discussion forward.

Halfway through the class period, the professor pauses the conversation. She goes to the podium computer.and clicks on a few links, and soon a video-

Figure 3. Handheld Computers in Class

Photo: Joe Mehling, Dartmouth College

conferencing session is displayed on the right-hand screen. She has arranged to have a colleague of hers "drop in" on the class to discuss a point that is in the colleague's particular area of expertise. The class has a conversation with the expert, who is at large research institution more than 500 miles away. Students listen to the expert's comments and are able to pose questions using one of the three cordless microphones available to the class. On the left-hand screen, the visiting professor shows some images and charts that help explain the concepts under discussion.

The professor concludes the day's class by showing a lab sign-up form, available on the course's Web site. Sandra is able to access the Web page almost instantly with her handheld computer and succeeds in signing up for lab times that work well with her schedule. It was good she didn't wait, for within 10 minutes of the end of class, the other students in her class have signed up for most of the slots, conferring with friends using chat programs to ensure that they sign up for the same lab slots.

Scenario 2: Using the Virtual Learning Space

When the class concludes, Sandra turns to her neighbor to ask about several points the professor made in class. This attracts two other students, who enter the conversation. As the discussion continues, they are joined by the professor, who is heading out. Since another class is beginning to file in, the professor suggests they move outside the room to continue the discussion. They find one of the "discussion pockets" unoccupied and move in. The discussion pocket is the college's term for a small, curved space with a table and bench to accommodate a meeting of four or five people. Found outside the newer classrooms, they are handy for informal, spontaneous discussions. Sandra's group moves into the pocket and for the next 15 minutes continue their "spill over" discussion of the class.

After this informal discussion concludes, Sandra heads to the library; she has an hour until her next class and needs to get some work done. She finds some table space, pulls out her laptop, books, and iPod and sets to work. She checks on her e-mail and sends some responses. Three friends "drop in" on her via the chat program, and she spends a few more minutes conversing with all three on separate subjects. That done, she fires up her iPod to listen to some music she downloaded using her subscription to the official campus online music service.

Now she begins work on a term paper for a history class. She rummages through the library's online collection, looking for a map she needs to illustrate a

Figure 4. Technology in the Library

Photo: Will Faller, Vassar College

point about 19th-century Asian history. She finds what she is looking for: although the map image is held by the library at a college on the other side of the country, Sandra has access to these resources. She is able to retrieve the map and insert into her document. She then traces arrows over the image to point out items important to the points she is making.

Again a friend drops in via chat, but this time it is about the joint presentation they are preparing for another class.

They are able to have an audio chat; Sandra's friend is in her dorm room, and Sandra is in a remote corner of the library where conversation will not disturb others. As their discussion progresses, they go to the course's Web site and launch the virtual whiteboard to diagram some concepts. They develop a conceptual diagram—drawing, erasing, and revising it until they agree the diagram is correct. They both download a copy. Sandra volunteers to work on polishing the diagram and will leave a copy of the final diagram in her share folder in her online portfolio "locker."

Sandra returns to work on her term paper and decides a half hour later to take a break. She again checks e-mail, chats briefly with a friend about their upcoming soccer game, and switches playlists on her iPod. Then she remembers that she needs to review some Italian newscasts for her Italian class. The files containing

Figure 5. IP-Based Chat

Photo: Joe Mehling, Dartmouth College

Figure 6. Virtual Workspace Anywhere

Photo: Joe Mehling, Dartmouth College

the newscast video are on her iPod, so she plugs her iPod into her laptop, finds the video files, and launches her viewer application. Plugging her headphones into her computer, she is able to watch the entire segment, making notes on parts she did not fully understand. She then checks the class's Web site and sees there is an additional set of video files for reviewing. She downloads these quickly onto her iPod. Noting the time, Sandra packs up her gear and heads off to her next class, stopping once at a stand-up e-mail station to see the latest messages that have arrived in her inbox.

Scenario 3: From the Information Commons to the Learning Commons

Had sophomore Martin come to the university at the same time as his older sister some six years earlier, he would have found, as she did, a computer lab. This was a large room, located in the basement of the science building, filled with benches and seats. At each seat was a computer. A set of documentation racks were on one side of the room; some documents were in short supply, while others were obsolete. On the other side was a help desk, staffed by students with a finite set of answers to the infinite variety of questions directed at them. Finding a free computer, particularly at the end of the term, was a challenge. Once you arrived at an available computer, there was little room for all your study materials: books, backpack, coat, and folders. The administration, anxious to maximize student access to computers, had crammed as many workstations as they could into the space.

While the computers worked fine for the most part (though cleaning them up after previous users was sometimes a chore), getting help was a problem. To get help—for the use of an application or for a research question—required going to the second floor for IT help or to the main floor of the library for research help. That meant leaving your computer unguarded, possibly to be claimed by another student equally hungry for computer time. So you ended up rarely going for help but instead muddled through as best you could, perhaps asking the student next to you when you were desperate.

But today Martin arrives at the first floor of the library and goes to a set of rooms collectively called the Learning Commons. At the threshold of the commons is the peer-tutoring room, a place where students can drop in and receive peer-based help with writing, research, or IT issues. Martin stops by to ask about incorporating MPEG-4 audio files into a PowerPoint presentation he's due to give next week for an anthropology course. At the same time, he is able to get some questions answered about relevant online journals for his research project in psychology.

Martin checks the time and heads to a work team pod—a small, horseshoe shaped table with a computer and large display—where he meets classmates from his chemistry course. The pod enables the work group to share the display and collectively work on materials. Martin works for an hour with three other students, reviewing drafts for their essays, checking online materials, and revising the Web site they are putting together for their collaborative project on the molecular properties of the surfaces of liquids.

Once that meeting is complete, he locates a free spot, pulls his laptop out of his backpack, and spends the half hour before his next team meeting doing a wide variety of things, including chatting with half a dozen friends about their party plans for the weekend. At the same time, he sends an e-mail to one of the TAs for the chemistry course, asking for clarification of an assignment. He also browses the Web, zeroing in on a Web site at another college that is relevant to his anthropology course work, as well as seeing if the latest CD from his favorite band is available through the Music Store. In a few minutes, he has purchased several tracks from it and downloaded them onto his computer.

Martin checks the time again. It's 10:00 p.m., and there's still a great deal to get done. He divides his time across several course assignments, numerous chat sessions, and reading (both from paper and from his computer screen). After a time, feeling drowsy, he goes to the Midnight Café, buys a soda and some chips, and returns to his work.

At 11:30 p.m., Martin packs his gear and heads to another part of the commons, the Media Studio, which offers a number of stations for students to use for more advanced work with video and audio. Martin is working with a team of four other students on an assignment for a film studies course. Their task is to find clips from a set of films that illustrate a particular filming technique and to explain why it is

Figure 7. Learning Commons

Photo: Roberto Marques, USITE/Crerar Computing Laboratory
Seminar Area, University of Chicago

Figure 8. Media Studio

Photo: Joe Mehling, Dartmouth College

effective. They rendezvous at a group station and spend the next hour reviewing films and identifying the clips they will use. They ask the student consultant on duty about whether it would be better to collect these in a single clip or as separate clips. By 12:45 a.m. Martin and his teammates have made their selections and given themselves tasks for the next phase of the assignment.

Martin calls up a Web page that contains a form for reserving one of the small group study rooms. He and some classmates have made an arrangement to meet with their anthropology professor. This meeting is to check on the progress Martin's group is making with their research project. The group wants the professor to review the video clips on their project Web site. Having found the reservation form, Martin is relieved to find that a room is available for the time they need; he reserves it. Noting it is now nearly one in the morning, Martin decides to turn in early for once (he has a language drill session at 7:45 a.m.). While walking back to his dorm, Martin prepares for the drill session by listening to some language lab audio files, which are streamed from the language lab server to his wireless iPod II.

New Learning Spaces

These scenarios show Net Gen students and faculty engaged in learning practices that are leveraged by IT, a process that requires either improving current practices or creating new ones. The underlying theme remains the same, however: cultivating learning practices consistent with learning theory and aligned with the habits and expectations of Net Gen students (and soon professors!) who have been "raised on" IT. The scenarios suggest the importance of integrating all learning spaces, formal and informal. For most higher education institutions, the lecture hall will not disappear; the challenge is to develop a new generation of lecture hall, one that enables Net Gen students and faculty to engage in enlivened, more interactive experiences. If the lecture hall is integrated with other spaces—physically as well as virtually—it will enable participants to sustain the momentum from the class session into other learning contexts. The goal is not to do away with the traditional classroom, but rather to reinvent and to integrate it with the other learning spaces, moving toward a single learning environment.

Building on these scenarios, Table 2 illustrates how Net Gen characteristics (such as the proclivity for group work) and learning theory might be supported by learning space design and IT. Learning theory is central to any consideration of learning spaces; colleges and universities cannot afford to invest in "fads" tailored to the Net Gen student that might not meet the needs of the next generation.

For example, start with the Net Gen students' focus on goals and achievement. That achievement orientation ties to learning theory's emphasis on metacognition, where learners assess their progress and make active decisions to achieve learning goals. Learning space design could support this by providing contact with people who can provide feedback: tutors, consultants, and faculty. This could, in turn, be supported in the IT environment by making formative self-tests available, as well as an online portfolio, which would afford students the opportunity to assess their overall academic progress.

Perhaps the most challenging aspect of these new learning spaces is the need for integration. As institutions create an anywhere, anytime IT infrastructure, opportunities arise to tear down silos and replace them with a more ubiquitous learning environment. Using laptops and other networked devices, students and faculty are increasingly able to carry their entire working environment with them. To capitalize on this, campus organizations must work collaboratively to create a more integrated work environment for the students and faculty, one that better serves the mobile Net Gen students as well as a faculty faced with the initial influx of these students into their ranks. This will involve not only libraries and IT organizations but also facilities planning and buildings and grounds departments. Development organizations may also become involved as institutions look for the resources needed to implement these new learning spaces.

Table 2. Aligning Net Gen Characteristics, Learning Principles, Learning Space, and IT Applications

Net Gen Trait	Learning Theory Principles	Learning Space Application	IT Application
Group activity	Collaborative, cooperative, supportive	Small group work spaces	IM chat; virtual whiteboards; screen sharing
Goal and achievement orientation	Metacognition; formative assessment	Access to tutors, consultants, and faculty in the learning space	Online formative quizzes; e-portfolios
Multitasking	Active	Table space for a variety of tools	Wireless
Experimental; trial and error	Multiple learning paths	Integrated lab facilities	Applications for analysis and research
Heavy reliance on network access	Multiple learning resources	IT highly integrated into all aspects of learning spaces	IT infrastructure that fully supports learning space functions
Pragmatic and inductive	Encourage discovery	Availability of labs, equipment, and access to primary resources	Availability of analysis and presentation applications
Ethnically diverse	Engagement of preconceptions	Accessible facilities	Accessible online resources
Visual	Environmental factors; importance of culture and group aspects of learners	Shared screens (either projector or LCD); availability of printing	Image databases; media editing programs
Interactive	Compelling and challenging material	Workgroup facilitation; access to experts	Variety of resources; no "one size fits all"

Conclusion

This description of learning spaces is suggestive rather than prescriptive. Learning spaces are complex, containing a multitude of variables. One of the key variables is the institution itself. Learning spaces are institutional in scope—their implementation involves the institution's culture, tradition, and mission. These institutional factors must be taken into account in order to design learning spaces to meet the needs of Net Gen students.

We must remind ourselves that today's students are only the "first wave" to exhibit Net Gen characteristics. Soon they will be graduate students and assistant professors, bringing their Net Gen work habits to the faculty ranks. In addition, faculty who are baby boomers and Gen-Xers are acquiring Net Gen characteristics as they become more facile with—and dependent upon—IT. Planning for Net Gen requirements cannot be dismissed as catering to a single generation. IT and the work habits that IT encourages are here to stay; planning for the Net Generation is tantamount to planning for the future.

No single magic formula will guarantee successful learning spaces on every campus. It is clear, however, that it will not be enough if we simply place projectors, computers, and DVD players in the classrooms. Nor will it be adequate just to provide scores of publicly available computers. Such tactics, in isolation, may have little impact. Learning space design is a large-scale, long-term project, involving building and maintaining consensus, curricular vision, emerging technology, and layout and furniture options, as well as intracampus organizational collaboration. Learning space design requires a collaborative, integrated approach, with an overarching vision that informs and supports specific projects.

The starting point for rethinking learning spaces to support Net Gen students begins with an underlying vision for the learning activities these spaces should support. This vision should be informed by learning theory, as well as by recognition of the characteristics of the students and faculty who use these spaces. An institution's specific culture, organizational structure, and fiscal circumstances enter the equation, as well. Once a vision has been established, the more concrete phases of planning can begin.

Acknowledgments

The author would like to thank his friend and colleague, Joan Lippincott of the Coalition for Networked Information, *for sharing insight and advice, as well as for her permission to use some of the ideas we articulated in our* EDUCAUSE Quarterly *article.*

Endnotes

1. American Psychological Association, Board of Educational Affairs (BEA), "Learner-Centered Psychological Principles: A Framework for School Redesign and Reform," revision November 1997, <http://www.apa.org/ed/lcp.html>.

2. National Research Council, *How People Learn: Bridging Research and Practice,* M. Suzanne Donovan, John D. Bransford, and James W. Pellegrino, eds. (Washington, D.C.: National Academies Press, 1999), pp. 12, 47; online edition available at <http://www.nap.edu/catalog/9457.html>.

Further Reading

American Association for Higher Education, American College Personnel Association, and National Association of Student Personnel Administrators, "Powerful Partnerships: A Shared Responsibility for Learning" (June 1998), <http://www.aahe.org/assessment/joint.htm>.

Robert B. Barr and John Tagg, "From Teaching to Learning—a New Paradigm for Undergraduate Education," in *Learning from Change: Landmarks in Teaching and Learning in Higher Education from* Change *Magazine 1969–1999,* Deborah DeZure, ed. (Sterling, Va.: Stylus Publishing, 2000), pp. 198–200. Originally published in Change, vol. 27, no. 6 (November/December 1995), pp. 12–25.

Jacqueline Grennon Brooks and Martin G. Brooks, *In Search of Understanding: The Case for Constructivist Classrooms* (Alexandria, Va.: Association for Supervision and Curriculum Development, 1993); online edition available at <http://www.ascd.org/portal/site/ascd/template.book/menuitem.ccf6e1bf6046da7cdeb3ffdb62108a0c/?bookMgmtId=4101177a55f9ff00VgnVCM1000003d01a8c0RCRD>.

Malcolm B. Brown and Joan K. Lippincott, "Learning Spaces: More than Meets the Eye," *EDUCAUSE Quarterly,* vol. 26, no. 1 (2003), pp. 14–16, <http://www.educause.edu/ir/library/pdf/eqm0312.pdf>.

Nancy Van Note Chism and Deborah J. Bickford, eds., *The Importance of Physical Space in Creating Supportive Learning Environments: New Directions for Teaching and Learning, No. 92* (San Francisco: Jossey-Bass, 2002).

National Research Council, *How People Learn: Brain, Mind, Experience, and School: Expanded Edition,* John D. Bransford, Ann L. Brown, and Rodney R. Cocking, eds. (Washington, D.C.: National Academies Press, 2000), <http://www.nap.edu/catalog/9853.html>.

Lennie Scott-Weber, *In Sync: Environmental Behavior Research and the Design of Learning Spaces* (Ann Arbor, Mich.: Society for College and University Planning, 2004), <http://www.scup.org/pubs/books/is_ebrdls.html>.

About the Author

Malcolm Brown is director of academic computing at Dartmouth College. In this capacity he oversees IT support for teaching, learning, research, classroom technology, and media production. He has been active with the New Media Consortium (NMC), serving as chair of the NMC Board for 2003–2004, and is on the project board for the NMC Horizon Project for 2005. One of his areas of particular interest is learning theory and its application in the classroom. He has presented on these topics at the EDUCAUSE and National Learning Infrastructure Initiative (NLII) conferences and has participated in NLII focus sessions as well as Project Kaleidoscope's planning workshops for National Institute of Technology and Liberal Education (NITLE) schools. Brown has also taught courses on topics in intellectual history in the Jewish Studies program at Dartmouth.

CHAPTER 13

Net Generation Students and Libraries

Joan K. Lippincott
Coalition for Networked Information

Introduction

The University of Southern California's Leavey Library logged 1.4 million visits last year.[1] That remarkable statistic illustrates how much a library can become part of campus life if it is designed with genuine understanding of the needs of Net Generation (Net Gen) students. This understanding relates not just to the physical facility of the library but to all of the things that a library encompasses: content, access, enduring collections, and services. Libraries have been adjusting their collections, services, and environments to the digital world for at least 20 years. Even prior to ubiquitous use of the Internet, libraries were using technology for access to scholarly databases, for circulation systems, and for online catalogs. With the explosion of Internet technology, libraries incorporated a wide array of digital content resources into their offerings; updated the network, wiring, and wireless infrastructures of their buildings; and designed new virtual and in-person services. However, technology has resulted in more modernization than transformation. There is an apparent disconnect between the culture of library organizations and that of Net Gen students. This chapter will explore how libraries might better adapt to the needs of Net Gen students in a number of specific areas.

Libraries and digital information resources can play a critical role in the education of today's students. Libraries license access to electronic journals, which provide key readings in many courses, and set up electronic reserve systems to facilitate easy use of materials. Libraries are an important resource for assignments that encourage students to go beyond the course syllabus. They provide access to the marketplace of ideas that is a hallmark of American higher education. Since much of the learning in higher education institutions takes place outside the classroom, libraries can be one important venue for such learning. The library can play a critical role in learning directly related to courses, such as writing a paper, and processes related to lifelong learning, such as gathering information on political candidates in order to make informed choices in an upcoming election. Libraries provide collections, organized information, systems that promote access, and in-person and virtual assistance to encourage students to pursue their education beyond the classroom.

It is difficult to generalize, but this chapter will use some characteristics of the Net Gen student that have been described by a number of researchers.[2a,b,c,d] Given that this generation of college students has grown up with computers and video games, the students have become accustomed to multimedia environments: figuring things out for themselves without consulting manuals; working in groups; and multitasking. These qualities differ from those found in traditional library environments, which, by and large, are text-based, require learning the system from experts (librarians), were constructed for individual use, and assume that work progresses in a logical, linear fashion.

What are some of the major disconnects between many of today's academic libraries and Net Gen students? The most common one is students' dependence on Google or similar search engines for discovery of information resources rather than consultation of library Web pages, catalogs, and databases as the main source of access. Since students often find library-sponsored resources difficult to figure out on their own, and they are seldom exposed to or interested in formal instruction in information literacy, they prefer to use the simplistic but responsive Google. Another disconnect is that digital library resources often reside outside the environment that is frequently the digital home of students' coursework, namely, the course management system, or CMS. Library services are often presented in the library organization context rather than in a user-centered mode. Libraries emphasize access to information but generally do not have facilities, software, or support for student creation of new information products. All of these disconnects can be remedied if appropriate attention is paid to the style of Net Gen students.

Access to and Use of Information Resources

When students use a wide array of information resources that they seek out on their own, they can enrich their learning through exploration of topics of interest. However, with the vast resources of the Web available, students must first make choices about how to access information and then which information resources to use in their explorations and assignments. Increasingly, students use Web search engines such as Google to locate information resources rather than seek out library online catalogs or databases of scholarly journal articles. Many faculty express concern that students do not know how to adequately evaluate the quality of information resources found on the Web, and librarians share this concern. Libraries need to find ways to make their information access systems more approachable by students, integrate guides to quality resources into course pages, and find ways to increase their presence in general Web search engines. Newly emerging services such as Google Scholar are providing access to more library resources in the general Internet environment. Libraries also need to be more cognizant of Net Gen students' reliance on visual cues in using the Internet and build Web pages that are more visually oriented.

The Library Versus the Web

Net Gen students clearly perceive the open space of the World Wide Web as their information universe. This is in opposition to the worldview of librarians and many faculty, who perceive the library as the locus of information relevant to academic work. Students usually approach their research without regard to the library's structure or the way that the library segments different resources into different areas of its Web site. Library Web sites often reflect an organizational view of the library (for example, how to access the reference department or online catalog); they do not do a particularly good job of aggregating content on a particular subject area. Students usually prefer the global searching of Google to more sophisticated but more time-consuming searching provided by the library, where students must make separate searches of the online catalog and every database of potential interest, after first identifying which databases might be relevant. In addition, not all searches of library catalogs or databases yield full-text materials, and Net Gen students want not just speedy answers, but full gratification of their information requests on the spot, if possible.

Recent surveys exploring college student use of the Web versus the library confirm the commonly held perception of faculty and librarians that students' primary sources of information for coursework are resources found on the Web and that most students use a search engine such as Google as their first point of entry to information rather than searching the library Web site or catalog.[3a,b] Several campus studies also examined where students gather information for a paper or an assignment. One study at Colorado State University yielded information that 58 percent of freshmen used Google or a comparable search engine first, while only 23 percent started with a database or index.[4]

The world of information is large and complex. There are no easy answers to providing simplified searching to the wealth of electronic information resources produced by a wide range of publishers using different structures and vocabularies. Students may perceive that librarians have developed systems that are complex and make sense to information professionals but are too difficult to use without being an expert.[5] However, as new generations of information products are developed, producers and system developers should try to address the information-seeking habits of Net Gen students. Libraries and the global service provider OCLC are working with Google so that information from peer-reviewed journals, books, theses, and other academic resources can be accessed through the Google Scholar search service. This is a step in the right direction, taking library resources to where students want to find them.[6a,b] Libraries also need to integrate more multimedia resources into their searchable content; this type of digital content is becoming increasingly important to Net Gen students, who may wish to study an audio recording of political speeches and incorporate segments into a term project as well as access books and journals on the topic. However, libraries typically incorporate information objects into their catalogs only when those resources are owned or licensed by the library. Is this still a relevant strategy in a world of global access to information via the Internet?

Locating Quality Digital Information

Providing mechanisms for information seekers from academe to locate quality information resources in a particular subject area is also a challenge for libraries—a very important one. Many academic libraries provide "library guides" or pathfinders to quality information resources, available through the library Web site, but typically they are not heavily used. A limited number of subject disciplines have developed coordinated Web guides to information resources; a notable example is AgNIC (http://www.agnic.org), serving the field of agriculture. Some libraries are developing mechanisms to link subject pathfinders into course management systems for every course at the institution. This useful strategy brings the information to the place where students will be actively engaged in academic work. Librarians at the University of Rochester looked for new ways to bring quality subject resources to the attention of students. They recognized that "undergraduate students' mental model is one focused on courses and coursework, rather than disciplines." Therefore, they developed a mechanism to incorporate pathfinders into every course at the institution using the course management system.[7]

Both students and faculty believe that the library is doing a poor job with helping them discern which Web resources are suitable for academic work.[8] Libraries are addressing this concern by developing portals to catalogs, licensed databases, and Web sites that would meet the kinds of criteria used in building academic library collections and by working with such projects as Google Scholar.

Incorporating Visual Cues

Designing Web pages that are responsive to Net Gen students' style would also help guide students to appropriate content or help them when they have problems with searches. A study of high school students' Web searching revealed that students relied heavily on information displayed in graphic form on Web pages and often relied on graphics and visual cues to interpret the relevance of such pages.[9] Libraries and information service providers generally do not design their resources with such criteria in mind. Incorporating students on design teams and giving them the go-ahead to reenvision the way the library displays its resources would be a useful method of developing information that resonates better with Net Gen students.

To summarize, Net Gen access services will:

▶ Continue to integrate library information into Google or other popular access mechanisms
▶ Offer simplified and graphic ways for students to approach subject searches
▶ Integrate subject guides or pathfinders into CMS or other locations conducive to use
▶ Integrate searching of "open" Web resources and materials owned or licensed by the library

Library and Information Services

Librarians often take great pride in the personalized information services they offer to their constituencies and the classes they teach to incorporate information literacy into the academic curriculum. While many of today's Net Gen students have grown up with technology, they do not necessarily have the requisite knowledge or skills to use technology and digital information in ways appropriate to the academy. Librarians should persist in their efforts to find ways to help students learn about digital information, including important policy issues in this arena, such as privacy and intellectual property. They should consider updating some of their methods for teaching students, incorporating gaming technology, or developing more visually oriented instruction aids, for example. One-on-one services offered electronically should be tailored to students' characteristics, such as their propensity to work late hours and use a variety of technologies, including laptops and cell phones.

Fluency with Technology and Information Literacy

Are Net Gen students already so technology literate and information savvy that they have no need for instruction or personal assistance in using technology and library and information resources? We know that Net Gen students come to campus having played hours of video games, having spent much of their spare time surfing the Net and instant messaging their friends, and having used multiple electronic devices simultaneously. On the other hand, we hear complaints from faculty that students use inappropriate sources from the Web to support their ideas in term papers instead of peer-reviewed academic resources; that they submit multimedia projects that are superficial and full of glitz, not substance[10]—and that they no longer read, period.

When students graduate, their faculty in graduate degree programs and their employers expect that they will have a facility with technology and with digital information that the older generations do not have. New office recruits are often hired because of their Internet skill and are given projects that exploit their technology and information skills, developed during their college years.

In addition, today's college graduates live in a world where it is important to understand key information policy issues. Intellectual property, privacy, and First Amendment issues are fundamental to operating as an informed citizen in today's information society and directly affect the work of individuals who create, as well as use, networked information.

While Net Gen students generally can multitask, learn systems without consulting manuals, and surf the Web, they lack technology and information skills appropriate for academic work. Higher education institutions do not integrate or package technology and digital information skills instruction into the mainstream curriculum.

A National Academies report described a model set of skills for "fluency in information technology," which incorporates both information technology and literacy skills. The report's authors divided skills into three categories: foundational concepts, contemporary skills, and intellectual capabilities. They recommended that each university's subject area curriculum develop ways to incorporate instruction in these topics; however, they lamented that this is not currently the case.[11] The Association of College and Research Libraries (ACRL), a division of the American Library Association, has also developed guidelines for information literacy, but they have not been widely implemented by universities.[12] Technology and information literacy are generally perceived to be "library" or "IT" problems, not overall curricular issues.

At Southwestern University, a team of IT professionals, librarians, and faculty developed a student survey based on both the National Academies' fluency with information technology principles and the ACRL Information Literacy Competency Standards. Their findings revealed that while students rated themselves highly in their ability to find information on the Internet, they recognized that they floundered when they attempted to find materials appropriate for their research and wasted much time in the process. The students also expressed a desire for more technology applications to be integrated into their courses.[13] This model is being explored through a Mellon Foundation–sponsored project at the University of California, Berkeley, where selected faculty and librarians are working in partnership to incorporate information literacy skills and undergraduate research into large-enrollment courses with the goal of assisting students in developing skills that will serve them throughout their coursework at the institution.[14]

Delivering Service with Style

Information and technology literacy represents a content area in Net Gen students' education that has not been fully addressed. Separate but related is the "style" issue of how best to deliver this educational content and provide information and technology services to Net Gen students. Net Gen students work in information environments, and a very important one in college is the course management system. Libraries should develop tutorials, exercises, and guides that can readily be embedded in course materials within course management systems, and some are already doing this.[15a,b] They can develop games to teach these skills; TILT, the Texas Information Literacy Tutorial (http://tilt.lib.utsystem.edu/), developed by The University of Texas at Austin libraries, is an early example. Simulations such as Environmental Detectives (http://cms.mit.edu/games/education/Handheld/Intro.htm) can incorporate information-seeking skills into the game, reinforcing

Net Gen students' interest in figuring things out and working in groups. Libraries should explore blogs as a mechanism for students to exchange information on valuable information resources they find for particular course assignments. Blogs sponsored by the library might be particularly effective for graduate students beginning their dissertations and needing advice from peers and information professionals on locating materials for their literature reviews.

An emerging area of literacy is the need for students to increase their fluency with representing their knowledge in the digital, multimedia world. George Lucas stated that students need to learn a "language of screens" in order to be effective communicators today.[16] The Visible Knowledge Project, in which university faculty are working with multimedia content and developing assessment mechanisms to measure the effectiveness of their instruction, is also working on guidelines to assist faculty in evaluating student multimedia projects.[17] While Net Gen students often prefer creating a multimedia project rather than a term paper that is entirely text, they need assistance in understanding how to represent their knowledge in a form that is appropriate for academic work, just as they need to learn to write in a way that meets the standards of the academy.

Reference Services

Although libraries have offered e-mail reference services for a number of years, they were slow to adopt chat and sometimes developed sophisticated but complex chat software rather than the simpler systems typically used by Net Gen students. Librarians might need to change their mindset of employing the most sophisticated software that enables features they believe could provide improved service, such as permitting the librarian to demonstrate a search or review an information resource in one window while chatting with the student in another, in preference for software that students are more likely to use.

In one study where a library did use standard AOL Instant Messenger software, other roadblocks to student adoption were put into place. The librarians noted in their report on the service that they did not staff it during late-night hours when students were most likely to use the service and that they did not market the service in information literacy class sessions for fear that the response might overwhelm their capabilities. Instead, the service was not heavily used.[18] They did collect some responses as to why students took advantage of the service, and convenience was the main reason. One student reinforced why this type of service has appeal to the multitasking Net Gen students by replying that he had used the service instead of phoning the library so that he could continue working and browsing while waiting for an answer from the librarian.

Visual, Interactive Services

Students also like self-service, interactive Web sites, and it is surprising that libraries haven't developed visual representations of their services that students could explore. A survey by OCLC found that one of students' top suggestions for libraries was to offer interactive maps, study tips, and guides.[19] An example of that type of environment is a Web site developed by the British Museum as a "student's room" for an exhibit of Mughal, India, an ancient civilization.[20] Students see an office-style room that they can explore by clicking on components such as a globe, file cabinets, book shelves, and so forth. They are then led to museum resources including an atlas and primary resources from the museum's collections on the Mughal period. This type of model could be used for a library reference room and its resources.

Libraries could add value to key pages of their Web sites by including interactive tutorials on how to find information or how to judge quality information resources. Libraries could use part of their home page to highlight a "resource of the week," to better publicize information content that could likely assist students in their assignments. They could use customized mouse pads to advertise URLs for selected information resources.

Libraries also need to think about new services using mobile technology such as cell phones. They might allow students to reserve group study rooms and be alerted to availability via their cell phones, send simple text-message queries to library catalogs or databases, or check library hours via text messaging. Such services might be particularly valuable for students who live off campus.

How will we conceive and design these new services? Librarians should consult with students in the design phase of services and incorporate students on teams that make decisions about the implementation of those services. Making use of the imagination, creativity, technical skills, and perspectives of Net Gen students is the best way to ensure that new services will be responsive to both their needs and their style.

To summarize, Net Gen information services will:

▶ Use students on teams that design new services and environments
▶ Integrate services into course management systems
▶ Explore services for mobile devices

- Represent services and instruction visually and in multimedia modes
- Focus on partnership models
- Emphasize how to evaluate information resources
- Emphasize information policy issues

Environments

Although technology has transformed many campuses, physical spaces remain important in most higher education institutions. The library offers a venue where academic work can be carried out in a social context. As libraries renovate facilities to incorporate technology, they are also making them more suitable for student group work, informal socializing, and ubiquitous computing. Information Commons often provide space, workstations, and software that encourage both access to information and the capability to create new information products. Some Information Commons offer joint support to users from both the library and IT units. It is less common for libraries to rethink their virtual services to provide a better complement to their physically based services. Libraries have opportunities to alter their marketing strategies and their use of visual representations of information to encourage more and new creative uses of digital information resources.

Library Physical Spaces

As the Leavey Library at USC mentioned above demonstrates, students will flock to library facilities that offer environments conducive to Net Gen learners. What Leavey offers are hundreds of workstations in configurations that support both individuals and small groups, group study rooms where students can work together on projects, workstations equipped with a wide array of software that can be used for creation of new information products, and staff with both library and information technology expertise who can address subject-information requests and technology hardware or software issues.

Many academic libraries are following the Leavey Library model and are transforming part of their physical space into information commons, multimedia production areas, classrooms, or all three. For example, the University of Arizona's Learning Center has components that include a library information commons where students can work on workstations configured for individual or group work, develop multimedia projects, and get advice from reference librarians. Adjacent to the information commons are multimedia classrooms and a computer lab with support by Information Technology staff. The Indiana University information commons, developed jointly by the library and IT and situated on the first floor of the library, incorporates single and multiuser workstation areas, group study rooms, and classrooms and offers a wide range of services supported from a circular central desk staffed by library and IT staff.

While there is no one widely accepted definition of an information commons, generally it is a physical space, not always in the library, that incorporates many workstations equipped with software supporting a variety of uses, offers workspace for individuals and groups, provides comfortable furniture, and has staff that can support activities related to access to information and use of technology to develop new products. While information commons are usually developed for student use, some incorporate centers for teaching excellence or instructional technology support services for faculty.

These new types of library spaces communicate a welcoming attitude to Net Gen students. They are the opposite of old-style formal reference rooms where students were expected to sit on straight wooden chairs and work individually and silently, without access to technology. Instead, these spaces project a comfortable, relaxed environment, a celebration of technology, and an invitation to communicate. One editor wrote, after interviewing an architect who had designed a vibrant new library at the University of Nevada Las Vegas, "...try to think of your library as an environment rather than a facility—a place of interaction, learning, and experiencing rather than a place for storage and equipment."[21]

Library physical spaces continue to be valued places for building community in colleges and universities. Importantly, they also provide an atmosphere in which social and academic interests can easily intersect. When students were asked what they desired in an upcoming renovation of Teachers College at Columbia University Library, they replied that they wanted "a social academic experience."[22] Libraries can promote community by providing comfortable spaces for informal gatherings of students. Many libraries are adding coffee bars to their lobby areas or a building adjacent to the library; such spaces encourage students to continue conversations on topics of academic interest. Libraries might develop new ways of promoting community among students, related to course activity. For example, they may develop a message board or online mechanism for students to identify who else in the library building might be working on an assignment for a particular course if they need help from a peer or wish to study as a group.[23]

Integrating Physical and Virtual Environments

Most libraries have not yet learned how to effectively integrate physical spaces with virtual spaces and services. For example, the introductory screen on workstations in an information commons may have no description of the services or digital information products offered there. Vassar College has remedied this in their Media Cloisters (http://mediacloisters.vassar.edu/), where entering visitors are confronted with a brightly colored set of screens introducing student members of the multimedia team and advertising their areas of expertise.

How might libraries market services to Net Gen students, who are often visual learners? One possibility is to literally project information onto the walls of the information commons. In a changing display, libraries could develop programs to project pages of electronic journals, guides to subject fields or topics that many students are working on during a specific week, quality Web sites with good visual displays (for example, museum Web sites), and student or faculty multimedia information products. Such displays would alert students to the broad array of electronic information resources accessible through the library and could prompt student interaction with a reference librarian to pursue similar sources for their projects.

To summarize, Net Gen information environments will:

▶ Provide individual and group learning spaces
▶ Support access to and creation of information resources
▶ Offer staff and faculty development and training
▶ Provide staff with a range of technology and information skills
▶ Effectively market services to all groups of potential users
▶ Integrate physical spaces and services with virtual spaces and services
▶ Build community

Conclusion

Developing library content, services, and environments that are responsive to Net Gen students can be achieved by examining the characteristics of those students and making a conscious effort to address deficiencies and transform the current situation in libraries. Why should libraries and librarians adapt their well-structured organizations and systems to the needs of students rather than insist that students learn about and adapt to existing library systems? The answer is that students have grown up in and will live in a society rich in technology and digital information. By blending the technology skills and mindset that students have developed all their lives with the fruits of the academy, libraries can offer environments that resonate with Net Gen students while enriching their college education and lifelong learning capabilities.

Endnotes

1. Darren Schenck, "Super_Model," *Bibliotech USC: Annual Report Edition 2003* (Los Angeles: USC Information Services), p. 21, <http://www.usc.edu/isd/giving/private/documents/pubs/bibliotech_04.pdf>.

2. See a variety of resources including (a) Diana G. Oblinger, "The Next Generation of Educational Engagement," *Journal of Interactive Media in Education,* vol. 8 (May 2004), <http://www-jime.open.ac.uk/2004/8>; (b) Marc Prensky, "Digital Natives, Digital Immigrants: Part I," *On the Horizon,* vol. 9, no. 5 (October 2001); Marc Prensky, "Digital Natives, Digital Immigrants, Part II: Do They Really Think Differently?" *On the Horizon,* vol. 9, no. 6 (December 2001); Marc Prensky, "Overcoming Educators' Digital Immigrant Accents: A Rebuttal," *The Technology Source* (May/June 2003) (access Prensky's writings at <http://www.marcprensky.com/writing/>); (c) Ian Jukes and Anita Dosaj, "Understanding Digital Kids (DKs): Teaching and Learning in the New Digital Landscape," the InfoSavvy Group, June 2004, <http://www.thecommittedsardine.net/infosavvy/education/handouts/it.pdf>; and (d) "The Next-Generation Student: Report of the Microsoft Higher Education Leaders Symposium," Redmond, Washington, June 17–18, 2003.

3. (a) Online Computer Library Center (OCLC), "How Academic Librarians Can Influence Students' Web-Based Information Choices," white paper on the information habits of college students, June, 2002, <http://www5.oclc.org/downloads/community/informationhabits.pdf>; and (b) Sarah Lippincott and Martha Kyrillidou, "How ARL University Communities Access Information: Highlights from LIBQUAL+," *ARL: A Bimonthly Report,* no. 236 (October 2004), pp. 7–8, <http://www.arl.org/newsltr/236/lqaccess.html>.

4. Karen Kaminski, Pete Seel, and Kevin Cullen, "Technology Literate Students? Results from a Survey," *EDUCAUSE Quarterly,* vol. 26, no. 3 (2003), pp. 34–40, <http://www.educause.edu/ir/library/pdf/eqm0336.pdf>.

5. OCLC, op. cit.

6. See (a) the OCLC Open WorldCat program, <http://www.oclc.org/worldcat/pilot/default.htm>, and (b) About Google Scholar, <http://scholar.google.com/scholar/about.html#about>.

7. Brenda Reeb and Susan Gibbons, "Students, Librarians, and Subject Guides: Improving a Poor Rate of Return," *Portal: Libraries and the Academy,* vol. 4, no. 1 (January 2004), pp. 123–130, <http://muse.jhu.edu/journals/portal_libraries_and_the_academy/toc/pla4.1.html>.

8. Lippincott and Kyrillidou, op. cit.

9. Raya Fidel et al., "A Visit to the Information Mall: Web Searching Behavior of High School Students," *Journal of the American Society of Information Science*, vol. 50, no. 1 (January 1999), pp. 24–37.

10. Robert Zemsky and William F. Massy, *Thwarted Innovation: What Happened to E-Learning and Why* (West Chester, Penn.: The Learning Alliance at the University of Pennsylvania, 2004), <http://www.thelearningalliance.info/Docs/Jun2004/ThwartedInnovation.pdf>.

11. National Research Council, *Being Fluent with Information Technology* (Washington, D.C.: National Academies Press, 1999), <http://www.nap.edu/catalog/6482.html>.

12. Association of College and Research Libraries (ACRL), *Information Literacy Competency Standards for Higher Education* (Chicago: ACRL, 2000), <http://www.ala.org/acrl/ilcomstan.html>.

13. Sharon Fass McEuen, "How Fluent with Information Technology Are Our Students?" *EDUCAUSE Quarterly*, vol. 24, no. 4 (2001), pp. 8–17, <http://www.educause.edu/apps/eq/eqm01/eqm014.asp>.

14. Mellon Library/Faculty Fellowship for Undergraduate Research, UC Berkeley, <http://library.berkeley.edu/MellonInstitute>.

15. (a) Elizabeth Pyatt and Loanne Snavely, "No Longer Missing: Tools for Connecting the Library with the Course Management System," *eLearning Dialogue* (March 17, 2004), <http://www.syllabus.com/print.asp?ID=9094>; and (b) Brenda Reeb and Susan Gibbons, "Students, Librarians, and Subject Guides: Improving a Poor Rate of Return," *Portal: Libraries and the Academy, vol. 4, no. 1 (January 2004), pp. 123–130.*

16. *James Daly, "George Lucas: Life* on the Screen," EDUTOPIA, issue 1 (September/October 2004), pp. 34–40, <http://www.glef.org/magazine/ed1article.php?id=art_1160&issue=sept_04>.

17. Visible Knowledge Project, <http://crossroads.georgetown.edu/vkp/index.htm>.

18. Marianne Foley, "Instant Messaging Reference in an Academic Library: A Case Study," *College and Research Libraries*, vol. 63, no. 1 (January 2002), pp. 36–45.

19. OCLC, op. cit.

20. Mughal, India, interactive room and similar resources available from the British Museum, <http://www.thebritishmuseum.ac.uk/education/onlinelearning/home.html>.

21. Morrell D. Boone, "Library Design—The Architect's View. A Discussion with Tom Findley," *Library Hi Tech*, vol. 20, no. 3 (2002), p. 392.

22. Patricia Cohen, "Spaces for Social Study," *New York Times*, August 1, 2004.

23. This idea was proposed by a participant in a University of Massachusetts planning workshop for their proposed Learning Commons on April 6, 2004. For more information on the Learning Commons, see <http://www.umass.edu/provost/initiatives/learningcommons/>.

About the Author

Joan K. Lippincott is the associate executive director of the Coalition for Networked Information (CNI), a joint project of the Association of Research Libraries (ARL) and EDUCAUSE. Lippincott previously held positions at Cornell, Georgetown, George Washington, and SUNY at Brockport. She also worked in the Research and Policy Analysis Division of the American Council on Education and at the National Center for Postsecondary Governance and Finance. She has written articles and given presentations on such topics as networked information, collaboration among professional groups, assessment, and teaching and learning in the networked environment. Joan received her PhD in higher education policy, planning, and administration from the University of Maryland, an MLS from SUNY Geneseo, and an AB from Vassar College.

CHAPTER 14

The New Academy

Carole Barone
EDUCAUSE

Introduction

Something is happening to the academy—outside the consciousness of the majority of its members. A new academy is forming that

▶ acknowledges the changes manifested in the Net Generation,

▶ uses the power of technology to enable deeper learning,

▶ demonstrates the interplay of culture and technology, and

▶ changes the nature of interaction among the members.

Some within the academy are aware of these trends, but view them with trepidation because they represent a fundamental change in well-established assumptions regarding how faculty teach and how students learn, not to mention how the academy governs itself. Not engaging in thoughtful self-examination, however, may pose the greater threat.

Technology and pedagogy are converging in the learning landscape. Often this collides with the process, structure, governance, power relationships, and cultural values of the traditional campus. Efforts to transform higher education face deeply entrenched cultural, behavioral, and philosophical resistance. The decade-long effort to convince the traditional higher education community of the transformational power of technology (for example, through the work of the National Learning Infrastructure Initiative, http://www.educause.edu/nlii) has yet to yield the breakthroughs many anticipated.

The arrival of the Net Generation on campus is causing unrest in the classroom.[1] A wave of young people empowered to create knowledge, not merely absorb it, now flows in and out of the classroom, calling into question the convictions and processes that have served as the foundation of traditional higher education. It remains to be seen whether traditional higher education will adjust sufficiently to truly engage the Net Generation.

Alternative ventures targeting today's learners have begun to succeed in the traditional higher education market:

▶ Kaplan Higher Education offers undergraduate and graduate programs, both online and on campuses (http://www.kaplan.com/).

▶ Capella University is fully online (http://www.capella.edu/).

▶ Pepperdine University offers an online master's degree program in educational technology (http://gsep.pepperdine.edu/academics/education/ma-edtech/).

▶ American InterContinental University offers degree programs both online and at campuses in multiple states (http://www.aiuniv.edu/).

▶ The University of Massachusetts Online is adding five new degree programs for 2005 (http://www.umassonline.net/news/shownews.cfm?news_ID=62).

▶ The Apollo Group, the parent company of the University of Phoenix, projects an increase of 12 to 13 percent in its on campus enrollments and a 40 percent growth in its online enrollments over the previous year by the end of the first quarter of fiscal 2005 (http://www.bizjournals.com/phoenix/stories/2004/08/23/daily37.html).

These examples are indicators of enhanced confidence in the quality of the educational product offered online. In addition, the results of a study recently issued by the Sloan Consortium revealed that enrollments in online courses grew by nearly 20 percent from 2003 to 2004. The report concluded that this rate of growth far exceeds that of traditional higher education enrollments and "there is no evidence that online enrollments have reached a plateau."[2]

Confronting the Reality of Change

The growing impact of technology is evident in higher education. Technological change, and changes driven by the Net Generation, challenge—some would say threaten—higher education to assimilate the resulting roles, rules, and relationships in a new academy. That new academy must grow out of a traditional campus context that has successfully resisted such intrusions in the past.

When something happens that causes upheaval in our lives, our initial reaction is often denial. To some the emergence of a new academy constitutes just such an upheaval. Denial—and resistance to change—is believed to be a way of preserving the "academic values" that many see as central to their professional way of life. Habits and traditions are not academic values, however. Milton Greenberg discussed the "fantasies" or artifacts of higher education, such as the credit hour, in "A University Is Not a Business (and other Fantasies): "...the major higher education institutions are caught in a time warp. Teaching and learning tend to be served up in the same old containers, in the same old spaces, using the same old concept of fact-to-face interpersonal relationships."[3] Ironically, the only way to preserve true academic values, such as pursuing knowledge for the sake of knowledge, the process of discovery itself, or critical inquiry, may be to evolve from the familiar to the unfamiliar—in other words, to embrace the emerging new academy.

Higher education decisions are still governed by traditional expectations and mores. Perhaps we should take note of Langenberg reminding us, "... I am unaware of any cases in which successful buggy-whip makers made the transition to successful manufacturers of automobile-engine starters."[4] The presence of the Net Generation on campus and the growing acceptance of their "ways" in the external economic and social communities have yet to stimulate widespread transformation; traditional processes continue leading to traditional outcomes. Like the buggy whip, the traditional classroom lecture, the cultural values, and even the edifices associated with higher education seem to belong to another place and time.

Some traditional academics feel that the habits of the Net Generation result in a superficial grasp of their discipline and do not embody the gravitas of an "educated" person. Others claim that the Net Gen lacks "taste" in the choices it makes among online sources and resources. A growing number within the new academy, however, ask what traditional higher education is doing to engage the Net Gen in developing intellectual depth, sophistication, and good judgment in evaluating and using online sources of information. The Net Gen will not be intimidated into abandoning their preferences for interactive, easily accessible, Web-based information sources. They will simply work around the attempts to force them to revert to the traditional activities. If technology is enabling the development of their "information-age mindset,"[5] then technology is also a means of engaging these learners in a deeper learning experience.

There are options. Some traditional higher education institutions are trying to find the wherewithal to change from within. The longer traditional higher education remains in denial of the reality of the new academy, the less feasible transformation becomes. Higher education must avoid the mistakes of the business community. Resilience is preferable to resistance. As Hamel and Valikangas noted,[6] a transformation is a turnaround tragically delayed. Denial produces a sort of paralysis that makes it difficult to take the actions necessary to move from the past into a new reality.

Expectations

Historical perspective has a great impact on the convictions that both faculty and students bring to higher education. Many faculty members expect students who are like they were when they were students themselves, 25 to 30 years ago; they plan their courses and teaching methods accordingly. Meanwhile, because of the images of the "college experience" society continues to provide them, many incoming students still expect a classroom experience dominated by lecture halls and blackboards; traditional institutions reinforce these expectations regarding where and how students will be "taught." Most students still believe that this is how they should learn.

Students have daily encounters with technology and innovation in many areas of their lives; in fact, their social interactions may be organized around instant messaging, blogs, and other technology-based modes of communication. Students may use PDAs and wireless networks to stay in touch with each other, to get information, to vet their ideas and thought processes, Yet, they are not surprised by the mandate that they sit in classrooms and listen to lectures when they get to college—they just get bored and restless. Thus, it should be no surprise when they eventually—perhaps inevitably—begin to question the ways we ask them to learn, because those ways do not match with the interactive access to information and modes of communication by which they learn in other aspects of their lives.

Using data from studies conducted at Washington State University (WSU), Gary Brown argued that higher education is disassociated from reality "and nowhere is it more deeply rooted than in the perceptions of students."[7] This disconnect seems to be driving an increasing sense of disenchantment with the traditional approaches to teaching and learning. Data indicate that students enter higher education expecting the traditional learning environment, but also expecting to be intellectually engaged in, and challenged by, the learning process. Similar to the WSU study results, George Kuh reported that three years of data from the National Survey of Students Engagement[8] revealed that over the course of their undergraduate years, students become increasingly disengaged from, and disillusioned with, the higher education experience. Cynically, perhaps, they may do what they have to do to earn the grade, and then learn what they need to learn elsewhere ... and for the digital generation, "elsewhere" is the Internet.

Even those faculty deeply entrenched in established ways of doing things may be starting to feel that something is not working—that they and their learners simply are not on the same page—and therefore learning outcomes are suboptimal. Even though something may feel wrong in the formal classroom setting, most faculty have not yet made the transition to the alternatives presented by the new academy.

Faculty may use the Web to stay current with the latest thinking in their disciplines, but they expect to teach in a traditional classroom setting because that is the only way to ensure that students are learning the "right" things the "right" way. It is clear that some of our sacred cows, such as the lecture as a mesmerizing solo performance, "seat time" in the classroom, the academic calendar (which Milton Greenberg referred to as "a meaningless fiction"),[9] may not be able to make the journey to the new context of teaching and learning successfully. Perhaps they should not, given the new realities presented by our students, their use of technology, and their expectations for extending that use to support their learning.

Many faculty who attempt to adapt to the learning styles of the Net Gen expect to receive individual attention from the campus instructional support staff to make the transition. One-on-one consultation works fine when there are just a few brave pioneers experimenting with new modalities. The resource base breaks down, however, when the majority of faculty need ongoing instructional design and consulting services. Most campuses have fragmented support structures and few, if any, academically trained instructional design professionals. Few institutions have the budget resources to scale these support units to meet faculty expectations for individual attention.

It takes vision, courage, and communication to change expectations and to move toward behaviors manifest in the new academy, an example of which is the University of Central Florida (UCF). UCF's strategy is to offer groups of faculty within specific academic departments a blended course (part online, part traditional classroom setting) on how to teach a blended course. It is a worthwhile, scalable, and sustainable support strategy.[10] Faculty experience learning in the new modality as they learn how to transform their pedagogy to engage the Net Generation. At the same time, the necessary support services can scale in subtle ways. Faculty learn how to use standard, supported products, as well as how to adjust to a one-to-many model of support staffing. Thus, the UCF model serves as an example of how expectations, processes, and relationships need to change—and can change—in the context of the new academy. Such changes prepare a faculty that can reach the Net Generation on its terms—faculty who are ready to serve in the new academy.

New Context, New Academy

Thus far, the new academy has been described by inference. What does the term really mean? What are its key characteristics? Five characteristics separate the new academy from the traditional paradigm of higher education:

▶ The interplay of culture and technology (the socio-technological context)
▶ A multidimensional framework for action
▶ New cultural values
▶ A new style of leadership
▶ The relationship of learning to space

Socio-Technological Context

The interplay of culture and technology in the social environment is the dominant attribute of the new academy. All other aspects of the new academy stem from this dynamic. Understanding that technology's major impact has been social indicates that, in the new academy, the campus community must come to terms with a new identity expressed in new processes and behavioral conventions.

At the fall 2004 NLII Focus Session concerning learning space design, Carole Wedge, president of the architectural design firm Bulfinch Richardson and Abbott, spoke about the social aspects of learning and of "the compelling need for professionals and researchers to work collaboratively." From her perspective, social structures are increasingly enabled by and intermingled with technical ones in higher education. Indeed, the way many of us live our lives assumes "an integrated social, technical, and cultural environment."[11]

How institutions acknowledge the role of technology in their missions, actions, interactions, curricula, and instructional modalities sends an important message regarding the philosophy and form of the new academy. The following examples are instructive.

▶ The University of Central Florida's Web-enhanced course has become the instructional norm, according to Joel Hartman, UCF vice provost for Information Technologies and Resources. UCF studies show that students enrolled in "blended" courses "produce higher student learning outcomes … and [such courses] make more efficient use of classroom space.[12] Blended courses engage students in active learning experiences. UCF's extensive assessment program (http://pegasus.cc.ucf.edu/~rite), headed by Chuck Dziuban, has shown improvement in learning and retention among students in these courses.

▶ Because the desire for convenience is one of the hallmarks of the Net Generation, Carnegie Mellon Online offers courses specifically for its residential students (http://online.web.cmu.edu/public/about/courses/). Being able to fit a desired course into a class schedule depends on schedule conflicts, work schedules, learning style, or even when a student chooses to learn. Online asynchronous courses are convenient.

These examples illustrate that change is possible—not just through new organizations such as Kaplan and the University of Phoenix, but also in well-established institutions such as Carnegie Mellon University and the University of California. The sooner institutions begin to examine the implications of the interplay of culture and technology, the better they will be able to address the tensions created by this dramatic change—and take advantage of new opportunities it presents. Those campus communities that choose to remain in denial will be distracted by the tensions generated by the disconnect between the new realities of the Net Generation and the traditional institutional context.

New Decision-Making Framework

The pervasiveness of technology in higher education has affected all other components of the higher education environment, as well as the dynamic created by their interaction. Until the advent of the Information Age and the arrival of the Net Generation, the higher education community expected its environment to be characterized by static variables, linearity, logical progression, consistency, and incremental adaptation.

New computing and telecommunications technologies, however, have ushered in a new environment characterized by unpredictability and disruptive change. Unfortunately, the current governance processes of higher education, which evolved in an earlier context, are not well adapted to the more fluid, dynamic environment in which most institutions now find themselves. Decision making within higher education suffers from conventions and timetables that assume institutions have not months, but years, to adapt to changes in their environments.

In the just-in-time, technologically intensive world in which our institutions now must function, we know that these old assumptions simply do not hold. The academy's sense of time, and thus the ways in which it determines its actions and strategic directions, increasingly fails to connect with the world beyond the ivy walls.

The new academy is characterized by the complex interplay of agents, technologies, roles, communities, and rules. Paraphrasing from an earlier publication,

> Faculty, students, administrators, and campus leaders are the agents of change. Technologies, tools, and techniques are the instruments the agents have available to enable change in their realm of influence. Roles, relationships, and perspectives change as the technologies empower the agents in new ways. For example, students use e-portfolios to manage and own their learning, and they use wireless to discover new knowledge even while engaged in a traditional classroom experience. New technologies, tools, and techniques fundamentally change the nature of the academic program. Technology is enabling the formation and enhancing the effectiveness of many different types of communities that now coexist on campus. New communities form because members are using the tools. The interaction of agents using technologies, guided by rules in their roles within communities, has the potential to produce unanticipated, and often transformational, outcomes.[13]

For example, the introduction of wireless communication capability on a campus changes the dynamic in the classroom because students have instantaneous access to sources and resources. It changes the concept of community because wireless enables individuals to sustain relationships beyond (or even without) in person meetings. It changes power relationships and shifts the locus of control in the learning process from the faculty member to the student.

Instead of serving as safeguards of quality, traditional policies and guidelines such as class contact time stipulations become barriers when most learning takes place outside the traditional classroom setting. Governance practices that fail to take the dynamic in this new decision-making framework into consideration will stall progress toward a new academy. The campus community will eventually develop workarounds as a type of "shadow governance system" to enable the institution to continue to operate.

Cultural Values

The integration of technology into the fabric of life on virtually every campus will inevitably have a significant impact on campus culture, values, and governance—an impact on the institution's very understanding of its identity and mission. As a result of these impacts, a new set of roles, rules, relationships, and behaviors—not to mention a transformed sense of time—will emerge, recasting the institution in the mold of the new academy. The difference in cultural values between the traditional academy and the new academy may offer us the clearest picture of the shape this recasting will take. These cultural differences are shown in Table 1.

The critical examination of issues and proposed actions need not be constrained by the forms and expectations of governance models based on a stable, relatively unchanging institutional environment that, in many cases, no longer exists. By embracing the cultural values of the new academy, institutions can establish forms of shared governance that rely on dynamic, interrelated frameworks to enable the critical examination of campus issues in the compressed timeframes under which most must operate.

A variety of products support the work of online communities—tools that can enable the aggressive engagement of constituencies in a shared governance model appropriate to the new academy. For example, instead of monthly committee meetings, institutions could use Web-based forums to support widespread engagement of major stakeholders, leading to more rapid and well-informed decision making that still can command institution-wide support.

New Style of Leadership

Most campus communities expect relatively passive leadership. The "hands-off" leadership style resulting from traditional shared governance models does not lend itself to situations requiring dynamic change; it is better suited to preservation than to transformation. Since preservation of the status quo tends to be equated with protecting academic values, leaders have learned that maintaining their positions depends on ensuring that transformation takes place slowly—if at all—on their watch.

Most institutions, however, now face a constantly changing environment that demands active, enlightened, and sensitive leadership. In an interview John Hitt, president of the University of Central Florida, talks candidly about the journey he has taken to transform UCF.[14] He has found that institutional leaders can help their campus communities construct missions and identities that truly reflect the new realities in which they find themselves, and thus enable them to identify and act on viable opportunities.

Table 1. Cultural Values

Traditional	Socio-Technological
Linearity	Multidimensionality
Stability	Continuous change
Fixed structures	Flexible structures
Individualism	Collaboration
Consistency	Dynamic reconfiguration

Communication is a critical element of this new leadership style. It only occurs when leaders take the time to frame the issues in terms that are directly relevant to their campus communities. It is reinforced through the alignment of budgets and goals at all levels with a set of easily articulated, understood, and assimilated institutional goals.[15] Leadership makes alignment happen; alignment directs energy and resources toward agreed-upon goals. Transformation requires alignment.

Relationship with Space

If an institution is genuinely committed to embracing the new academy, then the way it designs and uses space must further the values of the new academy—values such as community, collaboration, and exploration. Space in the new academy is designed to support learning and research goals, not to comply with artificial space utilization criteria, such as number of tablet armchairs per square foot, percentage of seat occupancy per hour of the day and day of the week, and so on. Most classroom utilization criteria, space assignment protocols, and systems, however, are designed to achieve such nonacademic efficiencies rather than to assign space according to the pedagogic requirements of the course.

Learning spaces should support learning activity.[16] Learning activity is differentiated from teaching activity in that it is stems from the principles of deeper learning[17] and involves the active and social creation of knowledge, including engagement in problem solving and critical analysis, as well as the physical activity of forming and reforming groups. They should also reflect the institution's identity.

Flexibility, design for the future, ubiquitous wireless network access, small group spaces, social spaces, and "thought" spaces were among the ideas shared at the NLII focus session on learning space design.[18] Architect Carol Wedge advocated thinking of the campus as a system of spaces, resulting in a new approach to design, renovation, and building on campus.

MIT's Stata Center (http://web.mit.edu/buildings/statacenter/) provides a vivid example of aligning space design to learning goals. The Department of Aeronautics and Astronautics concluded that it needed to redesign its curriculum to prepare students for engineering practice in the 21st century. It became evident that a new learning space environment would be required to support the new curriculum. Technology, coupled with a new concept of learning space, serves as the enabler of learning experiences in the new curriculum.[19]

Evidence shows that new pedagogical approaches supported by appropriate space design have resulted in improvements in learning.

▶ North Carolina State University's SCALE-UP Program in physics (http://www.ncsu.edu/per/scaleup.html) is illustrative. Introductory physics students work in small teams, seated at round tables using computers in a space redesigned to support pedagogy that engages the Net Generation. The new design has produced a much higher student completion rate for the introductory physics course.

▶ The Virginia Tech Math Emporium[20] has demonstrated similar improvements in completion rates, using online modules and intense online testing accompanied by just-in-time help for students who encounter difficulties mastering the material. Virginia Tech also renovated space to accommodate the pedagogical design of the Math Emporium.

In the new academy, informal learning spaces take on new importance. Informal learning spaces with wireless capability suit the Net Generation's habits of being constantly connected, social, and interactive with peers. Establishing vibrant learning communities cannot be confined to class times or formal classrooms. A significant percentage of learning takes place outside the formal classroom, wherever people gather to interact—whether that is in a hallway or in a virtual community of practice.

Buildings designed for learning, such as MIT's Stata Center, the University of Arizona's Integrated Learning Center, or Stanford University's Wallenberg Hall, all include important features of space in the new academy:

▶ Flexibility within the formal classroom spaces (furniture on wheels, movable walls)

▶ Expansive areas in which people can interact informally

▶ Design elements that consciously promote interaction among the occupants

A focus on learning activity may necessitate changes in space planning projects, calling into question the traditional design approach that focuses on the shape of the room, the efficiency of the fixed seating arrangement, the instructor location, and so on. To align space projects with the institution's learning goals at all levels, building and renovation project managers need to understand the pedagogical principles the space should embody.[21] The stakes of getting space right (or wrong) are high; space requires huge resource investments (time and money). It is easy to design unsuitable or inflexible space if those charged with making decisions do not realize that a new academy is on the horizon. If a learning space is "wrong," the institution, its faculty, and its students may live with it for 50 years.

Institutional Resolve

Institutional resolve is expressed in alignment and trust: the alignment of action with stated goals and trust between leadership and the academic community. Adopting a culture of evidence bolsters trust, which enables institutional resolve. Gary Brown described the current state of resolve on most campuses:

> The student-centered banner, more bellow than bite, is, in most practice, pale language for the real need to transform ourselves and our culture into one that is centered in learning, oriented to the processes of learning rather than just the ends. In the coming days of wireless, blogs, swickis, wikis, gaming, and virtual realities, students will not be mere consumers of education; they will be critical allies in pioneering new ways of knowing and understanding.[22]

In building the culture of evidence necessary to understand and take advantage of significant trends, institutions cannot afford to "study the problem to death." Overindulging in evidence-gathering in the belief that everything must be precise runs the risk of preventing timely responses. The accumulation of evidence is frequently used—consciously or unconsciously—as a mechanism to slow or delay change. Institutions must seek a balance in their culture of evidence to avoid stranding institutional resolve on the rocks of absolute certainty.

Similarly, institutions can be strangled by convictions regarding their unique character. Such convictions (or delusions) of uniqueness have the power to blind decision makers to reality and cause them to reject extant evidence (about Net Generation students, for example), especially when it is externally generated. Assuming that national trends do not apply to a given institution carries the risk of inaction; confirming or disproving assumptions with data can galvanize institutional response.

Fundamental to the ability to transform the academy is the wisdom and humility to know students, their motivations, their goals, and their learning styles. Institutions cannot simply assume they know their students through the collective experience of faculty and administrators. They must create a culture of evidence. For example, after attending "Keys to Competitiveness," a workshop on the Net Generation by EDUCAUSE and the American Association of State Colleges and Universities (AASCU), an institutional leader from Lamar University noted, "The June meeting at the University of Central Florida ... sparked us to survey our freshmen. We left the June meeting a little less than convinced that our students are like UCF students.... [yet] our new students were surprisingly similar to UCF students in their use of technology and the expectations they have for institutional support."[23]

What we assume we know about students may not hold in today's rapidly evolving climate. To create the context and justification for a new academy at a given institution, the college or university must objectively define the characteristics of its student body in relation to teaching, learning, and technology. Only then can it harness that reality to drive the necessary institutional transformation.

Another facet of a culture of evidence is self-assessment. An institution must measure its progress as it moves toward transformation and creating its own "new academy." A rubric for assessing transformational change may help institutions in their own assessments.[24] The rubric challenges decision makers to use assessment to sustain momentum toward a changed state—the new academy. This type of assessment does not measure whether something "works." Transformative assessment measures progress toward a goal and helps an institution identify next steps. Because it represents an ongoing, iterative process, it is the ultimate expression of institutional resolve.

Conclusion

The discussion throughout this chapter—and the entire book—leads to a set of recommended actions:

▶ Confront the reality of the Net Generation of students.
▶ Decide that change is possible.
▶ Understand the dynamic interplay of culture and technology.
▶ Base decisions on values rather than traditions.

- Develop a culture of evidence.
- Align expectations with goals and actions at all levels.
- Determine priorities, make decisions, execute, and measure outcomes.

As Einstein observed, "The significant problems we face cannot be solved at the same level of thinking we were at when we created them." This is good advice for higher education as it addresses the learning needs of the Net Generation.

Endnotes

1. Diana Oblinger, "Boomers, Gen-Xers, and Millennials: Understanding the 'New Students,'" *EDUCAUSE Review*, vol. 38, no. 4 (July/August 2003), pp. 37–47, <http://www.educause.edu/apps/er/erm03/erm034.asp>.

2. See the Sloan Consortium survey report "Entering the Mainstream: The Quality and Extent of Online Education in the United States, 2003 and 2004," <http://www.sloan-c.org/resources/survey.asp>.

3. Milton Greenberg, "A University Is Not a Business (and Other Fantasies)," *EDUCAUSE Review*, vol. 39, no. 2 (March/April 2004), pp. 10–16, <http://www.educause.edu/ir/library/pdf/erm0420.pdf>.

4. Donald N. Langenberg, "Slow Progress in E-Learning Development Does Not Mean NO Progress at All," Letters to the Editor, *Chronicle of Higher Education*, September 3, 2004, p. B17; available by subscription at <http://chronicle.com/prm/weekly/v51/i02/02b01701.htm>.

5. Jason Frand, "The Information-Age Mindset: Changes in Students and Implications for Higher Education," *EDUCAUSE Review*, vol. 35, no. 5 (September/October 2000), pp. 14–24, <http://www.educause.edu/ir/library/pdf/ERM0051.pdf>.

6. Gary Hamel and Liisa Valikangas, "The Quest for Resilience," *Harvard Business Review*, September 1, 2003.

7. Gary Brown, "Getting Real in the Academy," *About Campus*, vol. 9, no. 4 (September/October 2004), p. 12.

8. George D. Kuh, "What We're Learning About Student Engagement from NSSE: Benchmarks for Effective Educational Practices," *Change*, vol. 35, no. 2 (March/April 2003), pp. 24–32.

9. Greenberg, op. cit., p. 13.

10. See <http://teach.ucf.edu/pathways.pdf> for a description of the UCF modalities.

11. See <www.educause.edu/2004Fall FocusSession/2672> for more information on the 2004 NLII Fall Focus Session. A summary of the focus session is available at <http://www.educause.edu/ir/library/pdf/NLI0446.pdf>.

12. See *The Key to Competitiveness: Understanding the Next Generation Learner—A Guide for College and University Leaders,* sponsored by AASCU, EDUCAUSE, and Microsoft, available on the Web at <http://www.aascu.org/book/default.htm>.

13. This argument pulls from and is further developed in Carole A. Barone, "A Framework for Action," *EDUCAUSE Review,* vol. 38, no. 6 (November/December 2003), pp. 104, <http://www.educause.edu/apps/er/erm03/erm03612.asp>.

14. Carole Barone, "Leadership, Goals, and Transformation: An Interview with John C. Hitt," *EDUCAUSE Review,* vol. 40, no. 1 (January/February 2005), pp. 24–32, <http://www.educause.edu/apps/er/erm05/erm0511.asp>.

15. For the UCF Mission and Goals statement, see <http://www.ucf.edu/aboutUCF/mission/goal.htm>.

16. 2004 NLII Fall Focus Session, op. cit.

17. For more information on the "NLII Map of the Learning Space" subsection "Deeper Learning and Learning Theories," see <http://www.educause.edu/DeeperLearningandLearningTheories/2623>.

18. 2004 NLII Fall Focus Session, op. cit.

19. See also Lawrence Biemiller, "MIT Splices Whimsy Into Its Architectural DNA," *Chronicle of Higher Education,* May 7, 2004; available by subscription at <http://chronicle.com/prm/weekly/v50/i35/35a02801.htm>. This article provides an informative description of the pedagogical links in the Stata Center's design.

20. Robert Olin, "Projects: Virginia Tech's Math Emporium: A Revolutionary Approach to Learning," *Mathematics Teacher,* vol. 93, no. 5 (May 2000), p. 442; find the article summary at <http://my.nctm.org/eresources/article_summary.asp?URI=MT2000-05-442b&from=B>.

21. *Change* magazine ran a feature section on new developments in campus architecture in the September/October 2004 issue, which also contained a resource review. See Jeanne L. Narum, "Transforming the Environment for Learning," *Change,* vol. 36, no. 5 (September/October 2004), pp. 62–66.

22. Brown, op. cit., p.17.

23. *The Key to Competitiveness,* op. cit.

24. For a quick reference on assessing transformation, see <http://www.educause.edu/ir/library/pdf/EDU0251.pdf>.

About the Author

Carole A. Barone is an EDUCAUSE senior fellow. Before joining EDUCAUSE in 1998, she was associate vice chancellor for information technology at the University of California at Davis. Prior to serving at UC Davis, she was vice president for information systems and computing at Syracuse University. She holds master's and doctoral degrees from the Maxwell School of Citizenship and Public Affairs at Syracuse University. Barone speaks and writes extensively on the relationship between technology and change. She coedited *Technology-Enhanced Teaching and Learning: Leading and Supporting the Transformation on Your Campus*, published by Jossey-Bass in 2001 as volume 5 in the EDUCAUSE Higher Education Leadership Strategies series. Barone received the 1995 CAUSE Elite Award.

CHAPTER 15

Planning for Neomillennial Learning Styles: Implications for Investments in Technology and Faculty

Chris Dede

Harvard University

Today's students have been described as having an information age mindset, being Millennials or members of the Net Generation. While this portrayal of generational learning styles can be oversimplified, the technology and media used by children during their formative years do have an influence on how they learn, as do the media used by adults. However, technology is no more static than people. The Internet is a constantly evolving infrastructure that now supports many media, including such disparate applications as "groupware" for virtual collaboration, asynchronous threaded discussions, multi-user virtual environments, videoconferencing, and mobile, location-aware wireless devices such as personal digital assistants (PDAs) with embedded global positioning system (GPS) capabilities.[1] Research indicates that each of these media, when designed for education, fosters particular types of interactions that enable—and undercut—various learning styles. Rather than describe the present (or the past), this chapter looks at the continuing evolution of computers and telecommunications and speculates on new learning styles emerging media may enable, as well as how higher education can prepare for this shift.

How Emerging Media Foster Neomillennial Learning Styles

Over the next decade, three complementary interfaces will shape how people learn:[2]

▸ **The familiar "world to the desktop."** Provides access to distant experts and archives and enables collaborations, mentoring relationships, and virtual communities of practice. This interface is evolving through initiatives such as Internet2.

▶ **"Alice in Wonderland" multiuser virtual environments (MUVEs).** Participants' avatars (self-created digital characters) interact with computer-based agents and digital artifacts in virtual contexts. The initial stages of studies on shared virtual environments are characterized by advances in Internet games and work in virtual reality.

▶ **Ubiquitous computing.** Mobile wireless devices infuse virtual resources as we move through the real world. The early stages of "augmented reality" interfaces are characterized by research on the role of "smart objects" and "intelligent contexts" in learning and doing.

Net Generation learning styles stem primarily from the world-to-the-desktop interface; however, the growing prevalence of interfaces to virtual environments and augmented realities is beginning to foster so-called neomillennial learning styles in users of all ages. The crucial factor leading to the augmentation of millennial learning styles with neomillennial characteristics is that the world-to-the-desktop interface is not psychologically immersive, while in contrast virtual environments and augmented realities induce a strong sense of "presence." This immersion in virtual environments and augmented realities shapes participants' learning styles beyond what using sophisticated computers and telecommunications has fostered thus far, with multiple implications for higher education.

How Immersive Presence Enhances Learning

Immersion is the subjective impression that one is participating in a comprehensive, realistic experience.[3] Immersion in a mediated, simulated experience (such as a virtual environment or an augmented reality) involves the willing suspension of disbelief. As an example, when watching a Harry Potter movie on an IMAX screen, the plot and characters coupled with visual and auditory input produce a sense of psychological immersion: the audience does not focus on the sensations of sitting in a theatre seat but instead on being present in a wizarding "world," observing a fascinating series of events. The example is weak, however, because the experience is passive, as opposed to the stronger immersion induced when participants shape an experience rather than just observe it.

The design of mediated-immersion simulated learning experiences depends on actional, symbolic, and sensory factors.[4] Inducing actional immersion involves empowering the participant in an experience to initiate actions that have novel, intriguing consequences. For example, when a baby is learning to walk, the degree of concentration this activity creates in the child is extraordinary. Discovering new capabilities to shape one's environment is highly motivating and sharply focuses attention.

Inducing a participant's symbolic immersion involves triggering powerful semantic associations via the content of an experience. As an illustration, reading a horror novel at midnight in a strange house builds a mounting sense of terror, even though one's physical context is unchanging and rationally safe. Invoking intellectual, emotional, and normative archetypes deepens the experience by imposing a complex overlay of associative mental models.

Beyond actional and symbolic immersion, advances in interface technology are now creating virtual environments and augmented realities that induce a psychological sense of sensory and physical immersion. Sensory immersion is relatively easy to foster in augmented realities, which are set in physical environments. Psychological immersion is achievable in MUVEs by design strategies that combine actional, symbolic, and sensory factors in manipulating an avatar to further the suspension of disbelief that the participant represented by the avatar is "inside" a virtual environment: the equivalent of diving rather than riding in a glass-bottomed boat.

For example, one design strategy to induce psychological immersion in virtual environments is using egocentric rather than exocentric frames of reference. As Salzman described,

> The exocentric frame of reference (FOR) provides a view of an object, space, or phenomena from the outside, while the egocentric FOR provides a view of the object, space, or phenomena from within. Imagine a dollhouse. As a human, you can peer at the house from a number of angles, you can reach into it to feel the rugs and furniture with your fingers, and you may even be able to stick your head inside; but you can only imagine what it would be like to be a doll living inside that house. You experience the dollhouse from the exocentric FOR. If you were the doll inside the house, you would experience the house and its furnishings from within—walking on the rugs, sitting in the chairs, and sleeping in the bed; but you would only be able to imagine what it would be like to be the human on the outside looking in. You would experience the dollhouse from the egocentric FOR. Each FOR would give you different kinds of

information about the dollhouse and it might shape what you come to know about that house.[5]

The research on virtual reality Salzman and I conducted on frames of reference found that the exocentric and the egocentric FORs have different strengths for learning. Our studies established that learning ideally involves a "bicentric" perspective alternating between egocentric and exocentric FORs.

We also researched how each of these three perspectives—the egocentric, the exocentric, and the bicentric—influenced participants' motivation and learning styles.[6] One major advantage of egocentric perspectives is that they enable participants' actional immersion and motivation more strongly than exocentric FORs, which are better suited for dispassionate observer roles. Another advantage of the egocentric FOR is that this perspective enables "situated" learning, while exocentric perspectives foster insights gained from distancing oneself from the context (seeing the forest rather than the trees). Bicentric FORs combine the strengths of each perspective.

Situated Learning and Transfer via Psychological Immersion

The capability of computer interfaces to foster psychological immersion enables technology-intensive educational experiences that draw on a powerful pedagogy: situated learning. Reports such as the National Research Council's study[7] delineate theoretical constructs for understanding teaching and learning. The major schools of thought cited are behaviorist theories of learning (presentational instruction), cognitivist theories of learning (tutoring and guided learning by doing), and situated theories of learning (mentoring and apprenticeships in communities of practice). Situated learning requires authentic contexts, activities, and assessment coupled with guidance from expert modeling, mentoring, and "legitimate peripheral participation."[8] As an example of legitimate peripheral participation, graduate students work within the laboratories of expert researchers, who model the practice of scholarship. These students interact with experts in research as well as with other members of the research team who understand the complex processes of scholarship to varying degrees. While in these laboratories, students gradually move from novice researchers to more advanced roles, with the skills and expectations for them evolving.

Potentially quite powerful, situated learning is much less used for instruction than behaviorist or cognitivist approaches. This is largely because creating tacit, relatively unstructured learning in complex real-world settings is difficult. However, virtual environments and ubiquitous computing can draw on the power of situated learning by creating immersive, extended experiences with problems and contexts similar to the real world.[9] In particular, MUVEs and real-world settings augmented with virtual information provide the capability to create problem-solving communities in which participants can gain knowledge and skills through interacting with other participants who have varied levels of skills, enabling legitimate peripheral participation driven by intrinsic sociocultural forces.

Situated learning is important in part because of the crucial issue of *transfer.* Transfer is defined as the application of knowledge learned in one situation to another situation and is demonstrated if instruction on a learning task leads to improved performance on a transfer task, typically a skilled performance in a real-world setting.[10] One of the major criticisms of instruction today is the low rate of transfer generated by conventional instruction. Even students who excel in schooling or training settings often are unable to apply what they have learned to similar real-world contexts. Situated learning addresses this challenge by making the setting in which learning takes place similar to the real-world context for performance in work or personal life.[11] Learning in well-designed digital contexts can lead to the replication in the real world of behaviors successful in simulated environments.[12]

Moreover, the evolution of an individual's or group's identity is an important type of learning for which simulated experiences situated in virtual environments or augmented realities are well suited. Reflecting on and refining an individual identity is often a significant issue for higher education students of all ages, and learning to evolve group and organizational identity is a crucial skill in enabling innovation and in adapting to shifting contexts. The social sciences see both the self and the organization as often fragmented, with complementary parts, rather than centralized and unitary. Identity "play" through trying on various representations of the self and the group in virtual environments provides a means for different sides of a person or team to find common ground and the opportunity for synthesis and evolution.

Immersion is important in this process of identity exploration because virtual identity is unfettered by physical attributes such as gender, race, and disabilities. Virtual environments based on games such as EverQuest (http://eqlive.station.sony.com/) and simulations such as Whyville (http://www.whyville.net/) illustrate how participants take advantage of fluidity in the identities they present. Simulations in virtual environments and augmented realities increase the value of these explorations by providing realistic feedback on how the real world responds to various patterns of individual and group behavior.[13]

But what is so special about the egocentric perspectives and situated learning now enabled by emerging media? After all, each of us lives with an egocentric perspective in the real world and has many opportunities for situated learning without using technology. One attribute that makes mediated immersion different and powerful is the ability to access information resources and psychosocial community distributed across distance and time, broadening and deepening experience. A second important attribute is the ability to create interactions and activities in mediated experience not possible in the real world, such as teleporting within a virtual environment, enabling a distant person to see a real-time image of your local environment, or interacting with a (simulated) chemical spill in a busy public setting. Both of these attributes are actualized in the Alice-in-Wonderland interface.

Immersion in Virtual Educational Environments

Most students now using MUVEs do so in the context of gaming. As Steinkuehler noted,

> Massively multiplayer online games (MMOGs) are highly graphical 2- or 3-D videogames played online, allowing individuals, through their self-created digital characters, or "avatars," to interact not only with the gaming software (the designed environment of the game and the computer-controlled characters within it) but with other players' avatars as well. These virtual worlds are persistent social and material worlds, loosely structured by open-ended (fantasy) narratives, where players are largely free to do as they please—slay ogres, siege castles, barter goods in town, or shake the fruit out of trees.... Thanks to out-of-game trading of in-game items, Norrath, the virtual setting of the MMOG EverQuest, is the seventy-seventh largest economy in the real world, with a GNP per capita between that of Russia and Bulgaria. One platinum piece, the unit of currency in Norrath, trades on real world exchange markets higher than both the Yen and the Lira (Castronova, 2001).[14]

Black noted that players of all ages are involved in many different MMOGs and in ancillary activities such as fanfiction Web sites, where people enamored with a particular game or book can add to its genre with their own writing.[15] (These fanfiction archives are substantial; Black documented a multifandom archive that contains hundreds of thousands works of original fanfiction, including over 20,000 Final Fantasy video game–related fictions and approximately 127,000 Harry Potter–based texts.) While the content of these games and activities often does not lead to knowledge useful in the real world, rich types of learning and identity formation do take place in these environments, fostering neomillennial learning styles based on characteristics of immersive mediated interaction. The research my colleagues and I are conducting on MUVEs for educating young people about higher order inquiry skills illustrates this.

The River City MUVE[16] is centered on skills of hypothesis formation and experimental design, as well as on content related to national standards and assessments in biology and ecology. We are demonstrating how students can gain this knowledge through immersive simulations, interactive virtual museum exhibits, and "participatory" historical situations. Students learn to behave as scientists while they collaboratively identify problems through observation and inference, form and test hypotheses, and deduce evidence-based conclusions about underlying causes.

The River City virtual world consists of a city with a river running through it; different forms of terrain that influence water runoff; and various neighborhoods, industries, and institutions, such as a hospital and a university (http://muve.gse.harvard.edu/muvees2003/). Through egocentric perspectives, the learners themselves populate the city, along with computer-based agents, digital objects that can include audio or video clips, and the avatars of instructors (see Figure 1). River City is typical of the United States in the late 19th century; the right-hand window in Figure 1 depicts how we use museum artifacts to illustrate building exteriors and street scenes from that historical period. In addition, throughout the world students encounter residents of River City and "overhear" their conversations with one another. These computer-based "agents" disclose information and provide indirect clues about what is going on in River City.

Content in the right-hand interface window shifts based on what the participant encounters or activates in the virtual environment (see Figure 2). In this case, the right hand window presents water quality data from one of eleven water-sampling stations in River City. Through data gathering, students observe the patterns that emerge and wrestle with questions such as, why are many more poor people getting sick than rich people? Multiple causal factors are involved, including polluted

Figure 1. Talking with an Agent

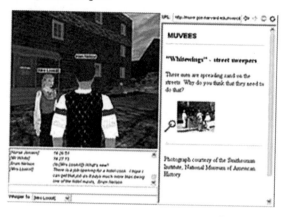

Figure 2. Collecting Water Quality Data

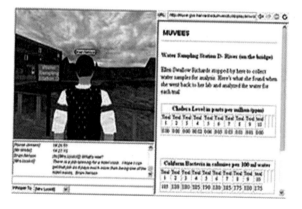

water runoff to low-lying areas, insect vectors in swampy areas, overcrowding, and the cost of access to medical care.

Dialogue is shown in the text box below these two windows. To aid their interactions, participants also have access to one-click interface features that enable the avatar to express (through stylized postures and gestures) emotions such as happiness, sadness, and anger. These interface features also allow looking upward or downward, as well as seeing the world from a first-person perspective or from behind one's own body in a third-person viewpoint. In addition, learners can interact with digital artifacts and tools, such as a virtual microscope in which the image from the microscope slide appears in the right-hand interface window.

Multiple teams of students can access the MUVE simultaneously, each individual manipulating an avatar which is "sent back in time" to this virtual environment. Students must collaborate to share the data each team collects. Beyond textual conversation, students can project to each other "snapshots" of their current individual point of view (when someone has discovered an item of general interest) and also can "teleport" to join anyone on their team for joint investigation. Each time a team reenters the world, several months of time have passed in River City, so learners can track the dynamic evolution of local problems.

Three strands of illness in River City (waterborne, airborne, and insectborne) are integrated with historical, social, and geographical content to allow students to experience the realities of disentangling multicausal problems embedded within a complex environment. In our research on this educational MUVE based on situated learning, we are studying usability, student motivation, student learning, and classroom implementation issues. The results thus far are promising:

▶ All learners are highly motivated, including students typically unengaged in classroom settings.

▶ All students build fluency in distributed modes of communication and expression and value using multiple media because each empowers different types of communication, activities, experiences, and expressions.

▶ Even typically low-performing students can master complex inquiry skills and sophisticated content.

▶ Shifts in the pedagogy within the MUVE alter the pattern of student performance.

We are now conducting large-scale studies to assess the strengths and limits of this educational approach, in particular how MUVEs shape students' learning styles.[17] Other researchers who study educational MUVEs designed for young people, such as Quest Atlantis (http://atlantis.crlt.indiana.edu/start/index.html) and Whyville (http://www.whyville.net), also are assessing how immersive virtual environments influence their participants' learning styles.[18a,b] These studies are documenting how storyline and players' progression through various levels of capability/power enhance motivation and integrate content and skills, as well as how identity play complements and extends learning. Research indicates that active learning based on experience (real and simulated) that includes frequent opportunities for reflection via bicentric frames of reference is both engaging and powerful for a broad spectrum of students.

Immersion in Educational Augmented Realities

An emerging interface that complements the Alice-in-Wonderland immersion of MUVEs is augmented reality via ubiquitous computing, in which mobile wireless devices immerse participants in virtual resources as they move through the real world. As one example, Hsi and colleagues have developed a device called eXspot intended to support, record, and extend exhibit-based, informal science learning at the Exploratorium, an interactive hands-on museum of art, science, and perception located in San Francisco.[19] eXspot participants visiting the Exploratorium carry a card with a radio frequency interference device (RFID) tag embedded. As various exhibits are viewed, these visitors can swipe the card on a RFID reader at the exhibit. At any time later, participants can view a museum-generated personal Web page listing the dates the museum was visited and specific exhibits swiped that day. Personal photos taken at the exhibits and online content about exhibits are also available. Research shows that many participants value this functionality and choose to access the Web page after leaving the museum.

As another illustration of ubiquitous computing for learning, Klopfer and colleagues are developing augmented reality (AR) handheld-computer simulations that embed students inside lifelike problem-solving situations to help them understand complex scientific and social dynamics (http://education.mit.edu/ar). Participants in these distributed simulations use location-aware handheld computers (with GPS technology), allowing users to physically move throughout a real-world location while collecting place-dependent simulated field data, interviewing virtual characters, and collaboratively investigating simulated scenarios.

For example, their Environmental Detectives AR simulation engages high school and university students in a real-world environmental consulting scenario not possible to implement in a classroom setting.[20] Students role-play environmental scientists investigating a rash of health concerns on the MIT campus linked to the release of toxins in the water supply. Working in teams (see Figure 3), players attempt to identify the contaminant, chart its path through the environment, and devise possible plans for remediation. As participants physically move about campus, their handheld devices respond to their location (see Figure 4), allowing them to collect simulated field data from the water and soil, interview virtual characters, and perform desktop research using miniwebs of data. At the end

Figure 3. Students in Augmented Reality

Figure 4. Handheld Location on Campus

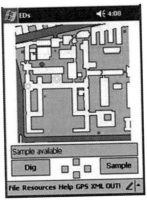

of the exercise, teams compile their data using peer-to-peer communication and synthesize their findings.

Initial research on Environmental Detectives and other AR-based educational simulations demonstrates that this type of immersive, situated learning can effectively engage students in critical thinking about authentic scenarios.[21] Students participating in these simulations indicated that they felt invested in the situations and were motivated to solve the problem. They moved nearly seamlessly between the real world and the information being presented to them on their handheld computers as they collected data from virtual scientific instruments and accounts from virtual experts and witnesses. Students were most effective in learning and problem-solving when they collectively sought, sieved, and synthesized experiences rather than individually locating and absorbing information from some single best source.

How Emerging Media are Fostering Mediated Immersion Throughout Life

Quite apart from educational innovation based on emerging media, people's daily use of new devices is shifting their lifestyles toward frequent mediated immersion, which in turn is shaping their learning styles toward neomillennial characteristics. Prognosticators such as Howard Rheingold[22] and William Mitchell[23] speculated about the impacts on individuals and civilization as new digital media pervade every aspect of life. For example, Rheingold depicted a future based on distributed networks of information, communication, and activity—as contrasted to the historic pattern of lifestyles centered on face-to-face groups interacting with local resources. Members of the same physical group may have very different personal communities as their major sources of sociability, support, information, a sense of belonging, and social identity. He sees these distributed communities, created through mediated immersion, as far-flung, loosely bounded, sparsely knit, and fragmentary.

Rheingold's forecasts draw on lifestyles seen at present among young people who are high-end users of new media, as well as the visions of researchers and businesses developing products and services based on virtual environments and ubiquitous computing. In a world composed of these high-end users with access to these new products and services, the following types of experiences would pervade people's lifestyles:

▶ Mobile wireless devices (MWDs), such as gaming devices, cell phones, digital music players, and PDAs would access media that are virtually connected to locations (such as street signs linked to online maps), objects (such as books linked to online reviews), and services (such as restaurants linked to ratings by their customers).

▶ MWDs would access every type of data service anywhere (such as banking and stock market information, weather, tickets and reservations, and transport schedules).

- MWDs would locate strangers nearby who have identified themselves as having common interests (such as people interested in dating and matched on desired attributes; friends of friends; fellow gamers; fans of a certain team, actor, or author).
- Rather than having core identities defined through a primarily local set of roles and relationships, people would express varied aspects of their multifaceted identities through alternate extended experiences in distributed virtual environments and augmented realities.

Rheingold painted a largely positive picture of this "social revolution" while articulating some concerns about privacy, quality of life, and loss of humanity.

The technology infrastructure necessary for these lifestyles is emerging. As Baker and Green[24] noted, one-third of U.S. households now have broadband access to the Internet. In the past three years, 14 million U.S. families have linked their computers with wireless home networks. Some 55 percent of Americans now carry cell phones, and the first data services—radio, photos, and short video clips—are starting to take off.

Mitchell's forecasts[25] are similar to Rheingold's in many respects. He too envisions largely tribal lifestyles distributed across dispersed, fragmented, fluctuating habitats: electronic nomads wandering among virtual campfires. People's senses and physical agency are extended outward and into the intangible, at considerable cost to individual privacy. Individual identity is continuously reformed via an ever-shifting series of networking with others and with tools. People express themselves through nonlinear, associational webs of representations rather than linear "stories" and co-design services rather than selecting a precustomized variant from a menu of possibilities.

Whether these forecasts of major shifts in society are accurate is uncertain. Probably, some people will choose the distributed immersive lifestyles Rheingold and Mitchell portray, while others will have less intensive interactions with new media that do not lead to dramatic changes in their activities or identity. More and more, though, people of all ages will have lifestyles involving frequent immersion in both virtual and augmented reality. How might distributed, immersive media be designed specifically for education, and what neomillennial learning styles might they induce?

Neomillennial Learning Styles Based on Mediated Immersion

Emerging devices, tools, media, and virtual environments offer opportunities for creating new types of learning communities for students and teachers. Bielaczyc and Collins indicated that:

> The defining quality of a learning community is that there is a culture of learning, in which everyone is involved in a collective effort of understanding. There are four characteristics that such a culture must have: (1) diversity of expertise among its members, who are valued for their contributions and given support to develop, (2) a shared objective of continually advancing the collective knowledge and skills, (3) an emphasis on learning how to learn, and (4) mechanisms for sharing what is learned. If a learning community is presented with a problem, then the learning community can bring its collective knowledge to bear on the problem. It is not necessary that each member assimilate everything that the community knows, but each should know who within the community has relevant expertise to address any problem. This is a radical departure from the traditional view of schooling, with its emphasis on individual knowledge and performance, and the expectation that students will acquire the same body of knowledge at the same time.[26]

Mediated immersion creates distributed learning communities, which have different strengths and limits than location-bound learning communities confined to classroom settings and centered on the teacher and archival materials.[27] In particular, distributed learning communities infuse education throughout students' lives, orchestrating the contributions of many knowledge sources embedded in real-world settings outside of schooling and fostering neomillennial learning styles.

The benefits of learning styles enhanced by mediated immersion in distributed learning communities are illustrated in Table 1.

Mediated immersion likely has other influences on learning style yet to be discovered, but these initial findings have a variety of implications for strategic planning and investment in higher education.

Table 1. Neomillenial Versus Millennial Learning Styles

Neomillennial Learning	Millennial Learning
Fluency in multiple media, values each for the types of communication, activities, experiences, and expressions it empowers.	Centers on working within a single medium best suited to an individual's style and preferences
Learning based on collectively seeking, sieving, and synthesizing experiences rather than individually locating and absorbing information from some single best source; prefers communal learning in diverse, tacit, situated experiences; values knowledge distributed across a community and a context, as well as within an individual.	Solo integration of divergent, explicit information sources
Active learning based on experience (real and simulated) that includes frequent opportunities for embedded reflection (for example, infusing experiences in the Virtual University simulation <http://www.virtual-u.org/> in a course on university leadership); values bicentric, immersive frames of reference that infuse guidance and reflection into learning-by-doing.	Learning experiences that separate action and experience into different phases
Expression through nonlinear, associational webs of representations rather than linear stories (for example, authoring a simulation and a Web page to express understanding rather than writing a paper); uses representations involving richly associated, situated simulations.	Uses branching, but largely hierarchical, multimedia
Co-design of learning experiences personalized to individual needs and preferences.	Emphasizes selecting a precustomized variant from a range of services offered

Implications for Higher Education's Strategic Investments

Table 2 presents speculations about how the emergence of neomillennial learning styles may influence higher education. Emphasis is placed on implications for strategic investments in physical plant, technology infrastructure, and professional development.

These ideas are admittedly speculative rather than based on detailed evidence and are presented to stimulate reaction and dialogue about these trends.

If we accept much of the analysis above, four implications for investments in physical and technological infrastructure are apparent:

▶ **Wireless everywhere**—provide total coverage of the campus; subsidize uniform mobile wireless devices offering convergence of media (phone, PDA, gaming, Internet)

▶ **Multipurpose habitats**—creating layered/blended/personalizable places rather than specialized locations (such as computer labs)

▶ Augmented reality—experiment with smart objects and intelligent contexts (via GPS and RFID tags and transceivers)

▶ **"Mirroring"**—experiment with virtual environments that replicate physical settings but offer "magical" capabilities for immersive experience

This is not to imply that campuses should immediately undertake massive shifts toward these four themes, but rather that students of all ages with increasingly neomillennial learning styles will be drawn to colleges and universities that have these capabilities.

Four implications for investments in professional development also are apparent. Faculty will increasingly need capabilities in:

▶ **Co-design**—developing learning experiences students can personalize

▶ **Co-instruction**—using knowledge sharing among students as a major source of content and pedagogy

▶ **Guided social constructivist and situated learning pedagogies**—infusing case-based participatory simulations into presentational/assimilative instruction

▶ **Assessment beyond tests and papers**—evaluating collaborative, non-linear, associational webs of representations; using peer-developed and peer-rated forms of assessment; employing student assessments to provide formative feedback on faculty effectiveness

Some of these shifts are controversial for many faculty; all involve "unlearning" almost unconscious beliefs, assumptions, and values about the nature of teaching, learning, and the academy. Professional development that requires unlearning necessitates high levels of emotional/social support in addition to mastering the intellectual/technical dimensions involved. The ideal form for this type of professional development is distributed learning communities so that the learning process is consistent with the knowledge and culture to be acquired. In other words, faculty must themselves experience mediated immersion and develop neomillennial learning styles to continue teaching effectively as the nature of students alters.

Table 2. Speculations About Higher Education Now and in the Future

Dimension	Now	Future
Location and physical infrastructure	Locations and physical infrastructures configured to accomplish specialized forms of activity (such as dorm room or apartment, classrooms, student center, library, computer lab) Direct physical manipulation of equipment in science lab	Wearable devices and universal wireless coverage mean access, information, computational power no longer tied to physical space (such as a computer lab) Most activities distributed across space and time, so tailoring space to particular purposes (such as library reading rooms) often no longer necessary Notion of place is layered/blended/multiple; mobility and nomadicity prevalent among dispersed, fragmented, fluctuating habitats (for example, coffeehouses near campus) Virtual simulations complement equipment-based science labs
Smart objects and intelligent contexts	Inert objects and contexts with information available only via signage Physical presence on campus only way of "being there"	Information virtually connected to locations (such as campus buildings linked to online maps) and objects (such as textbooks linked to course ratings by students) "Mirroring": Immersive virtual environments provide replicas of distant physical settings
Social group	Roommates, members of dorm or apartment, classmates	Far-flung, loosely bounded, sparsely knit, and fragmentary communities (independent of cohabitation, common course schedules, or enrollment at a particular campus)
Collaboration	Collaboration dependent on shared physical presence or cumbersome virtual mechanisms	Middleware, interoperability, open content, and open source enable seamless information sharing, collaborative virtual manipulation of tools and media, shared authoring and design, collective critiquing
Personal customization	Little or none	"Napsterism": recombining others' designs to personally tailored configurations[28] Customized services based on data mining for patterns of personal characteristics and behaviors

Cognition	Finding information Sequential assimilation of linear information stream	Seeking, sieving, synthesizing disparate sources of data Multitasking among disparate experiences and information sources Focus on associative interconnections among chunks of information Constant reflection on and sharing of experience Mind extended via distributed cognition, sensation, memory
Identity	Identity expressed in the context of face-to-face groups interacting with local resources	Virtual identity unfettered by physical attributes such as gender, race, disabilities Self continuously reformed via an ever-shifting series of distributed networking with others and with tools Self as an electronic nomad wandering among virtual campfires, no longer needing a local physical infrastructure to articulate identity
Instruction	Instructor designs and delivers one-size-fits-all content, pedagogy, and assessment Students are passive recipients	Learners influence design of content, pedagogy, and assessment based on individual preferences and needs Knowledge sharing among students as a major source of content Guided social constructivism and situated learning as major forms of pedagogy Case-based participatory simulations complement presentational/assimilative instruction
Assessment	Student products generally tests or papers Grading centers on individual performance Students provide summative feedback on instructional effectiveness	Student products often involve nonlinear, associational webs of representations (for example, authoring a simulation and a Web page to express understanding of an internship rather than authoring a paper that synthesizes expert opinions) Peer-developed and peer-rated forms of assessment complement faculty grading, which is often based on individual accomplishment in a team performance context Assessments provide formative feedback on instructional effectiveness

Conclusion

While generational descriptions can be useful, they also oversimplify. Differences among individuals are greater than dissimilarities between groups, so students in any age cohort will present a mixture of neomillennial, millennial, and traditional learning styles. Predictions of the future also carry risk. The technologies discussed are emerging rather than mature, so their final form and influences on users are not fully understood. A substantial number of faculty and administrators will likely dismiss and resist some of the ideas and recommendations presented here.

However, widespread discussion among members of the academy about the trends delineated above is important, regardless of whether at the end of that dialogue those involved agree with these speculative conclusions. Further, to the extent that some of these ideas about neomillennial learning styles are accurate, campuses that make strategic investments in physical plant, technical infrastructure, and professional development along the dimensions suggested will gain a considerable competitive advantage in both recruiting top students and teaching them effectively.

Endnotes

1. Chris Dede, Pam Whitehouse, and Tara Brown-L'Bahy, "Designing and Studying Learning Experiences that Use Multiple Interactive Media to Bridge Distance and Time," in *Current Perspectives on Applied Information Technologies: Distance Education and Distributed Learning,* Charlambos Vrasidas and Gene V. Glass, eds. (Greenwich, Conn.: Information Age Press, 2002), pp. 1–30.

2. Chris Dede, "Vignettes About the Future of Learning Technologies," *Visions 2020: Transforming Education and Training Through Advanced Technologies* (Washington, D.C.: U.S. Department of Commerce, 2002), pp. 18–25, <http://www.technology.gov/reports/TechPolicy/2020Visions.pdf>.

3. Carrie Heeter, "Being There: The Subjective Experience of Presence," *Presence: Teleoperators and Virtual Environments,* vol. 1, no. 2 (Spring 1992), pp. 262–271; Bob G. Witmer and Michael J. Singer, "Measuring Presence in Virtual Environments: A Presence Questionnaire," *Presence: Teleoperators and Virtual Environments,* vol. 7, no. 3 (June 1998), pp. 225–240, <http://mitpress.mit.edu/journals/PRES/ps00734.pdf>.

4. Chris Dede, Marilyn Salzman, R. Bowen Loftin, and Katy Ash, "The Design of Immersive Virtual Environments: Fostering Deep Understandings of Complex Scientific Knowledge," in *Innovations in Science and Mathematics Education: Advanced Designs for Technologies of Learning,* Michael J. Jacobson and Robert B. Kozma, eds. (Hillsdale, N.J.: Lawrence Erlbaum Associates, 2000), pp. 361–413.

5. Marilyn Salzman, "VR's Frames of Reference: A Visualization Technique for Mastering Abstract Information Spaces," unpublished doctoral dissertation (Fairfax, Va.: George Mason University, 2000).

6. Marilyn Salzman, Chris Dede, and R. Bowen Loftin, "VR's Frames of Reference: A Visualization Technique for Mastering Multidimensional Information," *Proceedings of the SIGCHI Conference on Human Factors in Computing Systems: The CHI Is the Limit* (New York: ACM Press, 1999), pp. 489–495, <http://portal.acm.org/toc.cfm?id=302979&type=proceeding>.

7. National Research Council, *How People Learn: Brain, Mind, Experience, and School: Expanded Edition,* John D. Bransford, Ann L. Brown, and Rodney R. Cocking, eds. (Washington, D.C.: National Academies Press, 2000), <http://www.nap.edu/catalog/9853.html>.

8. Chris Dede, Brian Nelson, Diane Jass Ketelhut, Jody Clarke, and Cassie Bowman, "Design-Based Research Strategies for Studying Situated Learning in a Multiuser Virtual Environment," in *Embracing Diversity in the Learning Sciences: Proceedings of the Sixth International Conference of the Learning Sciences,* Yasmin B. Kafai et al., eds. (Mahweh, N.J.: Lawrence Erlbaum Associates, 2004), pp. 158–165, <http://www.gseis.ucla.edu/~icls/ICLSshortproceed.pdf>.

9. Chris Dede, "Enabling Distributed-Learning Communities via Emerging Technologies," *Proceedings of the 2004 Conference of the Society for Information Technology in Teacher Education (SITE)* (Charlottesville, Va.: American Association for Computers in Education, 2004), pp. 3–12.

10. Jose Mestre, *Transfer of Learning: Issues and a Research Agenda* (Washington, D.C.: National Science Foundation, 2002), <http://www.nsf.gov/pubs/2003/nsf03212/start.htm>.

11. Chris Dede, Tara Brown-L'Bahy, Diane Jass Ketelhut, and Pam Whitehouse, "Distance Learning (Virtual Learning)," in *The Internet Encyclopedia,* Hossein Bidgoli, ed. (New York: John Wiley & Sons, 2004), pp. 549–560.

12. Janet H. Murray, *Hamlet on the Holodeck* (Cambridge, Mass.: MIT Press, 1997).

13. Sherry Turkle, *Life on the Screen: Identity in the Age of the Internet* (New York: Touchstone, 1995).

14. Constance A. Steinkuehler, "Learning in Massively Multiplayer Online Games," in *Embracing Diversity in the Learning Sciences: Proceedings of the Sixth International Conference of the Learning Sciences,* Yasmin B. Kafai et al., eds. (Mahweh, N.J.: Lawrence Erlbaum Associates, 2004), pp. 521–528, <http://www.gseis.ucla.edu/~icls/ICLSshortproceed.pdf>.

15. Rebecca Black, "Access and Affiliation: The Literacy and Composition Practices of English Language Learners in an Online Fanfiction Community," in process paper presented at the 2004 National Conference of the American Educational Research Association, San Diego (2004), <http://labweb.education.wisc.edu/room130/PDFs/InRevision.pdf>.

16. For more information on River City and the MUVEES Project, see <http://muve.gse.harvard.edu/muvees2003/index.html>.

17. Dede, Nelson, Ketelhut, Clarke, and Bowman, op. cit.

18. (a) Sasha Barab et al., "Making Learning Fun: Quest Atlantis, a Game Without Guns," to appear in *Educational Technology Research and Development;* (b) Chris Dede and Marielle Palombo, "Virtual Worlds for Learning: Exploring the Future of the 'Alice in Wonderland' Interface," *Threshold* (Summer 2004), pp. 16–20.

19. Sherry Hsi et al., "eXspot: A Wireless RFID Transceiver for Recording and Extending Museum Visits," proceedings of UbiComp 2004; to be published.

20. Eric Klopfer and Kurt Squire, "Environmental Detectives: The Development of an Augmented Reality Platform for Environmental Simulations," in press, *Educational Technology Research and Development.*

21. Eric Klopfer, Kurt Squire, and Henry Jenkins, "Augmented Reality Simulations on PDAs," paper presented at the national American Education Research Association (AERA) conference, Chicago, 2003.

22. Howard Rheingold, *Smart Mobs: The Next Social Revolution* (Cambridge, Mass.: Perseus Publishing, 2002).

23. William J. Mitchell, *Me ++: The Cyborg Self and the Networked City* (Cambridge, Mass.: MIT Press, 2003).

24. Stephen Baker and Heather Green, "Big Bang! Digital Convergence Is Finally Happening—and that Means New Opportunities for Upstarts and Challenges for Icons," *BusinessWeekOnline,* June 21, 2004, <http://www.businessweek.com/magazine/content/04_25/b3888601.htm>.

25. Mitchell, op. cit.

26. Katerine Bielaczyc and Allan Collins, "Learning Communities in Classrooms: A Reconceptualization of Educational Practice," in *Instructional Design Theories and Models: A New Paradigm of Instructional Theory,* Vol. II, Charles M. Reigeluth, ed. (Mahwah, N.J.: Lawrence Erlbaum Associates, 1999).

27. Dede, 2004, op. cit.

28. Mitchell, op. cit.

Further Reading

Helen Ashman, guest ed., "Special Issue on Hypermedia and the World Wide Web," The New Review of Hypermedia and Multimedia, vol. 8 (2002), <http://www.comp.glam.ac.uk/~NRHM/volume8/volume8.htm>.

Edward Castronova, "Virtual Worlds: A First-Hand Account of Market and Society on the Cyberian Frontier," *CESifo Working Paper Series No. 618* (December 2001), <http://papers.ssrn.com/sol3/papers.cfm?abstract_id=294828>.

Wynne Harlen and Craig Altobello, *An Investigation of "Try Science" Studied On-Line and Face-to-Face* (Cambridge, Mass.: TERC, 2003), <http://www.terc.edu/uploaded/documents/tryscience_execsum.pdf>.

Neil Howe and William Strauss, *Millennials Rising: The Next Greatest Generation* (New York: Vintage Books, 2000).

Diana Oblinger, "Boomers, Gen-Xers, and Millennials: Understanding the 'New Students,'" *EDUCAUSE Review*, vol. 38, no. 4 (July/August 2003), pp. 37–47, <http://www.educause.edu/apps/er/erm03/erm034.asp>.

Marilyn Salzman, Chris Dede, R. Bowen Loftin, and Jim Chen, "A Model for Understanding How Virtual Reality Aids Complex Conceptual Learning," *Presence: Teleoperators and Virtual Environments*, vol. 8, no. 3 (June 1999), pp. 293–316.

Don Tapscott, *Growing Up Digital: The Rise of the Net Generation* (New York: McGraw Hill, 1998).

About the Author

Chris Dede is the Timothy E. Wirth Professor of Learning Technologies at Harvard's Graduate School of Education. His funded research includes grants from the National Science Foundation, the Joyce Foundation to aid the Milwaukee Public Schools, and Harvard. Dede has served as a member of the National Academy of Sciences Committee on Foundations of Educational and Psychological Assessment, the U.S. Department of Education's Expert Panel on Technology, and the International Steering Committee for the Second International Technology in Education Study. He serves on various boards and commissions, including PBS TeacherLine, the Partnership for 21st Century Skills, the Association for Teacher Education, Boston Tech Academy, and the new Science of Learning Center at Carnegie Mellon/University of Pittsburgh, as well as federal educational labs and regional technology centers. Dede was the editor of Learning with Technology: 1998 ASCD Yearbook and coedited Scaling Up Success: Lessons Learned from Technology-Based Educational Innovation.

Index

Educating the Net Generation